Si,

Happy Christmas 2018 ...

from,

Huw.

V FORCE BOYS

Previous books by Tony Blackman

NON-FICTION

Flight Testing to Win
(Autobiography paperback)
ISBN 978-0-9553856-4-3
Published Blackman Associates 2005

Vulcan Test Pilot
ISBN 978-1-906502-30-0
Published Grub Street 2007

Tony Blackman Test Pilot
ISBN 978-1-908117-32-8-
Published Grub Street 2009

Nimrod Rise and Fall
ISBN 978-1-909166-02-8
Published Grub Street 2011

Victor Boys
with Garry O'Keefe
ISBN 978-1-908117-45-8
Published Grub Street 2012

Vulcan Boys
ISBN 978-1-909808-08-9
Published Grub Street 2014

Valiant Boys
with Anthony Wright
ISBN 978-1-909808-21-8
Published Grub Street 2014

FICTION

A Flight Too Far
ISBN 978-0-955385-63-6
Published Blackman Associates

The Final Flight
ISBN 978-0-955385-60-5
Published Blackman Associates

The Right Choice
ISBN 978-0-955385-62-9
Published Blackman Associates

Flight to St Antony
ISBN 978-0-955385-66-7
Published Blackman Associates

Now You See It
ISBN 978-0-955385-67-4
Published Blackman Associates

Dire Strait
ISBN 978-0-955385-68-1
Published Blackman Associates

Java Waters Run Deep
ISBN 978-0-955385-69-8
Published Blackman Associates

TONY BLACKMAN

V FORCE
BOYS

ANTHONY WRIGHT

ALL NEW REMINISCENCES BY AIR AND GROUND CREWS
OPERATING THE VALIANT, VULCAN AND VICTOR
IN THE COLD WAR AND BEYOND

GRUB STREET | LONDON

Published by
Grub Street
4 Rainham Close
London SW11 6SS

Copyright © Grub Street 2017
Copyright text © Tony Blackman 2017, © Anthony Wright 2017

A CIP record for this title is available from the British Library

ISBN-13: 9-781-910690-38-3

Design by Daniele Roa

Printed and bound by Finidr, Czech Republic

DEDICATION

*To all the operators, aircrew and ground crew, who helped
to make all the V Force aircraft an effective deterrent during
the years of the Cold War and beyond.*

CONTENTS

ACKNOWLEDGEMENTS

When Anthony and I finished *Valiant Boys* we were aware that we had missed some good contributions from operating crews for all the three V bombers and that we already had a couple of excellent articles we had not been able to use for various reasons. So this book fills in these gaps and covers not only the very serious issues which made the V Force so effective but also includes some lighter tales which the authors may or may not regret. The book just would not have been possible without Anthony contacting all the authors who contributed to this book and encouraging them to rake up their memories, long gone by, and to put pen to paper. Not only that but Anthony himself added a very splendid chapter revealing some interesting events, some of which are unlikely to figure in the annals of the Royal Air Force!

There are over twenty-five contributors to this book ranging from sizeable chapters to a few short stories. The first two chapters on training by Nigel Baldwin and navigation by Norman Bonnor apply to all three V bombers; they are both updated contributions of versions published in specialist publications. The other chapters are ordered by Valiant, Vulcan and Victor though Spike Milligan operated in all the types.

John Muston's account of dropping the final and largest H-Bomb from the Valiant is very special and remembering that the first aircraft of the V Force went out of service fifty years ago, we have been very fortunate to have contributions on Valiant tanking and also from Tony Yule giving us the lighter side of squadron life.

On the Vulcan we have an AEO's story and Jim Vinales is back again giving us a gripping account of successfully baling out of the aircraft. We also have some stories capped by Anthony Wright's memories including a very memorable dining in night.

On the Victor Dick Russell has given us his early history before he became a famous tanker instructor and operator; his memories are supplemented by Gary West and also by Peter Sharp's vivid description of what it is really like putting out a landing gear fire. There are some descriptions of lone rangers and a chapter on a friendly fire incident which luckily did not result in any damage. Then we have Mike Keitch's account of handling nuclear weapons and we finish with a crew chief on 617 Squadron. Finally, there is an addendum with Monty Montgomery explaining the confusion over the correct name for Black Buck 1.

The photographs are of course an intrinsic part of the book and hopefully we have acknowledged all the ones that we have received and there are some in the public domain. We apologise if we have used some that we have not acknowledged.

Anthony Wright and I would like to thank all the contributors to this book and to our publisher John Davies of Grub Street. We feel very privileged to have been able to put this book together.

Tony Blackman and Anthony Wright, May 2017

PREFACE

This book is about the three V bombers which were built to guard the United Kingdom during the Cold War. Like the earlier individual V bomber books, this one has been written by operators of the aircraft so that we have first-hand accounts of what it was really like to defend the UK in that period.

Two of the chapters are slightly different from previous books. The first by Norman Bonnor explains how all the three aircraft types navigated to their targets. Such is the speed of advancing technology that it seems incredible today that all the aircraft had to navigate during the Cold War were some very early analogue computers, a sextant for looking at the stars, a drift and ground speed device and a very poor compass; no GPS, not even the earlier Transit or Omega systems. We have put this detailed chapter in this book because it is important that the equipment should be described, that the challenges facing the navigators should be appreciated and the way they solved the problems should be recorded.

The other very important and unusual chapter in this book is the detailed description of the nuclear armament that was used, the way the bombs were handled and the complete safety that was applied at all times. Having said that, Mike Keitch tells some very amusing and challenging stories of how he, as a junior NCO, had to move the weapons not only across the airfields but also across the country. Again it is important that these facts should be recorded and not left to historians to write third-party accounts.

As in the previous books one cannot help but be impressed reading of the long hours spent by the crews, ground as well as flight, sitting in or by their aircraft at the readiness platforms waiting to be scrambled to start a third world war. Thankfully it never happened but might well have done if the crews had not been there, waiting. The tedium was relieved by lone rangers flying to the United States, to the Mediterranean and to the Far East.

There are also two chapters on the early days of flight refuelling, one with the Valiant and the other with the Victors K1 and K2. The chapters are a reminder that the UK was very early amongst the world's air forces developing air-to-air refuelling. Finally, there is the story of a Falklands friendly fire incident which shows how easily things can go wrong in a wartime situation; interestingly it has been very straightforward getting the stories from the Victors that were being fired on but next to impossible getting first-hand accounts from the naval guys who launched the missiles!

CHAPTER 1

V FORCE TRAINING

Training the V Force for its primary and secondary roles – low level tactics against the Soviet bloc

Air Vice-Marshal Nigel Baldwin

Nigel Baldwin's first operational posting was in April 1963 (after the RAF College Cranwell, 4 FTS at RAF Valley (Vampire T11s) and 230 OCU RAF Finningley) as a pilot officer co-pilot on the then brand new Vulcan B Mk 2 on IX Squadron at RAF Coningsby. After two years there, he went back to the OCU for a captain's course and arrived with his new crew, as a flight lieutenant, on 35 Squadron at RAF Cottesmore (as a twenty-three year old); for the record he was one of the youngest captains.

After three years, he was posted to be the ADC to the AOC 11 Group at RAF Bentley Priory. After that, in 1970, he did the OCU course again, and went to 35 Sqn at RAF Akrotiri as a squadron leader flight commander.

After that he went to the RAF Staff College Bracknell as a student and then was staff officer to the SASO at HQ Strike Command for two years.

He then completed the OCU yet again, and in 1977 became OC 50 Squadron at RAF Waddington during which tour he led the Strike Command Vulcan team on Red Flag 79/2 at Nellis AFB, Nevada – the first all-night Red Flag. He finished his Vulcan B Mk 2 career with 2,700 flying hours on the aircraft.

He completed two tours in the USA: the first as a wing commander at the US Air War College at Maxwell AFB, Alabama; the second, as a group captain, as an International Fellow at the US National Defense University in Washington DC. He is a founder member of the RAF Historical Society and chairman since June 1996. Here he tells how V Force training was carried out.

This is a lightly-edited version of a paper presented as a contribution to a Royal Air Force Historical Society seminar devoted to 'Training for War in Peace' held at the RAF Museum, Hendon on 26 March 1998 and originally published in the Society's Journal No 20, 1999.

The basic aim of the medium bomber force (MBF) training system was very simple: to produce crews able to carry out their primary mission, that is to say individual nuclear strikes within close timing and tracking tolerances.

All my experiences were gained in the Vulcan Mk 2 force – I helped to collect brand new aircraft from the factory in 1963 and, by the time I left as OC 50 Squadron at

Waddington in the summer of 1979, we were beginning to take the aircraft to St Athan for disposal. I began, of course, as everybody did, at the OCU – the Operational Conversion Unit, first at Finningley later at Scampton. That course took about four months – after sea survival training at Mount Batten, aeromedical training and decompression from 56,000 ft at North Luffenham, six week's ground school, two weeks in the flight simulator for the pilots and about eighty hours flying for the captain and AEO (a little less for the co-pilot and the navigators) over six weeks. Then a fortnight at Wittering learning about nuclear weapons.

The Classification and BTR Scheme

Once on a squadron, the focus became the Classification Scheme. This varied over the years but, broadly speaking, its foundation was the six-monthly basic training requirement (BTR) – an allocation of training exercises to be completed by each of the five crew members. For instance: so many airfield and runway approaches using ILS and GCA, some asymmetric, some without some of the powered flying controls or airbrakes; practice diversions; navigational exercises, with and without various bits of the equipment working; a variety of simulated bombing attacks – sometimes dropping practice bombs, sometimes 1,000 pounders; electronic warfare training runs through the facility at Benbecula where we could turn on some of the very powerful jammers the Vulcan carried in its tail. We also had to do a specific number of fighter affiliation exercises – in my case, usually with Lightnings and later Phantoms. Then there were overseas flights, participation in Group and Command exercises – and so on. As far as flying itself was concerned, the best I ever did was about 300 hours in one year but the norm was 240/250. I finished up with about 3,000 hours on Vulcans after four tours.

To top it all off, there was a seemingly endless succession of airborne checks (on all crew members) by the resident experts. There always seemed to be somebody in the back looking over shoulders or sitting in one of the two pilots' seats checking the other pilot and the crew. This came to a head with the annual visit of the Group Standardisation Unit (GSU) (the 'trappers'). It was this report that we knew the AOC read, and the various tyrants under him. The GSU spent a fortnight with each squadron in turn. They flew with about half of the crews, grilled the rest on their professional knowledge, observed some in the flight simulator, and went through the squadron's administration with a fine-toothed comb. If there was a can of worms hidden anywhere, they would find it, open it, empty it out, and examine the contents. These days we would call it 'quality control'. Much hung on the eventual debrief of the squadron commander and his flight commanders; even more hung on the eventual written report.

Going back to the BTRs – these were the dynamo that drove the squadron. The relevant data was laid out on large chinagraph boards in the flight commanders' office and those of the navigation leader, the QFIs/IREs, and the AEO leaders. Activities along the top, crews down the side – to create a matrix of boxes each of which had to contain a tick by the end of the six-month period. This 'tote', incidentally, provided an excellent indication of which crews were good at utilising their sorties fully.

The BTR system formed the basis of the crew Classification Scheme. This started with combat – which a crew was expected to attain within six to eight weeks of arrival (previous to that they were non-operational and thus not certified as being able to share in the nuclear standby burden). Declaration of combat status told everyone that a crew was capable of standing QRA – quick reaction alert – and, therefore, capable of going to war.

Combat star (or combat *) was the next step up and was usually attained when the crew completed satisfactorily a full BTR training period – so about nine months to a year into the tour.

Next came select – which required BTRs to be completed within more demanding limits; this was unlikely to be achieved until a crew was well into its second year, and sometimes not at all.

Top of the bill, and quite rare (perhaps one per squadron), was select star. This demanded even greater accuracy and all round professional and personal qualities. Selection required the commander-in-chief's blessing. There were supposed to be a few perks for select star crews such as first bite at the overseas ranger flight cherry.

So that was the structure we all worked under – and it was good. It gave everyone an increasingly demanding standard to aim for, it kept the lazy up to scratch, and it gave the enthusiastic first tourists a worthwhile target.

It was an article of faith in the V Force that the crew that flies together, dies together. In short, we were committed to operating as constituted crews (five-man crews that had been formed at the OCU stage, often on Day 1). This was one reason why there were so few select star crews. In theory, the five-man team had to stay together and do everything together for a whole three-year tour and the exigencies of the service tended to frustrate that; I, for example, had an RAF rugby player as my AEO and sometimes, it seemed, that the C-in-C, certainly the AOC, was needed to arbitrate on where the priorities lay.

In the short term, if the nav plotter broke his leg, for example, it could prevent the crew from taking its turn on QRA (and from completing its BTRs). The approved solution was to paper over the cracks by applying for a 'temporary reconstitution' and, having had its customary grumble, Group HQ would usually acquiesce. You could try cutting the corner, of course, and fly with a 'guest' nav radar, for instance, but this could lead to lengthy debates about whether the targets attacked counted at all and, if they did, to which crew? While these problems could be quite severe in the QRA days, a more relaxed attitude began to prevail once the primary deterrent role had been passed to the Royal Navy's Polaris fleet in 1969.

Today, a substantial element of ground training is carried out in sophisticated, digital, three-axis, full motion simulators. The V bombers were firmly rooted in the analogue era. Nevertheless, there were flight simulators for the pilots – advanced for their time, a reasonable reproduction of the two-navigator station complete with the radar, and an electrical trainer for the AEOs. But they were all located in separate buildings. Indeed, at one stage, there were only two Vulcan cockpit simulators which meant that pilots at stations without one had to spend a whole day at a different site every month in order to satisfy their training commitments. We never had one at Akrotiri in Cyprus so the rules had to be changed. As the force contracted, however, we eventually finished up with a full set at each base, and it proved possible to co-or-dinate the three isolated crew positions so that they could be made to work together, even if they were in different locations. It was a bit Heath-Robinson, with complicated wiring looms linking the sites. Nevertheless, on a good day, it became possible to 'fly' a war sortie as an entire crew, complete with threats and battle damage. And an exhausting and thrilling experience it was too.

Like the rest of the RAF, the V Force believed that any overseas flight, even one as humble as a weekend away at Wildenrath, yielded excellent training in airmanship and captaincy while more ambitious deployments by individual V bombers provided oppor-tunities to train over different terrain and to show the flag. During the 'retreat from empire' phase in the 1960s, the V Force went all over the place to prove that we had not withdrawn from the world stage. In 1962, for instance, V bombers visited twenty-four countries. This began an era of lone ranger flights to newly independent states in Africa, to Malta and to Libya, to Canada and to the United States and westabout across the Pacific; and a prolonged presence in the Far East during the Indonesian Confrontation.

Associated with the need to reinforce, particularly the Far East, air-to-air refuelling was introduced in 1960 but the withdrawal from east of Suez meant that the need for long-range reinforcement had more or less evaporated. Only limited training was carried out and very few crews were ever qualified, although the basic equipment was never removed. At one stage, when Skybolt was in prospect, serious consideration was given to maintaining V bombers on airborne alert using air-to-air refuelling. A series of trials at Waddington explored the feasibility of the idea but it proved impractical for a number of reasons (the cockpits were simply too small and cramped, and we did not have enough tankers; and the strain on the whole organisation was just too much). With the demise of Skybolt, the idea was abandoned.

Low Level Training

To counter the Soviet deployment of SAMs (Gary Powers had been shot down in 1960), the medium bomber force was obliged to adopt low level tactics. I flew my first Vulcan low level training sortie out of Coningsby as a IX Squadron co-pilot in March 1964. The existing handful of recognised low level training runs in the UK was rationalised and extended to provide a single route which started in Kent and ran clockwise right around the UK to end at The Wash just north of Scampton. The route could be joined and left at numerous points but it worked in only one direction. Inevitably, overfamiliarity began to undermine its value. It was also very limiting tactically, as deviations from the route were not allowed. It suited the V Force, however, as we were not really in the tactical business; our wartime task was to fly low, on track and on time. To do otherwise would have disrupted the whole of the tightly co-ordinated NATO strike plan. Those who flew smaller aircraft, such as Jaguars and Buccaneers, found the degree of confinement imposed by the rigid route structure increasingly irksome, but the fact that you could not see much out of a Vulcan's cockpit precluded any relaxation of the rules although later on some brave hearts did authorise flight in low level areas as distinct from pre-ordained routes. With the Vulcan, to keep aircraft fatigue down, we would fly about an hour at low level – mostly at 250 knots accelerating to 350 for the two or three bombing attacks. Most crews flew at 500 ft AGL but some of the more experienced were allowed down to 300 feet.

To provide a change of scene and a more demanding environment, we made excellent use of the almost empty wastes of Labrador in Canada operating out of a formal RAF detachment base at Goose Bay. This, then, was a very active forward Strategic Air Command base with a ramp full of KC-135 tankers on QRA and a resident squadron of F-102s (whose noses were frequently put out of joint by departing Vulcans which only needed a third of the runway to get airborne, could beat an F-102 to 40,000 feet, and out-manoeuvre it when it got there). Every crew spent about a week at Goose Bay every year, and the low level training was excellent. A little later, we set up a similar facility at Offutt AFB, Omaha, Nebraska – the home of HQ Strategic Air Command – and this allowed crews to fly low level and attack targets over the USA using the USAF's network of so-called 'oil-burner' routes. A crew did this about once, or perhaps twice, a tour.

Another opportunity for different low level training emerged by detaching to Luqa in Malta or El Adem to fly routes over pre-Gadaffi Libya. On the face of it, the terrain may appear to have had little application to the primary operational mission but remember that, in war, the pilots would have been flying blind (we had a screen which was designed to prevent us being blinded by nuclear flashes) and, to the rear crew (who couldn't see out anyway) the relatively flat and featureless desert, providing few unambiguous, discreet radar returns, was a reasonable facsimile of the western USSR. (I used to pontificate to anyone who would listen that the highest ground between HQ Bomber Command at High Wycombe and Moscow was Harrow-on-the-Hill. So why were we flying through, and sometimes into, the Welsh Mountains?)

The only V bombers to be permanently based overseas were the Vulcans of 9 and 35 Squadrons at Akrotiri for the first half of the 1970s. We (I was a flight commander on 35 Squadron) were a bit limited in scope – a high level navigation stage to Crete and back then once around the island at 500 feet AGL 'attacking', with an F95 camera, two or three village churches was hardly demanding. But, being assigned to CENTO, we did get into the Shah's Tehran to fly low level routes over the wilds of Iran, and into Masirah and Oman, occasionally Turkey and Greece, and my crew got as far as New

Zealand and Mauritius. But EW training was particularly limited, and we had to make the most of the ECM ranges at Stornoway whenever we got back to the United Kingdom – which we normally did twice a year.

Exercises

Apart from the BTRs, the routine was punctuated by formal exercises. For the UK squadrons, the regular Group HQ-sponsored monthly affair would require each squadron to field three aircraft to fly a simulated navigation and bombing profile. Although these events often began with a scramble take-off (to get a tick in the BTR box), these activities were always pre-planned. The real test was Exercise Mickey Finn – a no-notice exercise, usually once a year – but if the first one didn't go well, Command HQ could and would order it done again. Mickey Finn required the recall of all available crews, the generation of the maximum number of aircraft, dispersal of the entire force to its wartime launch bases where they sat on ORPs, at fifteen minutes' readiness, for a couple of days or so.

After being called to cockpit readiness several times (and, although you could make a reasonable guess, you never really knew which one would be 'for real'), we would eventually be scrambled. Dispersals were usually released individually, crews then flying a simulated war mission. One year, however (probably 1967?), the whole lot were scrambled at once. More than 100 Vulcans and Victors were airborne within four minutes. It worked but it gave air traffic kittens, and the next problem was to get them all safely down again. The subsequent 'sortie' involved everybody flying time-wasting 'trombone' patterns to establish a reasonable degree of separation at the group dispersal point through which we all had to funnel for recovery to our main bases. The lucky ones were home within the hour, but some were much later.

Bombing and Navigation Competition

The other high point of the annual calendar was the Command Bombing and Navigation Competition. The rules were constantly being changed (not least, we thought cynically, to make sure that visiting SAC crews could not possibly win) and the level of participation varied. In some years, all crews took part, while at other times it was only representative crews, selected after a fly-off at squadron level. Just how useful all this activity was is questionable. It was supposed to stimulate innovative approaches and, in the early days, it probably did, but once the best techniques had been devised, the competition really became a diversion of effort, not least because it placed a great deal of emphasis on celestial navigation which was, in truth, no more than a get-you-home aid. We were supposed to be training for war, and you could not realistically go to war on astro, certainly not at low level. But looking back on it from a distance, I now realise that the annual competition with SAC had a political importance way beyond our irritations in the crew room.

NATO

Now a word about NATO: although the first V bombers, the Valiants of 207 Squadron, had been assigned to SACEUR as early as 1960, it was not until May 1963 that the whole of the MBF was put at its disposal. At squadron level, however, this had very little impact as training was still a wholly national affair, command and control continued to be exercised from High Wycombe. Although wartime targets were now allocated by SHAPE, the details were administered by HQ Bomber and later Strike Command. Nothing seemed to have changed. SACEUR did not make much impression at squadron level until the late 1970s when its Taceval policy obliged us to paint everything green, fill sand bags, and carry our NBC kit with us. While we had certainly been assigned to SACEUR, and we had to accommodate the occasional NATO officer, we largely conducted our affairs in 1980 in very much the same way as we had done in 1960 – right down to the bomber controller giving the same launch instructions over 'the bomber box'.

Red Flag and Night Low Level Training

Although it was still an impressive air display performer, by the late 1970s the Vulcan was rapidly becoming obsolescent. It still had one more shot in its locker, however, and it proved possible to much enhance the aircraft's ability to operate at low level at night and in bad weather. In 1978, the USAF invited the RAF to take part with the Vulcan in the first all-night Red Flag. As OC 50 Squadron at Waddington at the time, and under the critical gaze of the SASO – Air Commodore Mike Robinson – I was told by HQ 1 Group to select four aircraft from the fleet, six aircrews, and a small team of expert technicians, work them up in the UK and at Goose Bay, then participate in Red Flag 79/2 – and, "by the way, don't have an accident". There were to be no technical enhancements to the kit, so it was really a question of getting the most out of what we already had: a rather basic terrain following radar (TFR) which we had bought off the shelf ten years before and that had languished largely unused in the Vulcan's cockpit not least because pilots had preferred to look out at the ground passing by instead of keeping their heads down on instruments. Once we concentrated on it, however, and improved its reliability, it served us well. It was neither drift nor bank stabilised, nor could it anticipate the need to give a fly-down command as you approached the crest of a ridge. It simply looked at where the nose was pointing – which was not necessarily where the aircraft was going.

The pilots overcame these limitations by close co-operation with the rear crew (and that is why the crews were selected with such care). So long as the nav radars could provide frequent accurate fixes, the plotter's kit (essentially Decca Doppler resolved around a very accurate heading reference system) permitted the aircraft's progress over the ground to be monitored with precision; the nav plotter was able to provide a commentary forecasting, for example, when the TFR would give a fly-up demand and anticipating the need to push over, with the other navigator providing advice on radar 'cut offs'. Compared to the Tornado's fully automated system, this was a tactically limited approach (you had to stay on the pre-planned track) and one which was totally hands-on and very labour intensive. But in 1978 we did not have any Tornados – and the system certainly worked – the key being mutual confidence back and front. We worked up both confidence and experience gradually and certainly impressed our American hosts at Nellis AFB when we flew through the mountainous Red flag ranges contour flying at night at 1,000 ft – well below the B-52s and most of the F-111s.

For all that, I do not believe that it was a realistic approach for other than very competent crews. It was absolutely essential that the navigators had the maturity and confidence to say if they had any doubts at any time. Unfortunately, you could not simulate this technique and, to be proficient at it – and you had to be proficient – required a lot of practice. This meant lots of night flying with all the attendant problems of noise, anti-social hours and so on, although, on the plus side, we found that night low level flying was very economical in terms of airframe fatigue. It is also questionable whether it would have coped with really rugged terrain (although we did do it over Wales and the Lake District) but, as I have said before, there is not much high ground en route to the Soviet Union.

After Red Flag, my crew went back to Goose Bay to fly routes there at 800 ft at night then we went to Offutt in Omaha to fly some of the USAF routes at 500 ft over some lakes and 800 ft over the plains – while the HQ 1 Group SASO sat in his office at Bawtry biting his finger nails. My most gripping memory of the time was flying several hundreds of miles low over the flat terrain of Labrador on a pitch black night – unlike anywhere else we had flown, it was absolutely jet black – a phenomenon impossible to find in Europe. On one occasion, we flew in solid cloud for what must have been twenty minutes or so without realising it. I don't think I told the rear crew at the time.

Conclusion

The ultimate question, of course, is: did the V Force do the right training? Could we have done it? Could we have got through the Soviet defences at low level to the target on time? I suppose that all training turns out to be flawed to some degree when the system is actually put to the test. Operational experience would certainly have revealed that some of our techniques could have been improved – except, of course, that in WWIII it would have been a one-shot system. My own view, given reinforcement by our experience on the night Red Flag and by subsequent night training, is that our training was essentially right and, remembering all the peacetime constraints, that we did about the right amount of it. We had both quality and quantity enough to ensure that a proportion of us would have been able to reach our targets (several hours before SAC would have got there incidentally) especially if we had been launched at night or in poor visibility by day. I think that that was still true right to the end of the Vulcan's life. Whether we would have got back to base, I am not so sure – but I never lost any sleep over that problem nor did most of my colleagues.

Nigel went out to Tengah, Singapore with 35 Squadron for four months during the Indonesian Confrontation March/June 1966.

The view from the officers' mess at Gan. *(Nigel Baldwin)*

CHAPTER 2

V FORCE NAVIGATION

The V Force: 1955 to 1966
Navigation at 50,000 and 500 feet

Air Commodore Norman Bonnor FRIN FRAeS

The V Force had to navigate into Russia and to other targets without GPS and modern computers. **Norman Bonnor,** *an expert navigator, explains the tools available and how the aircraft achieved their required accuracy. Norman was a nav radar in the V Force and later he commanded RAF Waddington; he went on to become deputy commander of the NATO AEW Force. On leaving the RAF he became a key member of the Royal Institute of Navigation serving as president 2002/2005 and here follows an extract of a paper he gave to that body.*

The first V Force aircraft (Mk 1 versions of the Valiant, Vulcan and Victor) entered service in the late 50s, each equipped with a true airspeed unit, Green Satin Doppler radar, a ground position indicator (GPI) Mk 4, the navigation and bombing system (NBS) which included the H2S Mk IXA ground-mapping radar, a radar altimeter, a periscopic sextant but, apart from a standby compass in the cockpit, their only heading reference was a single G4B gyro-magnetic compass. These were the navigation aids intended for use in the aircrafts' war role of strategic bombing. To meet peacetime requirements, particularly for standard instrument departure and arrival procedures, other navigation equipment included: a radio compass, the instrument landing system (ILS) and Gee Mk 3 later replaced by TACAN; I don't intend dealing with the use of these latter aids except to say that we also used the radio compass for reception of Consol and, more importantly, to keep in touch with Test Match scores!

The major innovation when compared to earlier medium bomber aircraft of the RAF (e.g. Lancasters, Halifaxes and Lincolns) was the real time input of accurate drift and groundspeed from the Green Satin Doppler radar into the computations of a fully inte-grated navigation and bombing system. The NBS was a very complex group of analogue computers, which relied on the use of 'chopper' amplifiers to cut up DC signals repre-senting various parameters into pseudo AC for amplification. Among its many features were the calculation of forward throw and trail of a selected weapon and the output of accurate steering commands to the computed release point with an automated release signal; gone were the days of 'pressing the tit'. Unfortunately, the system was large and very heavy involving many 'black boxes', or perhaps these are better described as 'black dustbins', most of which having to be installed in the pressurised cockpit. The Green Satin Doppler was very reliable and, apart from occasional unlocking problems over calm seas and the inherent errors caused by sea surface motion, its velocity and drift accuracy easily met the long-range dead reckoning (DR) requirements of strategic bombing. The same could not be said of the G4B compass. A great deal of effort was devoted to calibrating the compass using twelve-point ground swings with Fourier analysis to smooth out observational errors and confirm the quality of the results, but large cross-track navigation errors were still very obvious in the

Green Satin Doppler radar and ground position indicator Mk 4.

(Norman Bonnor)

air despite the use of the NBS automatic variation unit which continuously applied a local variation value to the compass output. But before delving more deeply into the problem of compass errors, I should briefly describe the roles of the aircraft crew and the navigation techniques we used in those early days of the V Force.

Initially, most V Force captains were experienced bomber types with at least two tours under their belts but, within a few years, selection was opened to some of the first co-pilots who had joined the force straight from training and now had up to three years experience of the aircraft and role. By the mid 1960s, most co-pilots came straight from training and included a proportion of young ground engineers on a flying tour to broaden their appreciation of aircrew needs; an excellent scheme which was unfortunately abandoned when their flying training was seen as too expensive for the time they spent on aircrew duty. One of the co-pilot's primary tasks was management of the fuel system and, as a third of the aircraft's weight without weapons was fuel, this involved C of G management as well. Some ground engineers also filled the air electronics officer's seat; the AEO's role was a mixture of signaller, air engineer and defensive systems operator in that he looked after long-range communications on the HF single side-band radio, he managed the electrical and hydraulic systems and controlled the radar warning systems, chaff dispensers and the multitude of high-powered jammers we carried.

The navigation team: nav radar and nav plotter positions in a Vulcan.

(Norman Bonnor)

The nav team comprised a nav radar, who had undergone a ten-month training course at the Bomber Command Bombing School at Lindholme on radar scope interpretation and the detailed operation of the NBS system, and the nav plotter who, in those early days, had

completed at least one previous flying tour with above average assessments. To navigate to the target area, the plotter used a traditional flight plan proforma, a Lambert's Conformal plotting chart, a separate navigation log (although 'log on chart' techniques were adopted at an early stage), and the usual paraphernalia of Douglas protractor, Dalton computer, 4H pencils etc. During sortie planning, the nav radar used 1:250,000 topographical maps to select suitable radar fix points for the en route phase, and large-scale maps and aerial and radar scope photographs to study the target area and to select offset aiming points for the target which usually was not a significant, individual return on the radar; two offset selections were available – internal and external. To help identify the target and related offsets, he would draw an outline with a fine marker pen of the predicted radar echoes on a piece of acetate and, during a bombing run, he would hold this overlay on the plan position indicator (PPI) to 'map match' the radar picture and ensure the range and bearing markers were placed over the correct offset or target using the small joystick controller, the CU626. The offset distances were measured or calculated as accurately as possible in yards and set on the NBS as northings and eastings. Here was the second reason why compass errors were so important to the nav team; these offsets were measured against a true north datum, so any error in the true heading used by the NBS appeared directly in the bombing results. For example, using an offset 10,000 yards from the target (not a particularly long one) a degree of heading error would introduce more than 150 yards bombing error over and above any aiming, ballistics or other errors.

A new V Force crew arriving on a squadron from the appropriate Operational Conversion Unit was qualified to fly the aircraft safely and efficiently but not yet operationally; their first task was to complete a number of training sorties, some ground training requirements and to study their assigned NATO and national war targets before they could be declared 'combat ready'. This was the first step on a complex six-month training schedule to achieve, retain or improve their Bomber Command classification as a 'constituted' crew. All V Force crews had to be a 'constituted' group of five individuals who, because of the highly classified nature of the war role, the nuclear weapons, and the target materials, had been 'positively vetted' before starting their OCU training.

Bomber Command imposed three navigation modes or techniques on the nav team for combat readiness training: primary, secondary and limited. Primary allowed full use of all aids including radar fixing which made staying within about a quarter mile of track and timing to better than five seconds very easy; in fact, the technique was too easy, and we hardly needed to practise its use. Secondary assumed loss of the radar picture for fixing to simulate a more 'stealthy' penetration of enemy defences so denying the H2S transmissions for AI fighter or missile homing, but the Green Satin drift and groundspeed inputs were still available. This meant using other methods for updating present position with the emphasis on astro as the war role demanded autonomy. For navigators from an earlier era, I should point out that visual 'on-tops' are not usually

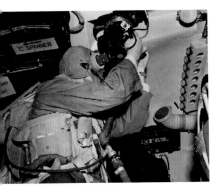

The nav radar taking an astro sight in the Victor.

(Norman Bonnor)

available or very accurate from 50,000 feet. The V Force took astro techniques to their limit; the traditional three-star fix was largely abandoned in favour of sandwich fixes formed from along and across track position lines by averaging at least five one-minute sextant shots (in effect 300 individual measurements) with complex corrections applied for turning and longitudinal acceleration errors. A good crew would achieve errors of three to five miles at the terminal point of a 1,000-mile navigation stage using the secondary technique. Limited technique took away the Green Satin inputs as a simulated failure, leaving the true airspeed feed and wind vectors set manually on the NBS. This was clearly more difficult, but if the high level winds were reasonably stable, a good crew would be inside ten miles at the end of 1,000 miles. Almost all the plotters I flew with used track plots for all three techniques including limited where fixes or most probable positions (MPPs) were used to calculate 'delta' values of the N/S and E/W wind vectors to update the NBS settings manually.

Achieving good track keeping and timing accuracy was not just an end in itself; to maintain credible deterrence, the bomber force was required to prove its capability to penetrate the extensive early warning and air defence systems of the Soviet Union. This capability relied on a co-ordinated attack plan on a broad front to saturate the defences using mutual support jamming of the many types of Soviet surveillance radar and air defence communication systems; this required very accurate track keeping and timing so that no gaps appeared in the jamming that might reveal individual bomber aircraft. Height finding or fixing, very important for accurate bombing, was conducted over the sea or over flat terrain of known height as close to the target as possible using the radar altimeter to update the millibar setting on the barometric altimeter sub-system within the NBS.

For weapons training, a few practice bombs were dropped on ranges around the UK coast and overseas, but these exercises were treated as academic training only. Most radar bombing practice was conducted as simulated attacks against radar bomb scoring units (RBSUs) which were modified AAA tracking radars with an accurate plotting capability based near the major city complexes of London, Manchester, Newcastle and Glasgow as well as a unit in East Anglia. They each covered a range of up to forty targets of varying difficulty; crews could book attack times before take-off or call for an opportunity attack; bomb release was simulated by the end of a tone transmitted by the aircraft on UHF radio which automatically lifted a pen on the radar plotting table; the RBSU staff then used their tracking radar's values of the aircraft's track, speed and height to calculate the forward throw and trail of a simulated weapon and estimate the impact error, which was reported to the crew using a 'code of the day'.

But back to our real problem, the gyro-magnetic compass. The crews knew it was the weak link which is why so much attention was paid to reducing residual deviations by elaborate ground compass swings. However, at squadron level, not much was known or understood about compass errors caused by flying rhumb line headings at 500 knots. On XV Squadron, we elected to air swing the compasses of all our Victor Mk 1A aircraft using astro as the reference. To do this with sufficient accuracy, we fitted 'Vernier' scales to the sextant azimuth rings and calculated the sun's azimuth to 0.1 of a degree by interpolating the values in the yellow band AP3270. To our amazement, all eight of the squadron aircraft showed a very similar pattern of errors, with apparent residual deviations of over two degrees on SW headings; no wonder we were suffering large cross-track navigation errors. Later, when I left the V Force to complete the staff and specialist navigation courses, I learned how to calculate these hang-off errors caused by the time constant of the compass control loop and the real and apparent drift of the gyro.

Back on the squadron, we started using the air swing deviations, and our navigation performance and bombing results immediately improved. We also developed and used another technique to reduce the effect of compass errors on our bombing. This involved making the initial line-up on the target with an abeam offset so that any compass errors were manifested along track as range errors; in the late stages of the run (ten or fifteen seconds to release) the nav radar would tell the pilot to select the autopilot to heading mode so that it no longer followed the NBS steering command; he then switched to a second offset in the overshoot and took out the range errors on this new offset just prior to the release point. This method required good planning but paid dividends in the better results achieved.

Having solved the heading problem for high level navigation and bombing, the Soviets intervened by increasing their deployment of surface-to-air missiles. For some time, we had trained to defeat the SA1 and SA2 systems deployed around Moscow, and other major targets, by jamming their fire-control radars and by weaving our heading throughout the bombing run so that their prediction systems could not track for long enough to achieve a successful engagement. But by 1963, the SA3 was deployed in large numbers with almost complete coverage along the Soviet border and in depth around our planned targets or 'accounting line numbers' (ALNs) as they were known. To maintain the credibility of deterrence, tactics had to change; it was time to operate as individual aircraft and go low level to penetrate under the surveillance radar cover and below the effective height of the SA3 system; in reality, this meant not more than 500 feet above ground and lower over the tops of ridges and hills.

Low level navigation was new to most of us. At high level, the pilots had flown on instruments and, for the operational role, covers were fitted over the cockpit windows to shield their eyes from the flash effects of nuclear bursts; now some of the forward covers were removed, and the pilots were issued with an eye patch so that at least two eyes out of four would still be available after flying close to someone else's nuclear burst.

The low level navigation technique we developed involved the plotter giving a running commentary of the expected scene ahead from prepared quarter million topos which the pilots attempted to confirm whenever they were in visual contact. Meanwhile, the nav radar used terrain features in preference to cultural fix points to check and update the NBS position at regular intervals. Terrain screening on the radar picture was very pronounced below 500 feet, but, used by a skilled operator, could be adopted as a crude terrain-avoidance system. The important characteristic for a feature to show changed from what it was made of – metal or brick – to how high it was. Often a field pattern created by stone walls or hedges, or railway embankments, were much more prominent features than towns or industrial areas.

In the early 1960s, some of the Valiant aircraft went out of service as bombers and were converted to the tanker role, and the Mk 2 versions of the Vulcan and Victor entered service. At first, the better performance of the Mk 2 Victor and Vulcan meant that our primary attack profile was still at high level (up to 60,000 ft where the air is thin and the sky so dark blue that astro sights could be taken on the planets and brightest stars in the daytime), but soon the Soviet aircraft and missile threat meant that we joined our colleagues still on the Mk 1s at low level. Apart from slightly modified versions of Green Satin and NBS, the initial navigation fit of the Mk 2s was the same as the Mk 1s except for the compass. The G4B was replaced by twin gyro-magnetic compasses incorporated as part of the Smiths Military Flight System. Unfortunately, these suffered from very similar errors to the G4B but did have the added advantage that the pilots could now select to fly heading or track on a true or magnetic datum; I was never convinced that they really understood the difference.

The next change came with the introduction of the Blue Steel missile which gave a stand-off range of up to 150 miles at 50,000 feet or fifty miles at low level; with it came the GPI Mk 6, probably the most accurate analogue aircraft computer ever built, and the inertial navigation system (INS) of the missile itself. The aircraft could make use of the outputs of this system until the missile was launched. At last, an accurate source of true heading once the INS was aligned, but here was the rub; the deterrent role of the V Force involved rapid reaction from the famous four-minute warning from the Ballistic Missile Early Warning System at Fylingdales on the North York Moors, hence no time for a conventional fifteen to twenty-minute ground alignment. Airborne

Handley Page Victor B Mk 2 and Blue Steel.

(Norman Bonnor)

Ground position indicator Mk 6. *(Norman Bonnor)*

alignments had to be used; this was long before the very accurate GPS, and the rapid in-motion alignments of ring laser gyro INS now taken for granted by today's aircrew.

As well as the GPI Mk 6, some of the other equipments fitted in the cockpit for the carriage and operation of the missile were: the Blue Steel control panel (BSCP), the inertial navigator control unit (INCU) and the inertial navigator monitor unit (INMU) which was not a normal piece of military avionics. It looked more like a fancy multi-meter about 10" x 8" inset in the nav plotter's chart-table (central in the rear cockpit) with a Perspex cover so that it could be read without disturbing the chart and plotting instruments in use. This meter had a variety of scales with different readouts selected by a multi-function switch.

While the INCU and INMU were purely associated with the control and functioning of the missile's INS, the BSCP controlled and provided indications of most other functional aspects of the missile's operation including: the refrigeration system, fuel tank pressurisation, starting the auxiliary power unit (APU) and launching or jettisoning the missile. It also included many indicators relating to the position of the ailerons, foreplane and lower fin, nitrogen and hydraulic pressures and, one of its primary uses, monitoring of the temperatures in the two high test peroxide (HTP) tanks of the missile. This was crucial to safety as any contamination of the HTP (a super-oxidant) would make it boil and become a major hazard, particularly with a nuclear warhead nearby! This was why the QRA aircraft had to be visited by the alert crews at regular intervals throughout the day and night to confirm all was well, particularly when an aircraft/missile combination first came on state. The crew chief and other ground crew were not permitted to enter the cockpit once targeting materials were in place and the aircraft declared to Bomber Command. If I remember correctly, each operational missile on the station had to be flown once a quarter to meet Bomber/ Strike Command goals. When we flew with these so-called 'wet' missiles (without warheads of course) rather than training rounds, HTP temperatures were one of the items checked and logged every thirty minutes throughout the sortie. Should the HTP temperatures rise while airborne, the crew would divert immediately to the nearest

Inertial navigation monitor unit.

(Norman Bonnor)

'Blue Steel Diversion' airfield to offload the HTP into large tanks of water buried in the ground close to the operational readiness platform at the end of the runway. There were several of these specially equipped airfields around the country apart from the main bases at Scampton and Wittering. The co-pilot and nav radar were the offload crew who donned plastic suits after landing and connected hoses to the missile (this offload kit was kept in the visual bomb-aiming position); it was a very awkward operation with hard rubber gloves on and a face mask that kept steaming up! We had to practise this procedure regularly as a part of the six-monthly training requirements.

Although Blue Steel could be regarded as a 'fire and forget' weapon with autonomous guidance, a lot of work had to be completed by the nav team before launch. After a scramble take-off, which the first aircraft using a simultaneous 'combustor' start of all four engines could achieve within fifty seconds (I don't know of any fighter aircraft that can achieve such a time today), the INS alignment was completed by the nav team using the GPI Mk 6, the INCU, the INMU, the BSCP and the NBS in what can only be called a 'mandraulic' manner; i.e. each step was separately initiated, carefully monitored and required a large number of switch selections; very different to the automated alignment sequence of modern inertial reference systems. During the alignment process, the INMU meter was used to monitor various parameters including: gyro temperatures and rotation speeds, torqueing motor currents on the gimbal rings etc. A so-called 'LEDEX' pole switch and indicator on the INCU was used to activate INS alignment using a numbering system so, for example, LEDEX 1 turned on the gyro heaters, LEDEX 2 locked the gimbals to the missile frame (hopefully reasonably level), LEDEX 3 spun the gyros up to speed etc. In other words, the nav plotter manually selected each step of the alignment process (checking the indications as he did so); this process was totally automated for ground alignments of later INS used in aircraft such as the Phantom, Jaguar, Harrier, Tornado and now the Typhoon.

The penultimate LEDEX position put the INS into a mode where Green Satin Doppler velocities (N/S and E/W) were compared with the IN velocity outputs, and the differences used to torque the INS stable platform and its levelling gyros. The assumption was that the Doppler velocities were correct, and that if the IN velocities were the same then the platform must be at right angles to the local earth gravity vector. The INS was initially aligned in azimuth using the aircraft's gyro-magnetic compass reading corrected for variation, and then continually corrected throughout the sortie using a fix monitored azimuth (FMA) technique. This involved the nav radar using the H2S radar (either with the PPI or the rapid processing unit (RPU)) to fix the GPI Mk 6 as accurately as possible and letting it run using IN heading for 150-200 nm (about twenty minutes flight) in a reasonably straight line, when he fixed again. The assumption was that any cross-track error was caused by IN azimuth gyro error, and this was torqued out automatically by accepting the fix on the GPI Mk 6 with other settings made that represented the track and distance between the fixes. The GPI Mk 6 was the key element in the integrated navigation system having been designed specifically to act as the interface between the aircraft navigation system and the missile but, because of its complexity, it was removed from the Victor Mk 2 and replaced with the old reliable GPI Mk 4 when the aircraft were converted to the tanker role. Later, they were equipped with a Litton 211 omega navigation system and, during the Falklands War, with an AC Delco Carousel INS.

Goole

Scunthorpe

Comparison of the RPU radar image (left) with the normal PPI display.
(Norman Bonnor)

The FMA process, and clamping the IN velocities to Green Satin values, continued throughout the sortie or until missile launch. In the final preparations for launch, the last position fix was taken on a release point fix (RPF). The RPF was the basis for defining the target position. Distances (N/S and E/W in minutes and decimal minutes of latitude and longitude) between the RPF and the target (or more correctly the position of the airburst height above the target) were set on the GPI Mk 6 and transmitted to the missile during the pre-launch checks so that the missile guidance and autopilot would know the target position very accurately. As the launch point was approached, the nav radar used the RPF to make the last corrections and, once these were accepted, the nav plotter selected the missile INS to FREE. At this stage it was then running as a space-stabilised system based on the RPF with no further Green Satin or FMA updates. Of course to launch the missile there were other final actions to perform interspersed with the above, including: unfolding the bottom fin at the rear of the missile, withdrawing the motorized locking pin on the missile release unit, pressurizing the fuel and HTP tanks, starting the missile auxiliary power unit etc.

The nav plotter activated the final launch switch, and the missile would hopefully fall away under gravity. To prevent the rocket motor firing too close to the launch aircraft, a 100-foot lanyard remained attached to the missile and, when this separation distance was reached, a pin was extracted that enabled the kerosene fuel and HTP to flow onto a silver catalyst screen in the Spectre rocket motor. Ignition was almost instantaneous and a thrust of 24,000 lb was now pushing a missile weighing 16,000 lb. You have to remember that Blue Steel was a pretty 'slick' aerodynamic shape and, at launch, the canard foreplane was set at fifteen degrees nose-up, the maximum angle. So, as it fell away, it stayed pretty well under the aircraft and gradually pointed its nose up until the motor fired when a 1.5:1 thrust to weight ratio rapidly accelerated it to Mach 2.5 in a steep climb, hopefully without colliding with the launching aircraft.

In training, missile guidance accuracy was assessed by simulating missile launch and allowing the INS to run free while the aircraft performed a manoeuvre designed to emulate the same effects on performance as the missile's high Mach number flight profile would impose after a real launch. By this stage, the Victor Mk 2 had been fitted with a side-scan radar capability and a rapid processing display unit. When in use, the H2S scanner was locked at ninety degrees to aircraft track (port or starboard) and radar video diverted from the normal PPI display to a low afterglow cathode ray tube across which photographic paper was drawn at a speed proportional to the groundspeed of the aircraft. The exposed image was developed by passing the paper over two slots through which developing and fixing chemicals were sucked. Although it sounds hazardous to employ hot and corrosive chemicals in a pressurised aircraft cabin, the system was successful in that the radar image produced was much sharper and with a much wider spectral range than the normal high afterglow PPI; of course, it also produced a permanent image which allowed the nav radar time to study the returns more carefully before making any updates.

The RPU was only fitted to the Victor Mk 2; I believe this small-scale introduction was really aimed at developing the technique for the ill-fated TSR2 in which an RPU-based side-scan navigation radar was the primary fixing aid. The Vulcan Mk 2 aircraft that were not selected to carry the Blue Steel missile were retrofitted with a twin-gyro platform that provided similar heading performance to an INS rather than the poor accuracy of the gyro-magnetic compass.

In many respects, the Valiant, Vulcan and Victor and their fully integrated navigation systems were ahead of their time and allowed the RAF to skip over a generation of strategic bombers based on piston-engined aircraft with pressurised cockpits such as the B-50 Washington or Stratofortress. It was a major step to jet-age strategic bombers which, although designed for operation at ultra-high level also performed very well in the low level role. However, a major part of the V Force success as a deterrent was down to the skill and flexibility of the aircrews, and the quality and resourcefulness of the supporting ground crews and operations staff; I am proud to say that I was part of it on both XV and 100 Squadrons flying the Victor Mk 1A and Mk 2.

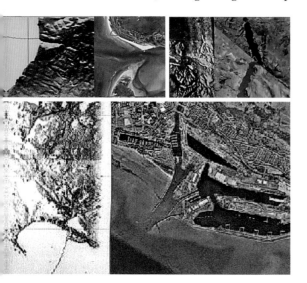

Some examples of RPU images versus Google Earth. From top left: the Dovey Estuary, Ullswater and Swansea Harbour. *(Norman Bonnor)*

CHAPTER 3

THE LAST UK H-BOMB

John Muston

*The V Force existed to deliver nuclear bombs and it was necessary to develop not only the aircraft and the method of delivery but also the weapons themselves. **John Muston**, nav radar, tells his experiences dropping the last and largest UK H-Bomb from Christmas Island and then goes on to describe his subsequent years flying in the Valiant. He left the squadron in 1961 before all the Valiants were grounded after seventeen years in the RAF and became a marketeer selling the latest industrial computers with great expertise. Having done that and being very flexible he bought and ran a very successful golf course. No substitute for RAF training!*

I arrived at the Valiant conversion unit at Gaydon in June 1956. I was the youngest nav radar to join the V Force and had reached this stage in my career after being in the RAF for just over four years. To my surprise, at the pre-entry procedure before I was conscripted at eighteen for National Service, I was advised that my educational qualifications meant I could train as aircrew. During initial training at Kirton in Lindsey, after twelve hours flying in the Tiger Moth biplane, it was agreed by all concerned that it would be safer for everyone to train me as a navigator. This I did, first at Air Service Training Hamble on the Anson 21 and then Hullavington on the Varsity. After receiving my navigator brevet I was posted to HQ Transport Command Upavon to finish my training.

A few weeks later I applied for a short service commission and spent three months on the communications flight flying in the three Anson 19s, two Chipmunks and a Proctor. I also took the opportunity to join a 53 Squadron Hastings flight to Singapore which memorably resulted in an emergency two-engine landing at Istres near Marseille. Obviously realising we would be there for some time we enquired if there was a pub nearby and were advised that there is always one just outside French military establishments. When we duly visited it we quickly twigged that it doubled as a brothel as the ladies had the price chalked on the soles of their shoes – somewhat of a shock to a green nineteen year old. Soon after this I was posted to Swinderby for a quick refresher course followed by the bombing school at Lindholme before joining 207 Canberra Squadron at Marham. A very agreeable year in the crew of Barry Mather with Tony Norman as the other navigator ensued. We soon achieved the top rating, especially satisfying as at the outset we were all under twenty-one. Surprisingly to me I was then posted to do the year-long course to learn the mysteries of the navigation and bombing system (NBS) to be installed in all V bombers. By far the best part of that year was the three months on 83 Squadron at Hemswell on Lincolns, learning to use the H2S radar developed during the war. A great experience was a trip to Aden with an exceptional all NCO crew, a total of forty-five hours. After the course came a brief but enjoyable spell at Marham flying in all sorts of aircraft with an old friend from 207 Squadron Bruce Sheppard. Now it was time for the real thing.

Soon after arriving at Gaydon I met Flush (his initials are WC) Conning who I knew, at least by sight, from Canberra days so we naturally teamed up together. We soon worked out that there were fifteen people on the course, i.e. three crews. Captains were a wing commander, squadron leader and a flying officer, the latter we thought strange as all Valiant captains were supposed to be vastly experienced. Anyway the wing commander swiftly hoovered up the most senior in each category quickly followed by the squadron leader who chose the next most senior. The flying officer then approached us and said, "Would you two young'uns like to fly with me?" We looked at each other and could not believe our luck as this flying officer had two rows of medal ribbons including the DFC and AFM! His name was Tiff O'Connor and he was legendary. We later learned that his CV included 1,000 bomber raids, a record number of strikes against the Japanese, evacuating casualties from jungle clearings in a Tiger Moth biplane, a record number of hours on Mosquitos, A1 QFI, the list is endless. As a master pilot he could concentrate solely on flying, but eventually the pension differential persuaded him to accept a commission. Our air electronics operator (AEOp), Brian Matthews, unusually a sergeant, a likeable and efficient operator who fitted in well, also joined us. Tiff's co-pilot was Stan Job who he knew from Canberra days at Scampton.

Prior to the Valiant flying I did a sortie with the wing commander doing let-downs in a Canberra. I think he was checking me out. I found him to be calm and confident and also very approachable. We sailed through the course, only one incident sticks in my mind. I think it was on our third sortie that Tiff said "Hello?" followed shortly by "Put on parachutes". We cannot now recall what the problem was but obviously it was sorted. However thereafter, if he ever said hello, we all had kittens in the back.

I can't remember when it was that we realised we three crews were all destined for the same squadron with Wg Cdr Hubbard as the CO. Even hazier is when we were aware that this squadron was tasked to test Britain's H-Bomb. The newsreels of the time said that those taking part were all volunteers. I certainly know that no one ever gave me the option. I also know that if they had I would have volunteered like a shot! The squadron was 49 with the motto 'cave canem' (beware of the dog), with a proud history, notably flying Lancasters in the war. We duly arrived at RAF Wittering in September 1956. From the start it was obvious that in our boss we had a man who was a born leader; the squadron was his life. A bachelor, whose only constant companion was his dog

'Crusty', he managed to foster a team spirit in both aircrew and ground crew that I never saw the like of before or since. Everyone was made to feel important and his enthusiasm was infectious.

We settled into a training routine and were shortly joined by two crews returning from Australia where they had successfully tested the A-Bomb trigger device for the H-Bomb. Captain of the dropping aircraft was Squadron Leader Ted Flavell who became the flight commander of B Flight of which we were part. He was well known for being the captain of a Canberra whose radar bomb aimer set his coordinates for the Theddlethorpe bombing range off the Lincolnshire coast a whole unit out. Then with unerring accuracy he dropped a 25-lb practice bomb down the toilet bowl of the gents in The Prussian Queen pub a few miles from Louth. A customer who had chosen to relieve himself against an outside wall nearly did something more drastic! It cost the crew a considerable sum for repairs and a whole barrel of beer for the regulars and nothing more was said.

The main purpose of our training routine was to perfect the aiming technique required. The weapon was set to explode at 8,000 ft and over the sea to minimise damage and radiation from fall out. As the depth of the sea at the target was 3,600 ft it could not be moored. Thus a timed run from a land marker was made. Runs were made over the marker so that, by extension, the release point would be reached one-and-a-half miles later. The release button was pressed on the marker and the bomb fell after eleven seconds. Eventually practice made nearly perfect. We used this method at Orfordness, sometimes dropping 10,000 pounders to satisfy the powers that be of our accuracy. The Valiant provided a superbly stable bombing platform even at our operating height of 45,000 ft. It did occur to me that after the year-long NBS course the equipment was not even to be installed in our aircraft.

The main training problem for me was the dreaded dinghy drill. If for some reason we could not release the weapon, we were not to land but would fly over one of the navy ships on a predetermined track and bale out at 10,000 ft. The aircraft would fly on and automatically nose forward into the sea at a set position. To simulate this we were helicoptered to about a mile off Newquay beach and made to jump out from what seemed like a ridiculous height. This was no doubt great entertainment for the beach crowd but, being a non-swimmer, terrifying for me. I provided some merriment for the chopper crew as they reckoned I had the Mae West and dinghy inflated before I hit the water and came up like a cork sitting waiting to be rescued. I had to do it all again at Christmas Island – at least the water was warmer.

Over the next few months we did a lot of bombing sorties at the Wainfleet, Chesil Bank, and Jurby ranges as well as Orfordness. In April 1957 four crews left for Christmas Island; inevitably they were the most senior captains. The main task for the remaining crews was to ferry the actual weapons from the UK to the island. This had to be accomplished in under twenty-four hours. Reserve crews and aircraft were positioned en route at Goose Bay, California and Honolulu. The fitting of underwing tanks avoided the need to top up fuel in Northern Ireland prior to the Atlantic leg and also the intermediate stops in Canada or the USA. The weapon-carrying crews changed at these locations. Sometimes the stays were for several days and I vividly recall catching a Greyhound bus to San Francisco to hear such jazz 'greats' as Dave Brubeck, Muggsy Spanier, and Earl Hines all in one night. Eventually we did the final leg to the island. We were only there one day so did not fully experience it; this would come later. It is worth noting that during the whole exercise, which lasted seventeen months, we never had to change aircraft, underlining the extraordinary reliability of the Valiant.

As far as the tests were concerned the first three, which were off the uninhabited Malden Island, produced disappointing results. This obviously caused some embarrassment politically, and to the scientists, so the next test in November 1957 was actually not an H-Bomb but a massive A-Bomb, still the biggest of that type. Then, in April 1958 relief all round; the test worked to the tune of two megatons.

Then it was our turn. We took off from Wittering on 23 July 1958, arriving at the island four days later. It is the largest coral atoll in the world and is situated 1,000 miles south of Hawaii, just north of the Equator and close to the International Date Line. It is part of the Line Islands and is administered by the Gilbert (now Kiribati) Island Group some 1,000 miles to the west of the capital Tarawa. It is therefore splendidly isolated and ideal for the purpose. It had never been permanently settled, the porous coral making water capture and storage difficult. We lived in pairs in a huge tented area with the odd gerbil-like creature in the tent folds and marauding large land crabs for company. We had boards at the entrance to keep them out. One particularly large specimen decided an underground tunnel was needed so began to excavate a hole outside the entrance. When we flew we were given a large container of undrinkable black coffee, which we found an ideal use for by pouring it down the hole. The sight of this creature spluttering to the surface was hilarious and did put it off for good. Morning ablutions were primitive consisting of a line of about twenty seats, open to the elements, with a sort of outlet underneath. The worst scenario was to get between two old crusty army majors who would carry on a conversation across you as if it was the most natural thing in the world. Flies were a major problem and to combat them an Auster aircraft would spray everywhere with DDT twice weekly (we made sure there was no washing out on those days). However, despite all the inconveniences, with typical British stoicism and humour we still enjoyed ourselves. There was an outdoor cinema, I remember seeing the Sputnik crossing the sky, tennis was possible in the evening and there was some fifty yards of waist-deep water inshore of the reef full of marine life. The food was reasonable and the bar, though limited for choice, very welcome. If we felt really energetic we could always play the Fijian detachment at volleyball. This was futile as every one of them was a man mountain.

We started training quickly, first checking the bombsight as usual and then using the mission procedure at the target prepared. This target was only accessible by helicopter so when it was our turn to plot the impacts we enjoyed this method, especially when we saw a school of giant manta rays. Flush and I got to our respective positions and checked the radio between us, and then the aircraft. On the first run I put my lunchbox by my side and concentrated on the job in hand. Having plotted the impact and passed the result to the aircraft I looked down to witness a veritable army of hermit crabs marching off with my sandwiches.

We soon learned that a new system of bomb release was to be tested. This consisted of plotting the aircraft on the ground and feeding the required track into the ILS. The ground controller would do the countdown and all the bomb aimer had to do was to press the button at zero. This naturally did not please Pete Woolcock, the bomb aimer of the other crew, and I at all. What was the point of all that practice? Unfortunately the system proved to work remarkably well and each crew dropped 10,000-lb bombs by both methods.

The first test was of an atomic trigger suspended from a balloon. I met an old friend Robin Adams and scrounged a trip with him doing a sea search for unauthorised shipping in a Shackleton Mk 1. I have nothing but admiration for those crews, doing an endless square search, usually seeing nothing and yet keeping alert for fourteen noisy hours.

On 2 September 1958 came the first of the two H-Bomb tests. We took off first and then Squadron Leader Bill Bailey followed. As the grandstand crew Tiff positioned us slightly behind and to one side of him. The radar method of release was to be used. Everything seemed to go very smoothly and we pulled away shortly before release and saw the flash through chinks in our blackout shields, and felt the blast some time later. We learned that the test had been successful and the bombing error was an amazing ninety yards. Obviously this was hugely better than anything achieved previously.

Interestingly those results were never revealed.

And so, early on 11 September 1958, we climbed into XD827. After the air conditioning hose was removed it soon became very hot as usual. Just as dawn was breaking we took off from a deserted airfield. All personnel had been positioned at the furthest possible point on the island from the explosion, some twenty-eight miles away. As we were climbing away to our operating height of 45,000 ft the ground controller informed us that because of a failure of the radio link between them and the radar unit the drop would have to be made visually; as you can imagine I was delighted. We did a practice run to ensure that all systems and the bomb itself were functioning normally and finally Flush positioned

UK's last H-Bomb test. *(John Muston)*

me on track at around forty-five miles. I soon picked up the marker on the north of the island (as usual spot on) and very few small corrections had to be made. There was some cloud that occasionally obscured the markers but the final marker at the southern point soon appeared and after one more correction the final seconds were rock steady. I pressed the release button and after the delay saw the weapon fall away, big, black, shiny and falling normally. Tiff then turned through 135 degrees as tightly as possible in the rarefied air while I struggled from my prone position in the nose to my normal seat. Blackout shutters were positioned and we had just levelled out on to the escape heading at seven miles distance when we perceived the flash. The blast wave caught up with us with a large jolt at twenty-eight miles followed by a smaller one at thirty-five miles from the blast reflection off the sea. Eventually we turned around and it was an awesome sight; already the top of the mushroom cloud was higher than us. We felt that it had all gone well and we duly let down and landed. The task force commander held a reception for us where we made full use of the refreshment provided. We later learned that our error was 260 yards. As this is the only visual error ever published and as Wg Cdr Hubbard was heard to say that "the more you practise the better you get", we thus assumed that ours was by far the best. Tiff was awarded the AFC and I the C-in-C's commendation for our efforts. Years later I saw a DVD made by AWRE that showed our run on the ground radar with our tracking identical to theirs.

John Muston receiving the C-in-C's commendation from the Wittering station commander Group Captain Alan Boxer. *(John Muston)*

One week later we were on our way home. Flush and I used to alternate the navigation on overseas trips so that I could keep my hand in. The only thing I recall from the journey is the final leg from Goose Bay. I have never been so cold and it was not until we reached our cruising height that I could write. To our great surprise, when we arrived at Wittering we found that – and this is typical of the man – the squadron commander had arranged for our families to be there to meet us as we taxied into dispersal.

Not long after, we learned that all tests in the atmosphere were to cease under the new Test Ban Treaty. Our aircraft would be fitted with NBS and we were to revert to the normal V Force role. A quick refresher course brought us up to speed on the equipment. There was much sadness in the whole squadron that our unique identity would be lost. To try to prolong the camaraderie that we enjoyed, Wg Cdr Hubbard suggested we form a club to be called 'The Megaton Club'. We all enthusiastically agreed. It is a measure of the team spirit we had that it survives to this day. This is largely due to our corporals, particularly of B Flight and especially Fred Venning. These remarkable men all seem to be still alive and never appear to get any older. Being of a certain age we have had several 'final' reunions and are optimistically planning another one.

Things were never quite the same in the period that followed. There was a new commander, of proven skill in the standard V Force role but who did not engender the enthusiasm of his predecessor. Things like cocktail parties and interaction with the ground crew went by the board, and it was as if the previous two years were to be forgotten.

At about this time we had a change of co-pilot. Stan went off to play with bigger toys in the shape of Thor missiles. In his place came John Ford; young, handsome and with a sports car. Not content with this he was a good pilot and we enjoyed having him in our team. Flying largely consisted of simulated NBS attacks and long-range sorties using only astro-navigation. The standard required was testing with no error more than three miles and one minute at the start of the bombing run after four hours. In time we achieved the select crew rating. In the first year there was a two-week detachment to Malta where Flush took over the visual bombing at the El Adem range in Libya. We also had an enjoyable lone ranger to Nairobi, made particularly so as the brother of our crew chief Colin Mather owned a coffee plantation not far away. He and his Kenyan staff treated us handsomely and provided a unique experience for us all. I flew with another crew to Bahrain and on the return journey we night-stopped at El Adem. That evening only the crew chief Bill Caple and I were in the bar when we were informed of a fuel leak from our aircraft. It transpired that a tank change was needed which Bill did with limited support from me. This took all night and, having signalled for a replacement, we advised the captain in the morning. The following night we fitted the new tank, finishing again in the morning. At no time did anyone come to see how we were doing or commend us for our efforts. This would never have happened in the old days.

In the autumn of 1959 the squadron was chosen to do flying displays for the Queensland centenary celebrations in Australia. Four crews were selected with us as reserve.

Tiff never complained, but as squadron QFI I would have been a bit peeved. We all flew out via Cyprus, Karachi and Sri Lanka to RAAF Butterworth on the Malaysia/Thailand border (conveniently only a short ferry ride to Penang). One amusing incident was when the nav leader miscalculated the time of dawn at Karachi by an hour, which resulted in an embarrassing wait: Valiants could not use paraffin-lit runways. After this we spent over twenty hours in a Hastings transport to RAAF Amberley, near Brisbane, via Singapore, Brunei and Darwin. At least we now appreciated the vastness of Australia and how little there is in the middle. A surprise reception was laid on for us at Government House, which we really appreciated. Our services were not called upon and I must admit the displays were impressive. We followed the team in a Comet 4 to RAAF East Sale, Adelaide, Perth and Darwin and then back to Butterworth. Then came a great experience. We travelled by train to Singapore, changing at Kuala Lumpur, a journey now much publicised and expensive, but then quite primitive. We were given a primus stove to cook on and the carriages were pretty spartan. However it was a wonderful way to see the country, often on a single track and sometimes going right through the middle of small villages. At Singapore we were flown back to the UK courtesy of a British Airways Britannia.

In 1960 the main item of interest was a lone ranger to Salisbury (now Harare) taking in the Victoria Falls on the way. In those days it was a delightful city which makes it all the more sad to see it now. There was also a two-week detachment to Cyprus, a place recovering from very turbulent times but still such an interesting island to explore. Lots of sorties in this year were instrument ratings and a training, inevitable, Tiff being the squadron QFI, but not too exciting for us in the back.

It came to an end for me in March when Tiff and I were both posted. I had completed four-and-a-half trouble-free years with a total of almost 1,500 hours flying with the best pilot ever and an outstanding crew in Flush and Brian in the most reliable aircraft, the Valiant. Who could ask for more?

I enjoyed my final four years in the RAF, instructing at the bombing school at Lindholme and Ops at HQ 1 Group at Bawtry, especially the former, but did not apply for an extension as I felt the best days were over. Ten years in computers and eighteen in golf were adequate compensation.

In 2011 Flush and I went back to Christmas Island, now called Kiritimati and also now on the other side of the International Date Line. From being largely uninhabited it is now home to some 7,000 people of whom 2,000 are children. We were part of a small group there to distribute money raised from several sources to the schools. We were treated to singing and traditional dancing at every one and all the children looked very fit and happy with a refreshingly lively attitude.

The only recognisable things from our time were the ruins of the church and squash court. The officers' mess is now the dining room of the Captain Cook hotel. The huge tented area is a palm tree plantation and the southern part of the island which, when

The crew photo was taken at our reunion on the 40th anniversary of our drop of 11 September 1958. From left to right: John Muston, nav radar and bomb aimer; Brian Matthews, air electronics operator; John Conning, nav plotter; Tiff O'Connor – captain on haunches and Stan Job, co-pilot. *(John Muston)*

we left was totally bare, is now covered in vegetation. Eighteen million birds spend all or part of the year there and the lagoons provide large catches for the sport fishermen, mostly from the US. We stayed a week – the Honolulu-Fiji flight calls there every Wednesday. We were very reassured that, despite our best efforts, nature has a wonderful capability of restoring things back to normal.

On the day John dropped the bomb apparently there was a slight complication which presumably he didn't remember. Malcolm Winterburn was an electrician doing his National Service. He says that when the aircraft was taxiing out the main aircraft fuse blew and it had to return; understandably he said it was a nerve-racking experience having to travel the full length of a hydrogen bomb to replace the fuse.

CHAPTER 4

VALIANT
TANKING
John Roberts

John Roberts joined the RAF in June 1952 having been called up for National Service. However, he agreed to serve four years subject to passing aircrew selection. His four years extended a bit and he left the service in May 1964. He soon realised there were few opportunities to continue a career as a navigator. So later in 1964 he joined an international company on a retail management course and remained with them for the next thirty years, latterly in senior management, before retiring in 1994.

I started my air force career by going to the aircrew selection centre at Hornchurch where I was told that I would be a useless pilot but a good navigator. A period of basic training at Cranwell was followed by a posting to 3 Air Navigation School (ANS) Bishop's Court in Northern Ireland in November 1952. The course lasted ten months and consisted of twenty pupils all of whom made the grade apart from three. The final training flight before the passing out parade was a trip to Idris, about twenty miles south of Tripoli in Libya.

The following six months were spent at Cranwell and Kirton in Lindsey waiting for a posting to a bomber squadron. The vast majority of navigators were going to Bomber Command as it was re-equipping with Canberras. Most of us had asked for Transport Command but that understandably seemed to be reserved for navigators with more experience. After attending a bombing and conversion course I eventually joined 21 Squadron at RAF Scampton in September 1954 aged twenty. Our crew Sgt Tom Johnstone and nav plotter Dave Schofield were both married, and as ex-apprentices were worldly-wise in the workings of the RAF. To all in Bomber Command RAF Scampton had a special significance having been the home of 617 Squadron, the Dambusters.

The next two years were particularly happy, as life on a Canberra squadron was relaxed with the majority of crews in their early twenties. Although most of us did not own a car and had not even passed a driving test, an active mess life made up for any shortcoming or restrictions.

Another experience for most of us was the chance to travel abroad. The lone ranger was designed to allow crews to become acquainted with operating overseas without close support from their home base. In our case we went as far as Habbaniya (close to

Baghdad) via Idris, Abu Sueir and Bahrain; on the way home we even included Gibraltar. Towards the end of my time on Canberras we were suddenly told to gain experience of visual bombing from 40,000 ft, the normal being 20,000 ft. As usual no explanation was given but numerous rumours soon spread around the squadron. The bomb sight we used was essentially the same as that used in the Second World War but modified to cope with the higher speed of the Canberra. The results were spectacular but not what was envisaged. The target on the bombing range looked very small and instead of getting within hundreds of yards we were happy to keep the bombs within the range boundary. The combination of bomb sight, together with the ballistics of the 25-lb practice bomb being dropped from such a height, probably accounted for such inaccuracy. Although accuracy did improve it never reached acceptable levels. All was revealed some two months later when the Suez Crisis started. However, I had been posted to Gaydon so missed out.

I was posted to No. 232 OCU at Gaydon as training wing adjutant towards the end of October 1956 and spent the next two years there, and much to my surprise I enjoyed it. My main job was to organise the training programme for pilots, navigators and AEOs converting onto the Valiant, the first of the V bombers. A new course arrived approximately every two months and once I had gained experience with the programme, which tended to repeat itself, and got to know the instructors I had quite a lot of spare time. The instructors were quite happy for me to attend their lectures so I completed the navigators course but didn't take the exams.

My stay at Gaydon gave me a wider appreciation and insight into the running of the station. Squadron life was quite insular, particularly as a twenty-year-old navigator. As my two years were coming to an end, Wing Commander R Best, head of Ground Training suggested I might like to go on the NBS course so in October 1958 I moved to RAF Lindholme.

The sole purpose of this ten-month course was to teach you how to operate the bombing system which was standard in all three V bombers. It was also a navigation system but would have limited use in wartime as it would have exposed the aircraft's position. The other reason the course was so long was the need for the nav radar to be able to identify any system faults and still be able to complete the bombing mission. There were only three of us on the course and by coincidence one of them, Dave Schofield and I had been on the same Canberra crew; with only three of us it must have added to the overall cost of training. The nav radar was reckoned to be the most expensive crew member of a V bomber, quoted as £150,000, quite a lot of money at that time. In June, the next year, it was back to Gaydon to join up with the rest of our new Valiant crew. I had to complete the course despite having done it earlier, but I could relax, especially as the final examination had not changed and I had not forgotten the questions. I suppose the instructors thought it was not worth the effort to set new questions. Alan Fisher was the captain and he was already experienced having been

NO. 47 VALIANT COURSE

SGT BENNET   FLT LT HAYDEN   PLT OFF RUTHERFORD   F/SGT WALLACE
FLT LT ROBINSON   FLT LT FISHER   FLT LT ROBERTS

co-pilot to the 214 Squadron commander, Wg Cdr M Beetham. The co-pilot was Pat Skinner, nav plotter Chris Hayden who had completed a tour in Coastal Command and Fred Bennet the air electronics operator (AEOp). Unlike the rest of us Fred was non-commissioned.

On 16 November 1959 we all arrived at RAF Marham the base for 214 Squadron, motto 'Ulter in umbris' ('Avenging in the shadows') with the emblem of a nightjar, a bird which is active at night. Our introduction to the squadron was eased as Alan knew all the other crews. Training in the following few months was rapid due to Alan's experience and the fact that Chris and myself had completed previous tours as navigators. Also, I had flown in the Valiant during my time as training wing adjutant at Gaydon. Chris and myself both had experience and confidence in astro navigation which was still being regularly used in the V bombers in the 1950s. At this time 214 Squadron was still a normal bomber squadron, but had been converted to tankers and was trialling air-to-air refuelling. This meant we still had wartime targets and had to practise accordingly, but were not involved in QRA.

A typical sortie was a cross-country exercise of four hours or more culminating in a bombing run on a coastal range to drop a 25-lb practice bomb, or a non-range target, when the aircraft was tracked by radar and a radio signal indicated bomb release. In the case of a non-range target this was generally at about 40,000 ft and an accuracy of 400 yards was achievable, the results being passed back to base for analysis.

The daily routine was similar to the one I had experienced on a Canberra squadron. Briefing at 8am covered the current met report, the day's flying programme and any other information from the flight commanders. The one thing I did notice was navigators had more work to do on a V bomber than on a Canberra. The nav radar had target preparation; this involved studying the layout of a non-range target and making an overlay which would be the same as that viewed on the NBS equipment. This was eased as the NBS had the facility to introduce offset distances, and so aim at an easily identifiable point on the radar screen and yet still bomb the target. All this became routine with experience and with experience came confidence. Astro navigation, which I mentioned was still being widely used, was usually pre-computed before take-off and so reduced the work load once airborne, the aim being to fix your position every twenty minutes. This worked very well so long as the planned take-off time was achieved. Finally, study of war targets was a constant priority.

At the same time trials 306 and 306a/b were being conducted. Trial 306 was to assess the aircraft as tanker and receiver and 306a/b were rendezvous procedures and techniques. These trials had commenced in March 1958 and went on until May 1960. Prior to this there had been considerable debate within the Air Ministry as to the value of in-flight refuelling. In December 1957 Air Marshal E C Hudleston had written to the ministry stating "air-to-air refuelling would be essential for V Force tactical freedom and the deployment of reinforcements of Fighter Command overseas". The arguments within the Air Ministry concerned the additional cost of tankers and the reluctance of Bomber Command to the conversion of any V Force Valiants. When the final decision was taken sixteen Valiants were converted by April 1959. The US Air Force had approximately 1,600 tankers as the B-52 bombers could not reach their targets without refuelling. The initial view of many 214 Squadron personnel towards becoming a tanker squadron was 'gloomy and unpopular'. This view was also held by Wg Cdr Beetham.

The method of refuelling adopted was called probe and drogue. The Valiant was modified to include the equipment necessary to perform refuelling, a control panel alongside, and controlled by the nav radar, a hose drum unit (HDU), an additional fuel tank at the front of the bomb bay containing an extra 4,500 lb of fuel and also a water-methanol system which would provide extra engine thrust when operating on shorter runways and higher outside air temperatures, which often occurred overseas. The Mark 16 HDU was fitted at the rear of the bomb bay and the drogue trailed to a length of ninety feet behind the aircraft when refuelling. The refuelling was controlled by lights. An amber light meant the refuelling could commence, green that fuel was flowing and red that contact must be terminated. The lights would also allow refuelling to be undertaken in radio silence. The single hose had its drawbacks as this meant that only one aircraft at a time could be refuelled and required the aircraft being refuelled to make contact with the drogue. Once the drogue had been pushed a distance back into the tanker refuelling could begin. 45,000 lb of fuel could be transferred at a rate of 4,000 lb per minute. Disaster could result if the aircraft being refuelled made a poor attempt at contact and the end of its refuelling probe broke off and remained in the drogue.

All squadron pilots were trained in the role of tanker and receiver. This proved vital as eleven Victor tankers were needed to refuel the Vulcan when it bombed Stanley in the Falkland Islands. Training had originally taken place at Tarrant Rushton, the head-quarters of Flight Refuelling Limited, a company set up by Sir Alan Cobham in 1934, but now a school had been set up at Marham. Like all things in life some pilots were better than others. Night-time refuelling was much harder. The experience was like driving a car up a motorway, at times you catch up with the car in front rather quicker than expected and have to apply the brake. In an aircraft the only option is to throttle back and descend under the tanker and wait for it to overtake you and then try again. The warning horn indicating the throttles had been closed too far woke up many a rear crew member! We were lucky as Alan was an exceptional pilot. When AVM Dwyer visited the squadron in June 1960 our crew were selected to take him on a flight refu-elling sortie. We were sorry when Alan left us in January 1962 but pleased as he went on to complete the Empire Test Pilot's Course.

In 1959 as part of the trials a number of long distance overseas flights were com-pleted. Apart from proving the capabilities and advantages of inflight refuelling it gave experience to both aircrew and ground crew. In the early stages a ground crew was dispatched, and this continued for major exercises, but from 1960 if the exercise only involved a single aircraft the tanker crew had to be capable of looking after their own servicing. A crew chief, normally a flight sergeant who was a qualified engine and airframe tradesman, accompanied the crew. I feel the crew chiefs never really got the praise they were entitled to. I will relate later how they solved a problem we encountered.

The following is a list of some long distance and in many cases record-breaking flights:

Marham	Nairobi	7 hrs	40 mins	4,350 miles
	Salisbury	9 hrs	42 mins	5,320 miles
	Johannesburg	11 hrs	3 mins	5,845 miles
	Cape Town	11 hrs	28 mins	6,060 miles

Further flights were completed in 1960 to Offutt, Changi, Vancouver and Butter-worth. Wg Cdr Beetham and his crew were naturally involved in many of these flights. However, the longest flight was a round UK trip of 7,440 miles in 18 hours and 5 minutes by Sqn Ldr J Garstin and crew. Apart from the experience and record-breaking aspect of these flights a considerable amount of favourable press exposure resulted for both the squadron and RAF.

June 1960 saw several changes to 214. Wg Cdr Beetham was posted to No. 3 Group, Mildenhall and replaced by Wg Cdr P Hill as squadron commander. As the two trials 306 and 306a/b came to an end the Air Ministry decided that the Javelin, Vulcan, Victor, Lightning plus Royal Navy Sea Vixen and Scimitar aircraft should be modified so that

214 Squadron Valiant staging through Gan refuelling Javelins. *(John Roberts)*

they could be air-to-air refuelled. Wg Cdr Beetham had successfully seen the trials completed and now Wg Cdr Hill had to continue by introducing air-to-air refuelling to other parts of the RAF. For the squadron this meant a change in emphasis, now we would have to respond to the demands of other squadrons.

In June 1960, 23 Squadron flying the Javelin was the first fighter squadron to be trained in air-to-air refuelling. The pilots seemed to have few problems, and this was probably due to their skill in formation flying and the greater agility of the aircraft. The real test came in August 1960 when Javelins were refuelled to Akrotiri, Cyprus, and a greater test in October when four Javelins were refuelled to Butterworth and return. This involved staging through Akrotiri, Bahrain, Mauripur (Karachi) and Gan. Due to the Javelins not having the necessary navigation equipment they had to fly in formation with the tanker. We had previously carried out some four-hour cross-country exercises to acclimatise the Javelin pilots to longer flights. Our crew, with captain Flt Lt Alan Fisher, were involved and my logbook shows this exercise took from 1-23 October and involved 44 hr and 35 min of flying time. Maybe flying in a tanker was not so 'gloomy'!

Soon after this air-to-air refuelling training started with the Lightnings. They also had no navigation equipment and would, like the Javelins, have to fly in loose formation with the tanker when in transit. Their pilots also didn't experience any problems, but doubt had been expressed as to the feasibility of refuelling due to the difference in the speed of the two aircraft. This proved unfounded. In October 1962 Lightnings were refuelled to Luqa. On this deployment we were 'bounced' by two French air force Mystères over central France. After the 'second go' the lead Lightning pilot had obviously had enough and asked if we could refuel him again if necessary. On the answer 'yes' when the Mystères came round again he 'put on the power' and overtook them. That was the last we saw of them! The deployment planning for both the Javelins and the Lightnings had to be very precise. With a range of approximately 1,000 miles the need to ensure a diversion airfield was within reach was a constant priority – account had to be taken in case refuelling failed. Talking to USAF fighter pilots who had just crossed the Atlantic into Spain from the east coast of America, regarding what happened if they missed a refuelling, the answer was the US Navy had vessels below the 'refuelling bracket' and they would have to ditch and hope to be picked up. Their perception of risk for both pilots and aircraft was different to ours.

The main priority for refuelling training came from the Vulcans. The increase in Russian air defences meant that the V Force might no longer be able to take a direct route to a target. The first dry contact had been made by Flt Lt W S Green, 101 Squadron, Finningley, in XA910, on 29 October 1959. Following the final report of trials 306/306a/b this training accelerated and was to lead to a Vulcan of 617 Squadron flying non-stop to Sydney, Australia in 20 hours and 3 minutes, a distance of 11,500 miles at an average speed of 573 mph. This took place on 20/21 June 1961 and involved nine tankers. We did the first refuelling at Akrotiri and further refuellings took place at Karachi and Singapore. For the crew, captain Sqn Ldr M Beavis, this was the culmination of what must have been both a tiring but exciting period of training.

The demand for air-to-air refuelling was increasing and 90 Squadron at Honington started tanker training in August 1961, and by October they were operational. In April 1962 both 214 and 90 Squadrons ceased to be bomber squadrons. The change from a bomber to a tanker squadron meant navigation priorities also changed. Time was still important when making a rendezvous with Vulcans and Victors but did not apply with fighters. Once we had met up, close to our home bases, we then flew together in open formation. When in transit to an overseas station time was generally irrelevant. Having spent nearly a year on the NBS course much of my training was no longer required, as the NBS became solely a navigation aid. We did, however, pay more attention to astro-navigation. The maps of areas such as the Sahara Desert were still blank and annotated 'area un-surveyed'. Also we frequently had long transit routes over the Indian Ocean. For the pilots life was made a little easier as the auto pilot could be connected to the NBS system and the aircraft effectively flown by the navigators. However, they did have the added pressure of landing at unfamiliar airfields. Many airfields did not have the instrument landing system, the main landing system at that time. As a replacement we used the NBS and with practice, and crew confidence, it proved to be very accurate. Other changes for tanker crews was the amount of time spent overseas. Generally, in transit, we flew consecutive days until we reached our destination. Occasionally we had two days or more before starting the return flight to Marham. Such places as Akrotiri and Butterworth were especially pleasant. Gan was like a modern-day holiday in the Maldives and certainly better than QRA.

Exercise Chamfrom in 1963, which was the deployment of Victors to Tengah, and later Butterworth, also required considerable tanker involvement. At the peak eight Victors were detached overseas. The need for this was due to the increased tensions between the newly independent Malaya and the Philippines. A typical entry in my logbook shows us being refuelled by another 214 Squadron aircraft to Khormaksar, Aden, in 9 hours and 30 minutes on 29 June and then continuing to Gan the following day. Four days later we refuelled a Victor on its way to Butterworth, and after a further five days, a Vulcan of 101 Squadron, captain Wg Cdr Griffith and crew. This was on Exercise Walkabout and flew non-stop Waddington-Perth in 18 hours and 7 minutes. As an interesting aside, when this crew returned to Waddington someone decided that they should be tested for in-flight fatigue so they had to endure a further refuelling and ended up flying for more than 22 hours. We returned to Marham on 13 July via Khormaksar and El Adem having completed 34 flying hours. Ten days later we refuelled Javelins to Luqa, Malta and return. This exercise was of particular interest as the outward flight was at night. By now the demands from other squadrons for routine training and overseas deployments meant that tankers were busier than ever, and the limitations of the Valiant as a tanker must have now become more apparent. A comparatively limited amount of fuel that could be transferred and the single probe and drogue system had drawbacks. One of the major ones being the possibility of a malfunction which meant tankers often had to be duplicated.

Early in 1963 Wg Cdr K Smith became the new squadron commander, and Wg Cdr Hill moved to Gan as station commander.

Despite the squadron being busy there was still time for the old-fashioned lone ranger and this came to our crew with a vengeance in November 1963. The route was refuelled through to Nairobi and the single legs to Gan, Butterworth, Calcutta, Bombay, Bahrain, Akrotiri and back to Marham, all in two weeks. Flt Lt Jim Fulford was now our captain and he had joined us when Alan had started the Empire Test Pilot's Course in January 1962. We also had a new co-pilot, and once again he had settled down quickly and so we were a select crew. I cannot remember why we were selected for this trip and I don't suppose we questioned the decision. However, our euphoria was short lived. The station commander Gp Capt I R Campbell decided he would like to join us which meant the co-pilot would be excluded.

This caused a problem for us. Although communications between crew members was supposed to be formal – nav to pilot etc. – in practice, as it was obvious who was giving the instruction and who was receiving it, this was often ignored. Also, after years together we all recognised each others' voices. After much discussion we decided we would carry on as normal, except when we were talking to the group captain. We thought he must be aware many crews did not take the formal approach. In the end this worked out very well, or else he decided to be lenient with us. Maybe he also had a guilty conscience as wherever we landed we were met by the local station commander and that was the last we saw of him until the next morning. He did apologise to us as we were left to re-fuel the aircraft and do the general servicing. On all such occasions we had a crew chief who was the 'expert' and the rest of us did whatever he asked. We had an unwritten rule that no one would leave the aircraft until everything had been completed. In the morning the crew chief would generally be the first crew member to arrive at the aircraft as the rest of the crew had to get a met report and file flight plans.

The trip was proving to be an unforgettable experience, especially in India, and even more so when we got to Bahrain. Even in November it was hot, and just after take-off we were enjoying the cool air from the ventilation system, when a loud rushing noise came through the intercom and the aircraft started to over-pressurise. At 1,000 ft we were minus 3,000 ft in the cabin and it was very hot, later we found chinagraph pencils had melted and were just a hollow tube. A shout from Jim "emergency depressurise" soon brought the reply from me, the nav radar, "it's not working" followed by a further instruction from Jim "stand by to bale out". One quick circuit and we landed; my logbook records the trip as 10 minutes. An inspection of the aircraft found no fault in the pressurisation system, other than 'flood flow' must have been selected. Flood flow feeds air into the cabin in an attempt to maintain pressurisation if the aircraft has been hit by enemy fire and the cabin punctured. As we found out it is quite violent if the cabin has not been punctured. The next day we took off again, albeit a bit apprehensively, but everything was all right. The final report came back to the station commander Gp Capt Campbell, and he wrote with a sense of humour, "whilst this is the only logical explanation, I emphatically deny doing it". The switch to select flood flow being on the co-pilot's side of the aircraft!

Another activity the squadron got involved in was demonstrating air-to-air refuelling, particularly at Battle of Britain air shows. Sqn Ldr J Garstin, considered one of the most competent tanker pilots, was frequently involved. The tanker and the receiving aircraft had to hook-up prior to the fly-past as there was no guarantee that this would be achieved during the short time taken to over-fly the airfield.

I mentioned earlier the value of the crew chief and how in my opinion they were under-valued by many people. I will give an example. We had taken off from Butterworth and the undercarriage would not retract. After dumping fuel and flying around for a while we re-landed at Butterworth and then had to carry out a retraction test on the undercarriage. The only person with the required knowledge was the crew chief, the rest of us acted on his instructions mainly pumping-up the hydraulic jacks. The co-pilot was given the task of pressing the undercarriage button while the rest of us looked on. I am sure the crew chief was not worried but the rest of us had our fingers crossed. The sight of an aircraft the size of a Valiant being held up by the jacks was not something we saw too often.

My time in the RAF was rapidly coming to an end as I was only on a short service commission so 5 June 1964 was my final day. I was sorry to leave as twelve years in the RAF had been a tremendous experience and was to stand me in good stead for the rest of my working life.

CHAPTER 5

AN EXTROVERT PILOT

Tony Yule

Tony Yule spent his working life as a pilot, starting in the RAF with the Valiant and then going on to the VC10. After leaving the service he joined British Airways flying the Concorde followed by time with Air Europe, Ansett and Air Holland. Obviously an ideal member of any crew, socially as well as operationally.

My pilot training was completed initially at No. 2 FTS (Flying Training School) at RAF Syerston, Nottingham, on the Hunting Percival Provost, affectionately known as 'The Piston Provost'. My advanced flying was at No. 8 FTS, RAF Swinderby, Lincolnshire on the iconic de Havilland Vampire T11. The course was commenced on 13 March 1960, successfully completed on 17 November in the same year and I was posted immediately to No. 232 OCU at RAF Gaydon in Warwickshire, to start the conversion onto the Valiant BK1.

After three months the squadron moved to RAF Marham, Norfolk. The adjutant was away and I was assigned the role in his absence. In essence, the job was to keep the Form 540 (squadron history) fully up to date and carry out any incidental jobs as required by the boss.

During one idle afternoon, I decided to take a 'peek' in the large gunmetal grey filing cabinet. When I got to the bottom drawer I saw a list of tags with names on. I realised then that these were the files of all the squadron personnel so I decided to see my own file. Not the best move one can ever make. I certainly don't recommend anyone ever doing so, especially to look at your grading/assessment section.

Presentation of my Wings by General C Grover USAF – 18 November 1960. *(Tony Yule)*

We all know that A is excellent, B is above average, C is a pass, D is a dunce, but an E! What the hell is an E? It took almost fifty years before I learnt why I and others were tagged as such. Well, the E was for education. It seems from the qualities required, the only thing we lacked were the stated educational qualifications for entry into the RAF.

I learnt that during our initial officer training there would be educational tests and if we failed those – then basically we would have been chopped and a future military career over forever. Someone was watching over me as I scraped through those tests.

When I had been at 232 OCU at RAF Gaydon I had joined a crew of Eddie Edwards – captain, Brian Taylor – nav radar, Fergie Hunter – nav plotter and Phil Crawley – signaller.

I should point out that Bomber Command was not my first choice. In fact, the only thing I wanted to fly was the Hunter. My disappointment soon went away when I discovered RAF life at aged twenty and that I had joined a brilliant crew. We were to fly together until I gained my captaincy some three years later. Truth is, I remember very little of my time on the OCU or indeed my first three months on 49 Squadron, based at RAF Wittering.

One should remember that coming from a small private boarding school I had precious little knowledge of the real world. It became a simple matter of keeping a very low profile and learning the correct behaviour/etiquette from those already established in their careers. The most lasting point from the Wittering days was, in fact, on my very first night when I came down from my room in the officers' mess to go to the bar, which meant walking along the corridor and passing the main entrance of the mess. I was quickly aware of a small crowd of officers, standing there, all looking to the entrance.

As I entered the area the door burst open and a young man rushed in, cheeks full, a large hanky in his left hand and a lighter in his right! The next moment, this officer who I can see today in my mind, but no name comes to me, blew a mouthful of, as it turned out, lighter fluid in the direction of those other officers, set the spray alight and became an instant flame thrower.

Now, having run out puff, he covered his mouth and face with the aforesaid hanky, which promptly burst into flames. Having forgotten or not noticed that it had become saturated with lighter fluid this caused some bad burns to his face and left hand. Of course all were cheering him on and when the seriousness of the situation became apparent, he was doused with water from the various flower vases in the area. Once again he was banned from the mess.

I later learnt that this was a regular item in his repertoire and that this was his first return to the mess, having been banned by the president of the mess committee (PMC) some weeks before, for having done the very same trick. Some intro to mess life for me!

The squadron was already preparing for the move, in June, to RAF Marham, affectionately known as 'El Adem with grass' and the crew joined in to help. In this time, we flew a limited number of details until on 27 June, we took XD857 to our new base, where

I was to stay until the summer of 1965. For me, life was just perfect. Single, loving flying, enjoying the mess and squadron social life, nothing could have been finer.

At this moment I should point out that I had not thought about a career in the RAF, I intended going to 'civvy street aviation' at the completion of my twelve-year contract, therefore had not considered things like, secondary duties, a must have, if one intended such a future in the RAF. I was therefore very surprised in the autumn of 1961, standing by the fireplace in the ante room with a plate of sandwiches in my left hand, cup and saucer in my right, when I noticed from the far end of the room, my flight commander, Sqn Ldr John Cheesbrough and the PMC, Wg Cdr John Langston, bearing down on me at high speed; there were no niceties, just a demand from the PMC, "Ah Yule, do you have a secondary duty?" "No Sirs" was my response. "Well you do now," said the PMC, "You're the bar officer from now on". I soon learnt that it involved me ensuring the smooth running of the bar, having adequate stock for all the functions in the mess, the monthly stocktaking and balancing of the books. Not a difficult task you might think but this bar was not run by qualified airmen from the base, but by two professional barmen, Jack and John, who knew the bar business inside out and ran rings round me in the first year of a two-year duty. However, these two likeable rogues made life very easy for me, so the books were always passed by the accounts committee.

During my first year as bar officer I became friends with the entertainments officer, who really hated his secondary duty. We shared the same office, became well acquainted such that I offered, for some unknown reason, to help him in the running of the mess entertainments. We liaised on the alcohol required and I watched and learnt how he organised the professional entertainers for each of the functions both big and small, through a dedicated entertainment agency, of whom I was to become very well acquainted a little later. This choice of helping him would become a big part of my future life in the RAF and outside the service, when I joined BOAC, the forerunner of British Airways.

I really took to the entertainment side of life and after I had completed a year of my duty, I approached the PMC and asked if I could take over his duty. The PMC's attitude was 'better one volunteer than ten pressed men' so I assumed the mantle of entertainments officer, which I took on at each RAF station and squadron where I could until I left the service.

The reader may remember in the Sixties, that gingham table covers and Chianti bottles, dripping with old wax, were 'de rigueur' in restaurants everywhere. I thus introduced them, holding a monthly Saturday steak night, in the smaller ante room adjacent to and what was to become, the old bar once the new bar was operational.

I was aware that the monthly functions were not always well supported and wondered why, since they were widely promoted in the officers' mess function sheet. It took a while to discover this lack of attendance was due to the wives who came with their husbands to the bar on Saturday nights being unaware of them.

I decided to write directly to the ladies of mess members, with a detailed programme of events. Slowly but surely, more and more people attended and the support for the functions became self-financing. One of the fun nights which surprised everyone, was a black tie dinner dance night. Normally dinner would be in the main dining room but I had encountered a local chippie who made the rounds of the married quarters each week. He sold cod, cut into three pieces, which I thought were a little small. I asked him if he would cut the cod into two bigger pieces, we agreed a price, a date and time to appear at the mess, on the agreed Saturday night, with his van backed up to one of the dining room windows, which were already closed and curtained, ready to serve fish and chips from his van to unsuspecting members and their guests.

When dinner was announced, the members entered the dining room to find bare tables except for bottles of ketchup, brown sauce, salt 'n' pepper and nothing else except to sit down at table for a short wait. Then to their complete surprise, one large curtain was drawn back to expose the chippie at the now open window. The members and guests were asked to queue at a window to collect their dinner in classic chip shop newspapers. I was told that this function was very well received.

That really sums up the social life that I was heavily involved with. The entertainment agency were brilliant with the money I had available from the large number of members who attended these functions and the agency provided me with a stream of top quality entertainers. I do thank the former entertainments member for showing me the ropes.

One could be forgiven for thinking that my life revolved around the social scene but, oh yes, I had a job to do! In fact, my role as a co-pilot with the crew turned to be a very rewarding one. I just loved the life. I became interested in the navigation plotting side of our trips and would watch keenly as Fergy Hunter planned each of the details we flew. Later, I would plan routes and occasionally Fergy would use one of the plots I had produced. That was a good feeling for me. Eddie Edwards was a great captain and I learnt so much from his relaxed approach to handling his crew. It would stand me in very good stead later when I too became a captain.

Squadron life changed somewhat and it seemed morale dropped too. I noticed it on the expressions of the faces of the more experienced crew members, but I could not fathom why. One problem area was the flight simulator. The training pilots were not so much instructors, more destructors, pushing the trainees in the simulator sessions to such a level, that you nearly always crashed at the end of the detail or were so heavily criticised, that you felt a complete failure.

One Canadian exchange pilot, John Jones, the day I was his co-pilot in the simulator, ended up on his training detail, having been pushed into a corner where the level of failures he had been subjected to, were so unreal that we eventually crash landed about two miles from touchdown! He was so angry, got out of his seat, turned to the instructor and said, "If this is the way you treat your f*****g pilots, then I'm taking the bus home" and stormed out of the simulator. Needless to say, there was an investigation and after much recrimination, a new training regime was instigated and life became better when we went for training in the simulator.

Morale was still not that good when the new boss arrived to take over the squadron. He picked up on the morale issue. As he was a wise man, he soon had a plan to make a distraction in order to raise morale. He became the tough boss at the weekly meetings in the crew room. The way he ran things, seemingly decisions were made without discussion! Sqn Ldr John Cheesbrough, the senior flight commander, jumped in and spoke up on a number of occasions, countering some of the boss's comments, in an attempt to make better changes for us all. We saw the boss relent on a number of occasions, accepting his flight commander's voice. We were happy to see we had a 'champion' in our midst which did the trick and morale improved. It was much later, when some of us learnt that it had been a deliberate plan by both leaders, to change the status quo. A good double act!

In the crew room of every squadron, there was a coffee bar designed by the squadron members. It seemed to us that as each new boss arrived, he wanted a different bar from the one that was liked by the previous boss. We duly rebuilt our coffee bar. On the counter of the bar, there was a frame with a piece of paper inside and on that list, were the names of those members who had not paid their coffee bar dues by the end of the month.

Life on the squadron was more or less a routine of flying navigation exercises ending up with a high level bomb run on the various dedicated ranges around the UK. These runs were simulated, no actual bombs were dropped. Once we arrived back in the circuit, it was the pilots' playtime in that we flew circuit patterns, radar approaches or visual approaches sometimes simulating an engine or double-engine-out scenario. It was all part of ongoing training.

I always wanted to know about the ATC controller's role, so I established contact with those officers and spent many an off-duty moment watching them work. These people were qualified as radar controllers too and would sit in front of their radar screens, and talk to the pilots making radar-guided approaches. If I remember correctly, there were three types of approaches we used, pilot-approach radar (PAR), ground-controlled approach (GCA), and standard-radar approach (SRA).

One of the controllers was called Don, if memory serves me correctly, and we became friends. He had a distinctive voice, such that whenever we returned to the circuit and he was on duty, I would always say, "Evening Don", or equivalent for the time of day. He would respond in similar mode and friendly contact was established. There was rarely any superfluous chat, just a personal bond being made. It was like that at many places I visited in the future.

One of the perks on the squadron was to make an overseas trip to a foreign base. These were known as lone rangers. It was away from base. A sort of 'jolly' yet included some training too. Usually on the bombing range at El Adem dropping 100 pounders which I was led to believe, behaved in a similar manner to the real things that we carried.

Eddie showed me the 'ropes' planning and operating such a trip and quite frankly it was very exciting for me in this period of my life. The trips were of some four to six days in length, staying over at RAF Luqa in Malta and El Adem in Libya. The flight time was a little over four hours, but as our aircraft were now fitted with underwing tanks, that gave us a much longer range if needed, with a flight time of some eight hours.

The underwing tanks held about 26,000 lb of fuel and had a jettison system that seemed second to none. We could, if needed, jettison 24,000 lb in some sixty seconds using compressed air from bottles inside the underwing tanks. The remaining 2,000 lb would take a further thirty seconds. We had to dump our fuel over The Wash on one occasion from about 2,000 ft. None of it reached the surface of the water as it evaporated so quickly.

On my first trip to Luqa, we had the following day off, so Eddie, on our first night, led the crew into 'The Gut' on a street called 'Straight', which was an area of night-time bars and entertainment of everything imaginable, yet by day, a simple working class district of tenement housing. Without the bright lights of the bars and clubs at night, the area by day was totally uninviting.

For me, my eyes were just wide open and I absorbed it all with relish, as Eddie took us to a bar called the Egyptian Queen, known as the 'Gypo Queen'. It was seedy and bustling with all forms of life. It was there that I first saw prostitutes in action. The 'niceties' as such, were full on groping before the couple involved took their leave to a room upstairs. I was to re-visit this area with my own crew a few years later.

The lone rangers were a regular occurrence, wherever they took you, giving me valuable lessons for much later in my career. The V bombers were introduced as the deterrent to prevent Russia taking an opportunist moment to attack the West. The reader should remember that in those early days, there were no surface-to-air missiles (SAMs) to shoot our aircraft down. There were only fighters which had limited high altitude operational ability.

The V bombers had the capability of reaching around 55,000 ft and technically, unstoppable should we have gone to war. Of course progress does not stand still and with the invention of the SAMs, the V Force was fast becoming redundant. Therefore, a new programme was introduced for the force to fly a high-low-high profile to deliver the weapon to its target. We became part of Strategic Command Europe (SACEUR). Why h-l-h? Well, it was assumed that if the V bombers were called to action, then it was full war conditions and we expected that there would be no UK to return to, so we would head off high level until within striking distance of the SAMs, descend to low level and fly to the target, drop our weapon, then climb to high level and head off to a pre-planned destination, in another part of the globe.

To achieve competency in our new role on the low level side, a training routine was set up where we flew a high level navigation exercise to a designated descent point to the north of Scotland. After descending to around 1,000-2,000 ft, we identified our entry point for the low level flight, on a prescribed route down the east coast until The Wash, initially at 500 ft until we were all proficient day and night. Flying at 500 ft anywhere over enemy territory, we stood the risk of being damaged/shot down by smaller weapons from ground troops. We also only flew at around 450 kt, therefore

Nuclear deterrent on the operational readiness platform at Marham. Big paint job when the deterrent went low level. *(Tony Yule)*

to have the element of surprise, we lowered our operations to 250 ft. Thus we re-trained and practised on almost every trip.

You may be wondering why we didn't hit the ground at night or in inclement weather. The success of the operation was entirely due to the skill of the nav radar, using his navigation bombing system from the high level mode into a radar system that was set to a given angle, that looked at objects in the direct path of the aircraft, such that if it looked solid, then the nav radar would instruct us to climb until he was sure he had a clear view on the other side of the object. Night low level was flown at 500 or 1,000 ft for safety. It was an operation of absolute trust between the pilots and navigators.

A big part of our time was spent on QRA having the ability to be airborne from a state of readiness, within four minutes. The QRA compound was on the other side of the airfield, yet close enough to the runway to enable the crews to achieve the airborne time. Ideally you would be called to operational readiness, sitting in your aircraft waiting for the message from Bomber Command. The three QRA aircraft, fully loaded, one from each bomber squadron, just stayed in the compound, heavily guarded by the RAF Regiment; also in the compound were the USAF custodians of the weapons, one assigned to each aircraft. If there was ever to be a QRA aircraft to fly, the crews would have needed a special code from Bomber Command HQ via a device on board, just for that purpose. The authentication would also be received by the custodian, who had his issued from another military source. If they didn't match, we didn't go.

The alert status on the base varied from day to day, as planned by Bomber Command, to test the station and crew's readiness to respond to the situation. However, every time there was an alert, it was the duty of one of the flight crew on QRA, to call base ops to check if the Q crews were involved. It was a formality as the answer was always negative, but we had to check anyway.

At the height of the Cuban missile crisis in 1962, Eddie's and the other crews were idly passing their time playing bridge, when the tannoy spluttered into life and the usual announcements calling the crews to operational readiness started blaring out. We carried on playing bridge just as usual. Ned Easy, the nav plotter from Dave Bridger's crew, strolled over to the phone and called ops to make the usual check to see if it applied to us. The response from the clerk in ops, obviously a little hassled with the situation responded, "Yes it did".

Oh man! We ran like hell to get into our aircraft showing all kinds of emotion. Once on board, there was just silence, each with his own thoughts of going to war and never coming back or to see your family and friends again etc., while we waited for that code to come through.

The custodian, with his weapon armed, was inside the aircraft also waiting. The wait was really quite long and in this period Eddie struck up a short conversation with the custodian. Then Eddie asked this man, "What would you do if I started the engines now?" Without any hesitation he replied in a very cold detached voice, "I would shoot you sir". Then before any further discussion could take place, our attention was drawn to the entrance to the compound by a young airman running like hell and waving his arm wildly, trying to attract our attention. It transpired that with all the tension on base with the Cuban crisis, the clerk in base ops, mistook Ned Easy's question to be from one of the regular squadron members that were being brought to yet another exercise readiness. That short twenty minutes or so being prepared to go to war, was very sobering. It never happened again I am glad to say.

As time passed, Eddie nominated me to complete the left-hand seat check (LHS) which was called the intermediate co-pilot's course (ICC). This would allow me to fly as pilot 1 (P1) with any nominated captain and, of course, Eddie was one of the nominated captains. From late 1962 I completed the course at the OCU and started to fly regularly as P1. This was to become invaluable when my conversion to full captaincy started on 106 Course in March 1964, some four months short of my twenty-fourth birthday.

Once again, my memory of the course is hazy except for one incident that has remained in my mind ever since. Prior to my first flight as captain with my own crew, all the rules regarding captains were explained to me, e.g. I must be the flying pilot until I achieved 200 hours as captain. Everything had been done and prepared for our flight. I had no idea what went on behind the scenes at station level when such flights were made. It seemed there were a few more observers in the tower than normal, to watch the proceedings. The principle being, if there's an incident and you witness it, then you cannot sit on any Board of Inquiry. Well, that was my explanation.

On this fine day, all things were done to the book and we taxied out to the take-off runway and were cleared to depart. I called for the pre-take-off checks, lined up on the centre line and when it came to the compass and tailplane indicator (TPI) selection, I should have said, "Compass to me, TPI to me". Instead, without knowing really why, yet in my mind naturally was, 'it's easier to command an operation while acting as co-pilot rather than have my full attention on flying the aircraft'.... I simply said, "Compass to you and TPI to you. You have control". The co-pilot started to point out that the rules...etc. when I interrupted him and said, "We're cleared to take off".

He advanced the throttles and we started accelerating down the runway building speed rapidly. On achieving 100 kt, there was a call from the flying pilot to state this fact when the non-flying pilot, me, checked both pilot's airspeed indicators to confirm that both were reading the same speed. I was shocked to see a 25 kt discrepancy and commanded "Stop" or whatever phrase it was and the co-pilot brought the aircraft to a slow speed and I said, "I have control", and taxied the aircraft to the end of the runway, turned right, came to a stop, well clear of the active runway and alongside a number of official looking cars. Inside these cars were the station's senior officers including the wing commander tech. As I climbed down from the aircraft, he approached me and demanded, "What was the problem Yule?" and I replied, "There was a 25 kt airspeed discrepancy Sir". His curt response was, "There f*****g better be" and he stormed off to his car.

Nothing more was said by him, but a week or so later, a flight lieutenant tech officer saw me in the bar one evening and quietly said to me, "You were correct Tony, it was 25 kt". Thank God that no one probed deeper!

My command course was completed at the back end of April 1964. I was posted back to 49 Squadron, went to see the boss to let him know that I had arrived, then to be assigned my crew. He welcomed me back and announced that he was going to be my navigator. My immediate thoughts were, who would be the captain, me a lowly flying officer and he being the wing commander? He must have read my face for he quickly said, "Tony, I have a squadron to run and you have a crew to run. I'll do my responsibilities here in the office, but when you want the crew for training, just come and tell me and I will appear. "Of course," he added, "You're the captain of the crew and responsible for the safe operation of the flight and I'm the tactical captain on the navigation side". I thought to myself, "What a good leader", feeling perfectly relaxed and pleased to be back amongst familiar faces.

There was one really big hurdle to overcome. On all the V bombers, the pilots had ejection seats and by now, the rear crew had power-assisted seats, which brought them to the semi-standing position, to be projected towards the open door, from where they would abandon the aircraft. Abandoning a Valiant was all fine and dandy for the pilots, but for the successful total abandoning of the aircraft by the rear crew members, the proviso for such a successful outcome meant that the aircraft had to be at a minimum height of 400 ft AGL with a speed greater than 90 kt. This fact was foremost in any captain's mind, for every take-off, should such a catastrophic failure happen, before you reached that 400 ft. I was told this in my early days on the squadron and it just stayed on 'the back burner'. It seemed that this topic was never discussed openly and captains made their own decisions whether they ejected or stayed to try and make some sort of crash landing. You can imagine how I felt when I met the crew for the first time to fly together for a short air test on 1 May 1964. I need not have worried as the guys came to my rescue by stating directly, "We've discussed this scenario and know the risks we face as crew members. Should we end up in this critical case scenario, our decision to you is, GO, if you can, as there's no sense in losing two valuable pilots too!" The matter was decided and there was no mention of it ever again. They were just superb, as it started my captaincy with clarity of mind.

I tried to be as effective a captain as possible, just as Eddie had been. The boss was true to his word and always turned up on time for target study or preparation for flights. Although the boss was on my crew, his duties meant he did not fly as often as he would have liked. He ensured we had an experienced navigator when he could not be present.

After this first flight, we did a spell of QRA for three days ending up on the 7th to fly for much of the day. On the night of the 6th, a Valiant from 207 Squadron was lost, close to the town of Market Rasen, killing all on board instantly. This incident was kept under close wraps so most people on the base were aware initially that there had been a major incident but not who or which squadron. I was later told that as I hadn't been seen for some days, rumour control was that I and my crew had 'bought it'.

I believe that in the next few months there was little to go on to find the cause of that crash. Then, after another major incident with another Valiant at the OCU, it appeared that fatigue failure might have contributed to or have been the cause of that crash at Market Rasen. In the meantime, life on the squadron was pretty much the same as it was when I was a co-pilot. I went back to running the officers' mess entertainments, while we just flew, did bouts of QRA and long periods of target study.

Then my crew had to plan a lone ranger and it so happened to be one of the same destinations that I did with Eddie. We planned the trip to Luqa for a night stop, layover for a full day, then El Adem and back for two days, each day dropping 100 pounders, before returning to Marham on the fifth day. Of course the reader will have guessed that the captain duly displaying leadership, would take his crew down the Gut at the first opportunity. This I duly did and I dressed quite smartly, a huge mistake, because when we arrived at the door to The Gypo Queen, the bouncers threw me out. What an indignity! However, I then took them further down the street to another bar of disrepute, where there was no objection to the dress style, as long as pictures of the Queen changed hands and drinks were purchased. We sat at a table and I was telling the lads…lads? Ha! I was still wet behind the ears and still used the cat's tongue to shave with, if there wasn't a harsh towel handy! Anyway, I was telling them all about Malta, when up came a very stunning young lady with an extremely short hemline, who promptly sat next to me on the large chair I was sitting on and snuggled up to me.

Bearing in mind I had just turned twenty-four the previous month, I was totally unprepared for her next move, which was for her hands to start exploring my legs from the knees upwards! I was 'bricking' it big time! The crew just had their eyes wide open as I ignored her antics completely, while nonchalantly continuing to drink and talk with them. I just brazened it out to give the impression I'd done all this before. It worked as she eventually gave up and cleared. Phew!

It was shortly after returning from our lone ranger back end of August 1964 that we learnt that the Valiant fleet was in the 'deep dark brown sticky stuff' suffering from fatigue problems. As a result of this, it was deemed necessary that all the Valiant squadrons, from around September 1964, would operate all aircraft to very tight limits, monitoring the new 'g' meters mounted above the nav's stations. Any excess 'g', according to the prescribed limits being exceeded, for whatever reason, and that aircraft would have to return to base immediately for investigation as to which part of the airframe had been affected.

Navigation trips with your own crew were now limited to four hours of flight time and for continuation training, two hours in the circuit, with two captains in the pilots' seats. It meant that I could have my own crew or I would fly right seat with another crew. This scenario continued until I completed my last two-hour trip in command, with my own crew and another captain in the right seat, on 7 December 1964.

It was around this time I believe that the decision was made to disband the Valiant force completely. It was a sad blow for us all and put HQ Strike Command as it was now known, in one almight quandary with all the pilots suddenly without work.

The co-pilots were satisfied fairly quickly as a number of Chipmunks were flown in to Marham and used for continuity flying from around January 1965. This turned out to be great for the many ATC cadets in the area who had lots of flying experience until all the co-pilots had been posted just about everywhere. The captains were also lucky, as in January 1965 we were trained on two Avro Anson aircraft, a Mk 19 and a Mk 21, which were attached to the Station Flight. We always joked that these were the station commander's personal aircraft. We flew these aircraft with one of the other captains, or even solo. I enjoyed the solo flying best. We primarily took or collected passengers who had business with the station or delivered items as were required elsewhere.

One Anson had a Gee navigation unit situated behind the captain's seat. This unit, an aid to navigation, was designed in WWII and used by a navigator, if he was carried on a flight. It was one of the checks required by the captain or navigator to ensure that the Gee unit was secure before flight, otherwise there was a risk that the unit could become loose and hit the head of the captain in flight and/or decelerating after landing. Yep, you got it! I suffered the ignominy of being hit on the back of the head, during landing on one of my solo flights. Didn't make the same mistake twice.

My time on the Anson and my life at 'El Adem with grass' ended soon after my last flight on 8 April. I was posted on 12 April, to attend No. 228 Course at the Central Flying School (CFS) at RAF Little Rissington, near Cirencester in Gloucestershire to become a qualified flying instructor (QFI).

CHAPTER 6

VULCAN AEOs REMEMBER

Richard de Verteuil, Geoff Lidbetter

The next few chapters are about Vulcan Mk 2s. In this chapter the AEOs are dealing with the Mk 2 electrical system which was completely different from the Vulcan Mk 1 and the Valiant; instead of 112V DC backed up by four batteries the Vulcan Mk 2 and the Victor Mk 2 used constant frequency 400 cycles/min AC backed up by a ram air turbine and an auxiliary power pack; the flying controls were electrically driven and relied on there being AC electrical power all the time; unlike the Valiant there was no manual reversion if the electrical power failed.

*This chapter has stories from both **Richard de Verteuil** and **Geoff Lidbetter**; Richard tells of his squadron experiences and took part in a lot of air displays. After leaving the RAF he joined Marconi Avionics becoming an expert in air data systems for helicopters. Retiring from GEC Richard became a teacher in mathematics and computing.*

My interest in flying began when as a twelve year old I saw three Canberras that were on a goodwill visit to Trinidad in the West Indies, where I was born. I saw these incredibly sleek aeroplanes across the airfield at Piarco, and said to myself, "Those are for me". In 1953 I came to a public school in England and my holidays were spent making and flying model glider aircraft. I had also by this time applied to go to Cranwell, but my father wanted me to have 'another string to my bow' and so in 1959 I went to the University of Birmingham, Edgbaston, to read Petroleum Production Engineering.

On the first day of freshers week, I entered the great hall and first on the right was the stall set up by the University Air Squadron (UAS). I signed up immediately and after my history of previous applications through Hornchurch came to light I was rewarded with acceptance as a cadet pilot, and soon commenced my flying training on weekends at RAF Shawbury on Chipmunks. I also continued my studies and completed my first year. In the summer break I went to Herefordshire where unfortunately I was involved in a motorcycle accident and had to forgo the UAS flying camp at RAF Martlesham Heath. At the end of my second year it was clear to me that I was not going to make it in petroleum and although I was accepted as a geology student, I decided to apply for a commission in the Royal Air Force.

On 2 October 1961 I joined No. 165 (UAS) Course at RAF South Cerney together with thirty other ex-university air squadron members and after completing the course I joined No. 2 Course at No. 1 FTS at RAF Leeming. The course had been tailored and shortened to suit UAS candidates who had completed at least three years flying, some of whom had as many as 400 hours on Chipmunks, and the pace of the course was beyond my piloting skills, having only eighty hours. After seventy hours on the Jet Provost Mk 2 it was decided that I would be more suited to retraining as an AEO, since my other main interest at that time and since has been electronics in its many forms.

So after a short sojourn at RAF Catterick, I joined a course at the Air Electronics School, RAF Topcliffe, and finally graduated with my AE brevet in September 1963. I was posted to the Maritime Operational Training Unit (MOTU) at RAF Kinloss and after completing a most interesting course on Shackleton Mk 2 aircraft, was posted to 201 Squadron at RAF St Mawgan on the Mk 3. That did not last long as it was decided that the squadron balance was not right and that the threat from Russia meant that the main tasking of Coastal Command should be concentrated in the Iceland/Faroes gap and therefore it made better sense to have three squadrons at Kinloss. So the MOTU was moved to St Mawgan and Nos. 201 and 206 joined 120 Squadron at Kinloss. This left 42 Squadron and MOTU at St Mawgan. Our crew received a new captain as our previous captain joined MOTU as an instructor.

While at St Mawgan I got my first introduction to the Vulcan. As was the practice, the V Force aircraft were dispersed periodically, and I was surprised one day to meet Wg Cdr Mike Darcy, OC 44 (Rhodesia) Squadron on the dispersal at St Mawgan. He remembered me as he had been wing commander training at South Cerney when I went through. Little did I know it, but we were to meet up yet again when I joined Bomber Command in 1970 where he was OC RAF Waddington.

My time on Coastal Command came to an end in May 1967, and after a further abbreviated tour I was posted to Wing Operations, RAF Kinloss. Then followed a tour as specialist operator on 360 RN/RAF Squadron at Watton and Cottesmore until September 1969. Interestingly, my arrival on 44 (Rhodesia) Squadron at RAF Waddington was to be the first tour I ever completed on the same station where it started. The OCU moved halfway through our course from Finningley to Scampton. My tour on IX Squadron, 1973-75 started in Cyprus and ended back at Waddington and it was there that I finally completed my service in the RAF back on 44 Squadron in December 1978.

Introduction to the Vulcan B Mk 2

I started my Vulcan Operational Conversion Course at RAF Finningley in October 1969 and I found the ground school to be very interesting, extensive and challenging. I had chosen to go to Coastal Command after Topcliffe to gain experience of doing my job while flying and having the advice and help of experienced air signallers and master aircrew. This was a good choice and by the time I came to the V Force I felt confident to carry out the very responsible duties of a Vulcan AEO. My ground and flying instructors were excellent, one having been my instructor at MOTU and the other later at the Ground Standardisation Unit as a trapper. Our crew's first flight was to end with a landing at RAF Scampton where the OCU was to be transferred.

On 11 December 1969 our crew, co-pilot, nav radar, nav plotter and AEO, myself, with an OCU captain Flt Lt John Le Brun, boarded XH534[1] and carried out the prestart checks. At this point the aircraft was being supplied with 115v 400Hz electrical power from the Houchin ground power unit and all electrical loads were being supplied via the synchronising bus bar, (sync bar), including the pilots' military flight system (MFS) which integrated the separate G4B compass and the artificial horizon displays and included the instrument landing system information.

The captain called the crew chief who was on the intercom system, plugged in externally, and said he was ready for engine start. The crew chief gave the all clear and the four engines were started. As the alternator outputs came up I switched them to their loads and the Houchin was disconnected electrically from the aircraft.

Just then, the co-pilot asked the captain, "Is that supposed to happen?" The co-pilot, Tony Burton, was an AEO who had retrained as a pilot after the Valiant V bombers had been scrapped, so he had some knowledge of aircraft systems. The captain called, "Chief! The horizon bar is slowly rotating and is now indicating upside down!" and to the co-pilot, "What is yours showing?" The co-pilot replied that his was steady, indicating level and normal. The only thing that had happened was that the alternators had taken over their loads. So the captain told the crew chief, "We can't take this aircraft like this, chief, let's shut it down. AEO, read the shutdown checks."

The crew chief reconnected the Houchin and it took over the aircraft supplies. The co-pilot said, "The horizon bar is rotating again, going back to normal". So the fault only manifested itself when the alternators were supplying their own loads. The captain said, "Well, we still can't take the aircraft like this so we'll shut down. Carry on with the shutdown checks." So we left the aircraft for the ground crew to sort out.

Next day we were allocated the same aircraft so obviously it had been repaired. We were briefed by the crew chief and what they found was that the supplies to the pilots' MFS displays had been swapped over and this had caused the horizon bar on the pilots' MFS to disagree.

The remainder of the course went fairly normally and I was eventually passed fit to fly without an instructor. However our crew captain failed the flying and was posted off to Bassingbourn as a Canberra instructor, having joined the V Force as a QFI recently from Flying Training Command.

---

1. 534 was the second Mk 2 Vulcan test aircraft first flown by the author (TB) on 7 July 1959 and reworked at St Athan.

On completion of the OCU course I was posted to 44 (Rhodesia) Squadron with the nav plotter Bob Wyer and Fg Off Plested the nav radar; the co-pilot Tony Burton went to 50 Squadron where he later gained a captaincy. On 44, I was posted to the boss's crew, Wg Cdr Bliss, nav plotter, and our captain was Nick Dennis, co-pilot Vic and Fg Off Plested was the nav radar. When Nick was tourex, we had Val Ventham posted in and he was followed by Dave Wadsworth who had been posted in from 101 Squadron. We also had a change of boss, and Wg Cdr Maurice Fenner joined the crew as nav plotter. So in my first tour we were lucky to get operational! I certainly have no recollection of getting any higher crew qualification.

There were however many benefits having the boss on the crew. In 1972 the squadron was detached to Singapore for Operation Bersatu Padu. We were stationed at Singapore Air Force, (SAF) Tengah and flew Malaysian low level routes. We also had a detachment to RAAF Darwin where we operated in the offensive role against the RAAF 73 Squadron Mirages. There we had an open day when we hosted some of the local primary schools, and made the evening news on Channel 7.

I think the radar operators and fighter jocks were quite surprised by the ability of the Vulcan to provide a jamming environment and 73, (whose emblem is a puma) produced a large cartoon that was put up in the officers' mess bar showing a puma mounting an elephant and the caption saying: "Now we'll do the jamming!" All in good fun and washed down by jugs of amber nectar – Australian drinking glasses are tiny. They deserve the name 'stubbies'.

The weather in Darwin was quite hot, and it was decided that the squadron would have a sports day sponsored by the aircrew with team games against the ground crew and a BBQ unashamedly cooked by K L, a brash young co-pilot, recently joined, and of considerable confidence in his ability to cook over an open fire and simultaneously down large quantities of Fosters in an ambient temperature about 90°F. It was therefore no surprise when young K L suddenly collapsed at the cookers complaining of being very hot. He was just saved from having more extensive injuries and a couple of us took him off to the showers to try and revive him.

Having stripped him and submitted him to warm and cold showers to no effect, we decided to call in the medics and an ambulance came and whipped him off to sick quarters. We later learned that an excess of alcohol combined with the heat of the day and heat of the BBQ had caused him to become severely dehydrated – he barely avoided a case of heat stroke that would have been very serious. After a night in sick quarters (SQ) he returned, rather red faced, to duty the next day.

Another benefit of being on the boss's crew was that of a long weekend on the Gold Coast. Wg Cdr Fenner had spent some time at the Australian Staff College and so he wanted to visit some of his acquaintances. We flew down to RAAF Edinburgh Field, the boss stayed at Edinburgh Field and the rest of us were then bundled into a hired car and given directions for Norwich, a large town in Queensland.

1972 had been quite a momentous year in Australia weather wise, and there had been a desperate drought in the interior that had caused a serious shortage of grazing and the premature culling of a very high percentage of the cattle, so meat was hardly in short supply. We arrived in time for dinner at a splendid steak restaurant where we chose our steaks from the cabinet and then we drove down to the Gold Coast. There the beaches had been damaged by the very high sea states generated by a recent typhoon. Saturday and Sunday flew by, and we saw the beach life savers at work and play. Soon it was back to Darwin and more flying before returning to Tengah.

I had now completed tours in Coastal, Signals and Bomber Command and was looking for a change of pace, yet again. Dave Wadsworth told me that the only way to get an overseas posting was to write a letter to the personnel staff at Adastral House volunteering to go abroad. I did this and was rewarded with a posting to Cyprus on IX(B) Squadron.

Cyprus and the Weapons Effects Demonstration

Flying the Vulcan in Cyprus in the summer months in particular calls for some very stringent rules. Temperatures hover in the high 90°F, and coolers help to keep the cabins cool on the ground. The normal sortie was a quick climb into the cabin, get

IX Squadron at RAF Akrotiri, 23 January 1974. From left: Sqn Ldr John Herbertson, capt OC A Flt, Fg Off Neil Ryder, co-pilot, Flt Lt Peter Tame, nav plotter, Fg Off Jill Tame, WRAF air traffic control officer at Akrotiri, Flt Lt Richard 'Dick' de Verteuil, AEO, and Flt Lt David Cherry, nav radar. Jill was Pete's wife. The flight was at night so she did not see much of the scenery. *(Richard de Verteuil)*

airborne within twenty minutes of closing the door, climb to high level for a cool down of the air ventilated suit (AVS), a navex with a navigation termination point (NTP) near the island and a descent to the low level route around the island, one or two simulated/ practice bombs at the range off Episcopi and then a couple of circuits and land.

Lone rangers were frequent to Tehran, Masirah, Shiraz, and back to the UK for delivery/collection of aircraft from Waddington. Aircraft were returned there for delivery to St Athan for major servicing. This also provided an opportunity for shopping, probably as important to the crew as the out-of-country low flying over the deserts of southern Iran. But more of this later.

Every year in Cyprus there was a weapons effects demonstration and flying display put on by the RAF at Episcopi. IX(B) Squadron was tasked with providing the 21 x 1,000-lb bomb demonstration on the range offshore at RAF Episcopi. As the Vulcan was now tasked primarily in the nuclear role, the only time any non-nuclear weapons were used was when 25-lb practice bombs were dropped on the range for scoring purposes. So it was necessary to find an aircraft that could reliably drop a full conventional load, and to do this the armourers were tasked with installing three bomb carriers and a full weapon release system that worked flawlessly. I am sure that the same problem had to be solved before the Vulcans went to Ascension Island during the Falklands War.

Our captain Sqn Ldr John Herbertson, who was also 'A' Flight commander, and our crew were tasked, with others, with carrying out many sorties during which a varying number of 1,000-lb bombs were carried and dropped/not dropped on the range. I do not know how many were dropped before a set of serviceable carriers were found and tested but I believe it did wonders for the depletion of the bombs in the stores that were past their use-by dates. Even 1,000-lb bombs have a 'use-by' date, it appears.

Eventually the great day came and we went off to drop the full load at Episcopi. I seem to recall that we released all twenty-one bombs, but only twenty exploded. I believe that may also have been the year that a Harrier ended its display by falling out of the hover. The pilot ejected before the aircraft hit the ground and exploded.

Our crew were also tasked with proving that in case of a scramble, the Vulcan Mk 2 could get safely airborne with a full fuel load on three engines in the high summer temperatures, and subsequently air-start the fourth. We did this a number of times working up from a minimum fuel load to a full one. Why this had not been proven before 1973 is a question to which I do not recall having heard an answer.

Further to these escapades IX (B) Squadron had one further memorable occurrence. On 23 July 1973, while operating out of Shiraz, an airfield in the south of Iran, a crew was on a lone ranger. On returning to land the aircraft suffered a total hydraulic failure. The undercarriage was lowered using the emergency air system, but the port main wheel failed to deploy. It was therefore put to the crew that the rear crew and Iranian observer could bale out at a safe altitude and the captain and co-pilot would then land the aircraft. The rear crew elected to remain in the aircraft and it was subsequently landed after burning off fuel and jettisoning the canopy.

On landing the captain held the port wing up for as long as practicable, but eventually it had to be lowered, causing the aircraft to swing off the runway. The bomb aimer's window broke and the scoop effect resulted in the cabin filling with dust. Everything else was going quite well until the aircraft came to a very wide and deep storm drain situated between the two runways which wrote off the nosewheel and remaining main undercarriage. It also broke the back of the aircraft. XJ781 was a total write-off. The crew all emerged unscathed through the cockpit and slid down the side of the nose. The two navigators in the rear had to be freed by the AEO as they had been trapped by the collapse of the desk. The captain was later alleged to have said if he had known about the ditch, he would have landed on the other runway. This might have resulted in less damage but it is likely that the aircraft would still have been severely 'bent'.

I had one last memorable flight while in Cyprus with IX (B) Squadron, whose unofficial motto was 'There's always bloody something'. On 20 July 1974 following the Greek military junta and its Greek Cypriot collaborators coup against the democratically elected president of Cyprus, Turkey invaded Cyprus and occupied the northern part of the island, forcibly expelling about 180,000 Greek Cypriots to the south. The British decided to remove the Vulcans of IX (B) and 35 Squadrons from Akrotiri, and the crews went with them. I stayed behind in the hospital as I had just suffered an accident on my motorbike and received extensive friction burns to my hands and left thigh. As a result of this the rest of my crew also remained in Cyprus.

On 21 July 1974 after the commencement of hostilities between Turkey and Greece, a report of a Greek task force off the west coast of Cyprus was acted upon by the Turkish air forces and a number of ships were attacked with 750-lb bombs. One of the ships, the Destroyer *D-354 Kocatepe* was sunk with the loss of fifty-four lives. This ship turned out be the subject of friendly fire and was in fact Turkish – the reports of a Greek flotilla were allegedly fabricated by the Greek Cypriot Navy Command. The RAF having the only search and rescue helicopters in the area were involved in carrying out search and rescue (SAR) operations, and the British were being helpful by relaying coded reports of progress through the American air base at Incirlik.

I was still in the RAF hospital and due to be discharged. I was approached by one of the wing staff and asked if I was fit enough to fly, and although the doctors were reluctant to release me to fly, I promised to be careful and not to cause further injury to my burns. I was the only currently qualified Vulcan AEO on the station and it was necessary to get an aircraft airborne to act as a radio relay to the USAF base at Incirlik, Turkey.

This relay was performed by our crew and we flew five sorties over five days carrying out maritime reconnaissance and radio relays. We set up a race track over the south-east coast of the island at fl400 and I sent the coded messages via HF to Incirlik. My

IX Squadron, Akrotiri 1973. *(Richard de Verteuil)*

instructions were to have the messages repeated back and after hearing my recorded voice on the 'repeat' I did not ask again.

Finally, a common description by Vulcan crews of the capabilities of the aircraft included the phrase 'The best five-man jet executive transport in the world – it gets you from one bar to another as quickly as possible'.

On one occasion our crew were tasked with flying from Cyprus to the western end of the Mediterranean to carry out electronic counter measures (ECM) and simulated high level bombing attacks against the US 6th Fleet. For this we had full tanks and two bomb bay tanks as well. On the return, having been 'shot down' by almost every ship in the fleet, and more than six hours in flight, John said, "this trip is dragging let's get it over". As was our standard operating procedures (SOP) on approaching Cyprus at about 200 nm range we would call Gata Radar, the air defence radar station situated on Mt Olympus, and report 'Four jet inbound to Akrotiri'. We were twice asked to confirm aircraft type, which we did, to be told that we were being tracked with a ground speed of M1.1 – they thought we must be a Lightning! The captain then admitted that we were doing M.92 and the plotter confirmed a tail wind of almost 200 kt!

As a direct result of the fracas in Cyprus between the Greeks and Turks, both by the way allies and members of CENTO, the Vulcan squadrons were returned to the UK in January 1975, IX to Waddington and 35 to Scampton. I had arranged with approval of the P staff to move on to another crew when my crew were tourex. Instead of three and a half years in Cyprus, we had one week short of two years! Foiled again.

Burst Eardrums on Holiday in Dixie

My third Vulcan tour was a return to 44 (Rhodesia) Squadron and I was crewed with the squadron QFI, Flt Lt Jon Tye, co-pilot Flt Lt Wilbey Crawford, nav radar Flt Lt Gordon Daniels and nav plotter Flt Lt Mike Feenan. I notice in my logbook that on arrival I flew on a number of flights that included air displays at RAF Finningley and RAF Leuchars guesting on another crew. My squadron acceptance check was actually carried out six weeks after joining.

The Tye crew started off as a training crew, and eventually achieved command category, lunched with the AOC 1 Group and in February 1976 we were selected as the Waddington Vulcan display crew. Jon had not flown a display as captain and after chatting to some of the OCU senior pilots, a routine was worked out and so we had to go off and do some practices. Eventually on May 2 we did our first display at Barksdale AFB, Shreveport, Louisiana as the guests of the US 8th Air Force. We also had to stand by the aircraft and talk politely to visitors and show selected people into the cockpit. Our captain also blagged us a visit to the SR-71 Blackbird hangar where we were able to climb onto the aircraft and peek into the pilot and rear crew positions. I was quite surprised to see that the pilot's instruments were conventional and rather similar to the Vulcan's; glass cockpits were still a few years away. The rear crew position from what could be seen can best be described as 'boring', just many panels of switches and an ejection seat. No radars, warning receivers or other super gizmos which one might have expected from that aircraft.

But the SR-71 up close is BIG. It sits in the hangar with ground crew rushing about and huge drip trays to catch the JP-7 as it pours out of the aircraft wings. The skin was a series of concave squares that tighten as the aircraft flies faster and eventually it stops leaking. The fuel is used to cool parts of the skin and to be preheated before injection into the engines. Its take-off the next day was mind blowing. It seemed to be on the ground accelerating like a bullet one moment and disappearing into the blue very soon after. The noise from the two huge reheated engines rivalled the Vulcan.

But I digress. We had come to fly a display and so we took our turn and roared off into the blue. After our series of low level turns, slow fly-pasts and wingovers, bomb doors open, undercarriage down etc. we climbed out doing the laid down climbing spiral to 4,000 ft. At this point we received a radio call.

"Can you extend your display as the next item is running late?" This was the USAF Thunderbirds flying the T-38 Talon.

We had nothing up our sleeves. I suggested "Fly downwind, descending turn at flight idle, approach runway descending and building speed to 250 kt then when in the middle of the crowd line, apply full power pulling up and climbing steeply to safe height then wingover and depart downwind and back for a landing when cleared."

"Okay, we'll do that," said Jon. So he did, and as we climbed out with full power and going up like a lift, there was a shout from the co-pilot; he had suffered a burst eardrum, and the medics delayed our return to Goose Bay by four days. But we kept that last manoeuvre in our display from then on. I am sure that it was appreciated by the crowd as it is really impressive to see the aircraft in a steep climb, hardly decelerating as it gets smaller and making a chest hammering amount of noise. We used to wing over at about 10,000 ft. It is interesting to note that the Vulcan display we did was quite slow, hardly ever more than about 250 kt pulling no more than 1.8 g and I remember seeing 89 kt on the ASI at the top of a wingover. The aircraft was also severely 'g' limited in order to extend its operational life and we seldom pulled more than 1.8 g; we had to record fatigue meter readings after every flight. The aircraft was usually fuelled to about 15,000 lb and this made the 80,000-lb thrust from the four Olympus 301 engines acting on an aircraft that grossed about 112,000 lb perform quite impressively. Take-off acceleration was very smart and I used to have to press against my desk to stop from sliding off my seat. I rarely strapped myself in for displays.

I also believe that Roly Falk was not the only pilot to carry out a barrel roll in a Vulcan, as late as 1978. Tony Blackman also admits to doing a very high number of displays where the aircraft was 'rolled off the top'. I remember well in my youth seeing the first display by Roly Falk at Farnborough where he rolled the aircraft after take-off. I was also there the day John Derry was killed in the DH110. I was with my aunt in the VIP enclosure and we were invited to meet him after his flight. Sadly it never did happen. My father and brother with two cousins and their father were on the hill where thirty people were killed by the starboard engine of the DH110. Having been in the artillery, my cousins' father saw the danger and told them all to run, and they were lucky to have escaped.

We flew a number of displays in the USA and Canada in 1976. 4 July was Loring AFB, Maine for the 200th anniversary of American Independence. We were hosted by and very well looked after by a B-52 crew. They took us out pistol shooting, and Jon, an ex-motorcycle trials rider, was given a trials motorbike in a quarry and showed them how it was done. We ended the afternoon with a BBQ where our plotter, Mike Feenan, surprised the Americans by calmly chomping his way through a stack of jalapeno peppers and we were given beautiful steaks in a Teriyaki marinade. We exchanged flying suits and aircrew badges. But we were not offered a look inside a B-52. I never did see the inside of one.

The weather on 4 July was awful, 1,000 ft cloud base and an occasional drizzle. No one was going to fly but Jon said we would do a flat display. After all we usually displayed below 1,000 ft except for the wingovers and climb out, so we did. The only other aircraft airborne that day were a couple of Air National Guard F-102 Delta Daggers that had been on readiness and were called out.

In August we flew three displays at Abbotsford International Air Show, Vancouver, Canada, and the Goose Bay Open Day. In June 1977 at the Jubilee Air Tattoo and fighter Meet at Greenham Common, Jon was awarded a special trophy for the display he put on. We also flew displays for the 44 (Rhodesia) Squadron Golden Jubilee, the IX (B) Squadron Open Day at Waddington, and a number of others at Exeter and North Luffenham.

In late 1977 our crew broke up and for my fourth tour I was re-crewed on 44 with the new squadron QFI, Sqn Ldr Tony Blyth, co-pilot Flt Lt Andy Leitch, nav plotter Flt Lt Dave Stannard, nav radar Fg Off Hill and found myself once more flying displays. In 1978 we flew four times for the Canadians at Toronto and a few more in the UK. On the return from Toronto to Trenton, a Grumman F-14 suddenly appeared on our starboard wing and Andy took a photo of it that was presented to me on my retirement. I have always considered the F-14 to be one of the best looking aircraft, with the Hunter, Canberra and of course the Vulcan.

A Flying Emergency in the Vulcan

My nine years on the Vulcan were approaching finality and I had never had any remarkable or memorable system failure, but in May 1978 our crew were on a training flight from Offutt AFB, Nebraska. We were to fly OB31, a high-low-high profile over the western training routes, known as oil burners. As was usual in May in that part of the United States, the temperatures were high and the low level was particularly bumpy.

The high level sortie was quite normal and the descent checks were carried out, No. 3 alternator was put on the sync bar and we entered the low level, flying at 500 ft AGL. At about ten minutes into the low level, a fire warning was seen on one of the port side engines, and in accordance with SOPs the two port engines were shut down and the emergency ram air turbine (RAT) automatically deployed which tripped the non-essential loads and reduced electrical power requirements in case of further failures.

As Nos. 1 and 2 engines were shutting down, I switched off their alternators and transferred their loads to the sync bar which had all the essential loads. At this point No. 4 alternator tripped off, followed smartly by No. 3. The RAT immediately took over the sync bar and valiantly tried to supply power for the entire aircraft essential loads.

For a few seconds there was no power within normal parameters to the aircraft systems and the flying controls. There was, in my opinion, no solution except to do a rapid reset of Nos. 3 and 4 alternators and hit the airborne auxiliary power pack (AAPP) start button. Fortunately the AAPP performed correctly and in about two seconds it took over the loads but for a short time there was no electrical AC power within limits and had there been any further delay the controls would have frozen. All of this was happening at 500 ft as the pilots were dealing with engine shutdown drills. There was no time for reading the checklist.

Having restored the electrical power I then checked the aircraft for any signs of smoke or fire using the periscope; everything looked fine and the pilots started a climb out and made emergency calls. We returned to Offutt keeping below 30,000 ft on two engines without any further problems; the AAPP had a thirty-minute limit on supplying power but I was forced to exceed this limitation in view of the fact that two of our alternators had tripped for no apparent reason and I was not willing to risk putting either of them on the sync bar.

Analysis after the return to Waddington suggested that a fault in the alternator load sharing circuits which are connected by the sync relays possibly caused the alternators to trip. Analysis by the ground crew on our return to Offutt discovered some possibly leaking seals in the hot air cross-feed system used for engine starting. The seals were replaced, but as there were no spare AAPP starter cartridges in the support pack, at Offutt or at Goose Bay, we had to wait for three days for them to send more from the UK before we could fly again. In the meantime the aircraft was taken to the end of one of the runways and the engines run at high power for an hour, much to the annoyance of the locals.

However, that is not the end of the story. Three days later we again tried to fly OB31 and at exactly the same point, about ten minutes into the low level, the fire warning light came on again. This time I went through a slightly different sequence, in slow time, did a normal AAPP start, checked for fire signs, none seen, and we returned to Offutt on two engines again. It was then decided that the most likely fault was a spurious warning from one of the two new transistorised fire-warning units recently introduced into service. Replacements were flown out from the UK and we finally successfully completed OB31 eight days after our first attempt. That had been a sixteen-day ranger, the longest and only the second delayed ranger I ever had.

At the end of 1978 I retired from the RAF having had seventeen great and enjoyable years of flying, round the world once, Hawaii twice and many trips to the USA, Canada, Australia, Singapore three times, and many points in between. I was doing a job in an environment that few others experience and I believe making a most worthwhile contribution to the maintenance of peace. I even had two flights in XH558 on 13 and 20 April 1971. Martin Withers DFC who was the captain of the Vulcan that bombed Stanley in the Falklands was one of the co-pilots who guested on our crew early on in my Vulcan experience, and was a fellow squadron member on 44 (Rhodesia) Squadron. I am proud to say that I met and worked with some of the finest professionals in the RAF, and it was a very sad day when I decided that I did not wish to become an air traffic controller.

I am presently a volunteer with the Royal Voluntary Service where I help 'silver surfers' and with equipment maintenance. I was lucky enough to see XH558 displayed twice in its last year flying at Headcorn and Shuttleworth and when it carried out its round the north final trip as it flew over my old school, Stonyhurst College, Lancashire.

Geoff Lidbetter joined the RAF as an aircraft apprentice in 1955, then transferred to aircrew in 1963 as an air signaller, flying Hastings of 24/36 Squadrons in Transport Command. Converting to air electronics operator (AEOp), he flew in Shackleton and Nimrod aircraft of 206 Squadron in Coastal Command. Commissioned as an air electronics officer in 1972 he spent the next eleven years on Vulcans.

The Neville Chute Trophy

Exercise Double Top was one of the many V Force annual inter-squadron bombing competitions. The following incident occurred in May 1979. Double Top consisted of a high level navigation exercise (Navex), leading into a low level route over SW England, culminating in an attack on a target located in the vicinity of Dunkeswell, Devon. For those who remember, there was a radar bomb scoring unit located at Dunkeswell airfield. Additionally, somewhere along the low level route, aircraft would be engaged by an electronic warfare missile threat simulator manned by staff on detachment from RAF Spadeadam, Cumbria.

I was the AEO on one of the 35 Squadron Vulcan crews participating in the exercise. Each crew carried an additional crew member, the umpire – we had a navigator radar from 617 Squadron. The umpire's primary duty was to ensure the pilots' explicitly followed target headings given by the nav rad whilst on the bombing run – particularly once the pilots had visually acquired the target. In order for the umpire to fulfil this role, it was necessary for him to stand on the step ladder leading up to the pilot positions.

Having completed the navigation exercise plus the majority of the low level section, the crew were intently focused on the bombing run, as we approached the target at 300 kt indicated airspeed (KIAS) flying between 300 ft and 500 ft AGL. Suddenly the captain called over the intercom "AEO look out of the periscope and check if the parachute door is open". I quickly raised the periscope and looked through the upper lens. The door was not visible, but equally I could not be sure the door was closed, because it was not within the periscope's field of view. Having completed the bombing run, it was time to climb out and return to Scampton. During the climb out, the captain explained the reason for his unexpected call on the intercom. When the nav rad called for bomb doors open, the pilot mistakenly moved the brake parachute selector switch from off to stream. Luckily, he quickly realised his error and set the brake parachute selector switch to jettison. Yes, there is a light alloy 'shear pin' which is positioned within the mechanism attaching the parachute to the aircraft. This shear pin is designed to shear and release the brake parachute when the aircraft speed exceeds 145-160 KIAS, which equates to a force on the aircraft/brake parachute of 103,000 lb +/- 5%. Fortunately for the umpire, who was standing unrestrained on the step ladder, except for holding on with his hands, or hand, a combination of the pilot's quick thinking in changing the brake parachute

50 Squadron crew Waddington after Halifax Building Society Public Relations sortie over Peterborough 27 April 1982 in XM569. Anthony Wright, nav radar; Pete Ollis, captain; Kevin Weeks, nav plotter; Phil Lawson, co-pilot and Geoff Lidbetter, AEO. *(Anthony Wright Collection)*

selector switch from stream to jettison and/or rupture of the shear pin, saved him from being thrown forward onto the cockpit instruments due to the aircraft's sudden and rapid de-acceleration. Needless to say, the only talking point amongst the crew during the transit back to Scampton was had the crew inadvertently got rid of the brake parachute?

After landing the captain's first transmission to the Scampton local controller was "Is the brake parachute door open?" Back came the controller's answer "Yes, it is open". Oh dear, the crew's worse fears had come true. To add to the crew's misery, we were disqualified from the low level phase, because the aircraft had briefly climbed above 1,000 ft AGL during the bombing run. Surprise, surprise!

On the squadron, I was well into my second stint as adjutant, which in retrospect was quite an interesting and informative secondary duty. Roughly a week after the brake parachute incident, I got a telephone call from Okehampton Police. The brake parachute had been found in open countryside. No harm or damage had occurred to human life or property – thank goodness. Somehow the Spadeadam detachment personnel had become aware of the incident, and following liaison with the Okehampton Police, Spadeadam agreed to retrieve the 'chute and deliver it to Scampton during their return journey to Spadeadam.

So in the end it all got sorted out. Needless to say the crew endured a lot of banter from our aircrew colleagues, who awarded us the Neville Chute Bombing Trophy.[2]

Lone Ranger to Trondheim

On the night of 28 April 1942, a Halifax of 35 Squadron took off from Linton-on-Ouse to attack the German battleship *Tirpitz* moored in Trondheim fjord. Whilst doing so, the Halifax was shot down by enemy anti-aircraft guns and crashed close to the small town of Stjordal near Trondheim. Of the six-man crew, there were no survivors.

During the 1960s, members of Stjordal community decided to create a permanent monument to the Halifax crew. They selected a huge granite boulder lying just outside the town and engraved on it the name, rank and role of each crew member. They contacted the RNoAF requesting the presence of the RAF at the service of dedication to be held on Saturday 23 June 1979. The RNoAF in turn contacted the RAF, who tasked 35 Squadron to send a Vulcan B Mk 2 and crew to attend the ceremony.

The deployment schedule comprised a transit flight from Scampton to Trondheim on the Friday, attendance at the dedication service on the Saturday, Sunday was a free day with a return transit to Scampton on the Monday – in essence a lone ranger. The squadron boss decided his crew would undertake the task. I was the lucky AEO. Trondheim was not a normal airfield destination in Norway, unlike Bergen, Bodø, Ørland, Oslo (Gardermoen) or Stavanger, which I had visited whilst serving in Coastal and Transport Commands. Prior to the outbound flight, the crew carried out the necessary pre-flight checks including fuel type availability, runway length, load classification number (LCN), approach/departure procedures, etc.

Upon arrival at Trondheim, the aircraft was marshalled onto a very new tarmac apron surface where it was parked. The engines were shut down, aircraft refuelled and 'put to bed' for the weekend. Having collected the rental car, the crew headed off for downtown Trondheim – only to discover the Noggies had booked the crew into a temperance hotel. Oh well, there were plenty of other venues to quench our thirst.

The service of dedication was held on the Saturday afternoon and, despite being a low key small town ceremony, was a most memorable and moving occasion.

Sunday being a free day, what were we to do? Having previously studied the appropriate en route chart for southern Norway, I recalled how close Trondheim was to the Swedish border, just seventy miles away. Why not drive across to Sweden and sample that country's way of life. The crew readily approved of my suggestion. We drove through the unmanned Norway/Sweden border crossing point and onwards to a medium-sized town called Storlien. The town was fairly quiet – it was a Sunday! On the return journey, before re-entering Norway, we managed to liberate a Swedish national flag.

---

2. Geoff swears the captain's name was not Neville!

Come Monday morning we packed our bags and headed for the airport. Unbeknown to the crew, over the weekend the Vulcan had steadily sunk into the newly laid tarmac. Upon arrival at the aircraft, both main bogey tyre surfaces had sunk approximately two to three inches below the surface. Rather than summon an aircraft tug, the boss decided to start all four engines and blast the aircraft out of the deep ruts. I cannot remember the precise throttle settings, but it sounded extremely noisy (the cabin entrance door was open) once all engines were running. However, luck was on the crew's side and the Vulcan escaped from the ruts. The flight back to Scampton was uneventful. To the best of my knowledge the Norwegians never complained formally or otherwise about the ruts.

Having flown on 44 Squadron, 35 Squadron and 50 Squadron Vulcans, Geoff was posted to 360 Squadron, the Electronic Countermeasures (ECM) Squadron, flying Canberras. As an electronic warfare officer (EWO) he flew continuously for eleven years, additionally carrying out planning and tasking duties for three years before retiring from the service as a squadron leader in 1994. Still with flying as his raison d'etre *he joined FR Aviation as an electronic warfare operator flying Dassault Falcon 20s for a further six years. This job took him over most of Europe and involved being the 'enemy' employing electronic warfare against RAF and NATO land, sea and air targets. Determined to continue flying, he then joined Phoenix Air, a US Company flying Learjet 35/36s for another eight years, operating throughout Europe, fulfilling EW tasks for NATO countries, which now included all the ex-Warsaw Pact nations except Albania. Stopping flying at 68, his passion for aircraft had not dampened – he is currently the AEO on Vulcan XL426 when performing taxi and aborted take-off runs at Southend Airport.*

CHAPTER 7

VULCAN BALE OUT

Jim Vinales

Jim Vinales was the navigator plotter on the winning Giant Voice team against the USAF in 1974 and was also in the Black Buck 2 crew. He has vividly described these events in Vulcan Boys. *Here he describes how he had to bale out in a Vulcan.*

Autumn 1969

John Smith was very happy with his posting. He was on his way to Phantoms and did we envy him. Spike and I enjoyed a beer with John in the living room of his married quarter and he made all the expected sympathetic noises. It was the autumn of 1969. Our Canberra squadron, 45 Squadron, at RAF Tengah in Singapore was to be disbanded early in 1970 and we'd be flying our aircraft back to the UK and then moving on to our next postings. For Spike and me that meant Vulcans. Horrors! The thought of a future tour, possibly more than one tour, stuck in the back of a Vulcan (the broom cupboard with the hoover running) did not appeal. Certainly, not when many of us were expecting Phantoms or Buccaneers, then new to RAF service. Spike was even more annoyed than I was. He'd been a navigator plotter and had been roundly insulted by a posting to Vulcans as a navigator radar. This was unheard of; the usual progress for a Canberra plotter was a posting on to Vulcans also as a plotter. It was well known that only brand-new navigators got posted into the navigator radar's seat on Vulcans; that, and returning old nav radars. Spike had been a bit of a naughty lad during his tour but he was a very able plotter and this insult was insufferable.

I, on the other hand, had been reasonably well-behaved (at least over the last two years of my Singapore tour) and, although a navigator observer, it appeared that I was ready for a posting to the Vulcan as a plotter. But that was not what I wanted. The boss had recommended me for fast jets and I thought I'd be in with a good chance for Buccaneers, maybe even Phantoms. But no, in fact, it would be thirteen years before I would end up in that back seat of the Buccaneer; ten years as a Vulcan plotter plus a ground tour in operations. But in 1969, that was not something I could have possibly known. All I knew was that I was on my way to Vulcans, to the black hole of Calcutta that was the rear cockpit of the Vulcan. No daylight allowed on the radar screens in the rear – so almost total darkness, relieved only by counterpoise lamps, for those who were unfortunate enough to spend their flying hours in the 'back'. As I drove away, I glumly thought how awful it would be. After three years of great fun as a navigator observer on the Canberra B15 with its rich variety of flight profiles and loads of travel in South East Asia, Australia and New Zealand, hell awaited! I really had little idea how my time on Vulcans would unfold. Boredom was expected, but I was quite unaware of the challenges that lay ahead.

8 January 1971 – Vulcan XM610

I stood at the back of the pan and looked up at the fin of the aircraft. On its side was the RAF registration number, XM610. Either side of the fin, the triangular wings spread out, casting a large shadow across the centre of the pan. The other four members of my new crew were already inside commencing their checks. I could afford to spend a few more minutes outside the aircraft before the checklist allowed power to the navigation systems. Of the other crew members, Flight Lieutenant Jim Power, the AEO, was the only one I knew reasonably well. I'd met him at the start of my Vulcan course at RAF Scampton in June of the previous year but had then been separated from him when our crew was split to fill vacancies in other crews on 44 Squadron. In early December, Jim and I had joined the Alcock crew who'd been on the course behind us at Scampton. We were about to carry out our fourth conversion sortie on the squadron. It would also be our first squadron 'solo' – no checking officers would accompany us on this flight. Flight Lieutenant Bob Alcock, the captain, had completed his tour as a co-pilot and, having served time in the right-hand seat, was now a qualified captain. His co-pilot was Flying Officer Peter Hoskins, a baby-faced graduate of RAF College Cranwell, which in those days trained cadets chosen as the future leaders of the RAF. Mild mannered and modest, he was, nonetheless, a very competent operator and would go on to forge an excellent career in the service. Flying Officer Rodger Barker, a tall blond Yorkshireman, was nav radar, now also starting his first flying tour.

Following my tour on Canberra B15s on 45 Squadron, I had recently been promoted to flight lieutenant and was now a freshly minted Vulcan nav plotter. I'd been first into operations that morning to finish planning this sortie. The plan would take us to above 40,000 ft, to a point to the north-east of Aberdeen, then a descent to low altitude by the Isle of May. We'd be coasting in to the east of Edinburgh, remaining at low altitude all the way back to the Waddington area and then climbing back up to 40,000 ft for a series of simulated bombing runs before returning to base, a sortie due to last about five hours. I'd noted the strength of the wind at low level as being above twenty-five knots. This was annoying as it would almost certainly mean we'd have to fly somewhat higher than the 500 ft above the ground we'd planned on the low level stage of this early conversion sortie. We were expected to do what we could to extend aircraft fatigue life, in this case by avoiding excessive turbulence over the hills. Squadron Leader John Laycock, our senior flight commander and authorising officer, had heard our brief and signed the authorising sheet. We were off!

I took one last look at the aircraft from the rear and marvelled at how impressive it really was, in spite of the 'cramped black hole' I was about to climb into. Dark it certainly was, but cramped? Come off it! Not to someone who'd just spent three and a half years in the back of a Canberra B15. More than enough room to swing a cat. What were all those guys at the OCU complaining about?

We roared down the runway, we three rear crew facing backwards and held back by our seat straps, and turned towards the north-east. The high level transit to the low level entry point was uneventful. Rodger and I were beginning to work well with each other and there'd be no problem making our booked slot time at the entry point to low level. Overhead the Isle of May we turned towards Bass Rock, giving it enough of a berth to miss the abundant bird life around it, and then crossed the coast, heading south, near North Berwick.

Bob looked ahead and saw the Lammermuir hills were covered in cloud – no go. He warned the rest of us that we'd have to climb out, at least temporarily. Four miles past the coast he applied power for the climb-out. The next event was something none of us was prepared for.

A huge explosion rocked the aircraft and left me temporarily stunned. What the hell! Had we hit the ground? Impossible! I was still alive. What on earth… "Fire in No. 1 engine! Fire in No. 1 engine!"

Bob shut the engine down and operated its fire extinguisher. In the back, Jim Power switched off the engine's alternator and looked out through his periscope – no signs of fire. One engine gone but loads of power in the other three – no problem. Rodger and I cast a glance at each other, relieved but not altogether convinced it was all over. Sure enough, the temperature on No. 2 engine was rising fast. "Fire in No. 2 engine!" Fire extinguisher activated, and "drop the RAT", the ram air turbine. This act electrically isolated all non-essential equipment. My navigation gear froze. No worries! Power was more urgently required to operate the flying controls and other essential equipment. No. 2 firelight was now out. I quickly worked out a best estimate of our position and passed it to Bob. "Mayday! Mayday! Mayday!" As Bob transmitted the Mayday call, Jim Power became aware of a flicker through his periscope. "The fire's not out, the fire's not out!" No. 2 engine fire warning light reappeared. We were going to have to abandon the aircraft.

Air traffic control offered Ouston, near Newcastle, as a diversion. No go! Far too small an airfield for the Vulcan. RAF Leeming, in the Vale of York, would be far better but that was still some distance away. There was no alternative. The rear crew would have to go. The two pilots had ejection seats but we in the rear did not. Bob levelled the aircraft out at 9,000 ft –"Prepare to abandon aircraft".

Rodger swivelled his seat and moved to the door at the floor of the cabin. I operated the manual depressurisation handle. "Jump, jump" came the order from Bob. Rodger pulled back the door lever and the door opened in a cloud of dust. Marginally after Rodger, I flicked the electrical emergency door opening switch. Had to make doubly sure the door opened against the force of the slipstream. Rodger adopted a crouched position and disappeared into the morning sky. I looked at Jim. He appeared to be having trouble untangling the little chains holding his mask. Keen to help him (the escape drill stipulated the order of escape as radar – AEO – plotter), I reached out to straighten the chains but they came free and Jim quickly tightened the mask to his face. He swivelled his seat and activated his assistor cushion. The seat restraining straps came free and Jim was pushed towards the door. He too curled up and slid quickly down the escape hatch. Unlike the Victor, the Vulcan was too narrow-bodied to allow for three swivel seats. Instead, the plotter's seat was a different, narrower, design and moved backwards and forwards on rails. I slid the seat back but did not activate the assistor cushion. I had no intention of trapping my legs under the chart table. I released my seat straps and moved to the right and down to the escape hatch. I caught sight of ground through the hatch and positioned myself to slide down the hatch. Strangely, I was conscious of the two pneumatic rams holding the door down, as I slid past them.

As I left the aircraft, the roar of the remaining two engines above me was immense. Almost immediately the parachute opened with a sharp crack. Where was that two-second delay? Annoyingly, my head was held down and I realised the parachute lines were coiled up and forcing my helmet down. This was not new to me; I'd experienced it several times in my early days in Singapore when I'd taken up sky-diving. Slowly, I found myself turning as the lines unwound. In the background, I could still hear the noise of the aircraft receding. Anxious to catch a glimpse of it, I looked over my shoulders and almost everywhere else but never managed to catch sight of it as it flew towards the south. It didn't help that my parachute had opened with me facing away from the aircraft. I suddenly realised I could see two colourful parachutes ahead of me. That didn't seem right. Surely our parachutes were white. I looked up at mine and saw it was also multi-coloured and only partly white. Later it was explained to me that all our aircraft had recently been fitted with the latest escape 'chutes with multi-coloured panels for both detection in peace and camouflage in combat. For a moment I thought I'd jumped straight into the centre of a sports parachute drop.

I looked down at the ground and saw a fertile valley 9,000 ft below me. With a bit of luck there'd be a soft landing in a nice green field. But I'd temporarily forgotten that strong wind from the south-west. Within a few minutes I could see that the nice green fields were being replaced by the brown and rocky uplands of the Cheviots. Ordinarily I would have released my dinghy and let it drop a few metres below me on its webbing cord. I decided against that. I'd rather retain the dinghy close to my bottom for better protection from any rock I might hit on landing. At 1,000 ft a minute, the drop seemed to take forever. But eventually, I could see the ground accelerate towards me. Oh Lord! Those rocks seemed big and everywhere. I was resigned to, at best, a broken limb. I could see I was being swept backwards and made no attempt to turn the parachute. In a basic emergency 'chute, without steerable panels, it would have been difficult anyway.

In any case, I was happy to let my dinghy cushion my backside should I hit a rock. And then, what luck! I drifted over the top of a hill and felt my progress slow as I hit the stiller air in the lee of the hill. The next moment I'd hit the ground and rolled over a few times on soft heather. I got up, unscathed. All around me I could see the menacing rocks but through sheer luck I'd managed to avoid them all.

I unhooked my various connections and quickly considered my immediate actions. Well, there was the parachute lying in a heap. I'd spread it out as a location aid. Somebody was bound to come flying by very soon, perhaps even the rescue helicopter. And, of course, there was SARBE, my personal search and rescue beacon. Oh, yes! SARBE!

A couple of years earlier I'd been in the officers' mess bar in RAF Kai Tak, Hong Kong, just about to head into downtown Kowloon with a couple of friends. I was enjoying a drink with Paul Burns, our observer leader on 45 Squadron, an experienced navigator who'd spent most of his service life on Javelin all-weather fighters. Paul had the dubious distinction of having ejected twice. The first time was over the sea off Singapore. He'd been quickly rescued by a fishing boat. The second time was considerably more painful for him. The aircraft had stalled on the approach to RAF Akrotiri, Cyprus. He'd ejected outside the seat parameters and had crashed into the ground before he'd separated from his seat. Only the decelerating effects of the seat drogue parachute had saved him from death, but the impact on hitting the ground had broken almost every bone in his body. Amazingly, little more than a year later, he'd been pronounced fit enough to return to flying on ejection-seat aircraft. "Jim," he said, "there's one thing I regret about those two events. In neither one was I able to deploy my SARBE. I was rescued too quickly in the first and was totally unable to do so in the second. A great pity, since the makers of SARBE will give any aircrew who uses their equipment in anger, a beautifully inscribed pewter tankard. If ever you have to bale out, make sure you activate your SARBE, even if you come down in the middle of the village green!"

Well, I certainly wasn't in the village green, I was in the middle of a desolate hilltop and I fancied that tankard. I stood the beacon on the nearest rock and set it beeping away for all it was worth. The rock would help increase the range of transmission, or so I'd been told.

I heard a voice coming at me from a distance. It was Rodger. He was down in the valley and had spotted me on the skyline. " Are you OK? I'm off to find Jim," he cried. "I'm fine, I'll stay up here and watch out for search aircraft," I answered back. He moved out of sight. Within minutes, a Varsity training aircraft appeared. It circled my position and I enjoyed myself by firing off mini flares at it. After some minutes, content that I was OK, it flew off. I was happy that he'd be relaying our position to the rescue coordination centre. A helicopter would soon be on its way. I was full of adrenalin and could not just sit down and wait. Instead, I rolled up my parachute, content that we'd been spotted, but it was too cumbersome to take with me. I left it where it lay and, dinghy pack in hand, started walking off in the direction I felt Jim to be. I had not walked more than a few hundred yards when a Whirlwind search and rescue helicopter suddenly appeared round the brow of the hill. The pilot spotted me and immediately slowed down and positioned the helicopter in the hover just above me on the hill. I ran the few steps up to the chopper and pulled myself into it, noticing that both Jim and Rodger were already in it. I had had the presence of mind to take my SARBE with me. Jim pointed at my beacon, reached out and disconnected the aerial. He was on intercom and had received instructions from the pilot to silence my SARBE. I looked at Rodger. He had a big bump over his left eye, obviously a heavy landing. I looked at Jim again and saw he had a trickle of dried blood by his right ear. The poor bloke had ended up in a tree desperately hanging on for dear life, like a koala bear. As he hit the tree, a small branch had penetrated his helmet and cut his ear. Fortunately, it was only superficial.

Back at the helicopter's base, C Flight, 202 Squadron, at RAF Acklington, we learned that both Bob and Peter had ejected and both were safe, although Bob's back had suffered in the ejection. Now the crew asked us to get back into the helicopter; they'd been tasked to take us to Ashington Hospital. At the hospital, a nice chap took my details and I asked him about his local town. "Do you mean to tell me you haven't heard of us before? Why, this is the home of Bobby and Jack Charlton!" I quickly apologised for my ignorance and made the excuse that as a Gibraltarian I'd lived in England only a total of three years.

Survivors: Vulcan XM610 8 January 1971. From left: Flt Lt James Power, AEO; Flt Lt James Vinales, nav plotter; Fg Off Rodger Barker, nav radar; Fg Off Peter Hoskins co-pilot and Flt Lt Garth 'Bob' Alcock, captain. *(Jim Vinales)*

Medical check complete, I stood up from the trolley bed, clad only in my boxer briefs, a little self-consciously. The briefs had been a gift from a girlfriend with a sense of humour; they were pink, a colour popular in the late sixties, and, had I known what was going to happen to me that day, I probably would have not worn them. But, unbeknown to me, there was worse. I had left the aircraft at a speed of about 230 knots, about double the speed at which paratroopers are normally despatched. Unsurprisingly, the parachute had opened with one hell of a yank! Underneath my flying suit, the back of my briefs had been torn from the elastic band to the bottom, my rear cheeks exposed to all and sundry. No wonder the nurses were having a bit of a giggle!

We three rear crew made it back to Waddington late in the evening and after debrief with the station doctors, we headed for the bar. A loud cheer went up as we entered the bar and we were soon surrounded by a whole stack of friends wanting to know our story. The beers kept coming but, with so much adrenalin in our systems, the alcohol was having hardly any effect. The beers tasted good and we basked at the centre of all the attention. The party lasted well past the normal bar closing time and it was into the early hours of the morning before we hit our beds.

Bob Alcock's back had suffered during the ejection and it was a few months before the crew could all fly together again. But fly together again we did and we went on to complete our tour, and never once moaned at having to do crew escape drills.

At that time Jim had a girlfriend, Margaret, who was a teacher at Tengah school. On hearing about the crash Margaret asked Rosemary, also a teacher and wife of Anthony Wright (co-author), who now worked in the War Room at HQ Far East Command, if he could find out any more information. He was able to forward the following message to Rosemary and then to Margaret.

```
V
1835: BOMBER:
    WINGATE, ENGLAND, JAN 8, REUTER -- AN AIRFORCE VULCAN
JET BOMBER, FORMERLY THE MAIN VEHICLE FOR BRITAIN'S NUCLEAR
STRIKE FORCE, CRASHED HERE TODAY DURING A ROUTINE TRAINING
FLIGHT NARROWLY MISSING THIS SMALL NORTHERN ENGLISH VILLAGE.
    ALL FIVE CREW MEMBERS SAFELY BALED OUT BEFORE THE BURNING
BOMBER LEAVING BEHIND A TRAIL OF THICK BLACK SMOKE DIVED FOR THE
GROUND AND EXPLODED IN A FIELD 100 YARDS (METRE) BEHIND
HERE.
    THE AIRFORCE ANNOUNCED LATER THAT A BOARD OF ENQUIRY IS
BEING SET UP TO INVESTIGATE THE CRASH.
    REUTER (ALL)
```
9 JAN 1971

Margaret

Have scanned UK papers but can't find anything on it! (Telegraph)

CHAPTER 8

VULCAN STORIES

Brian Cushion, Bill Downs, Monty Montgomery

Brian Cushion and Bill Downs were Vulcan pilots and they remember some incidents from their tours. Monty Montgomery describes some of his experiences as a co-pilot to Bill Downs before going on to greater things.

Brian Cushion *started his flying career as a Vulcan co-pilot and went on to be a QFI on Jet Provosts at Cranwell. From there he spent fourteen years on the Nimrod. After leaving the service he became an airline pilot flying DC9s, Fokker 100/70s and finally the A319/20/21 with British Midland.*

Prologue

Following completion of advanced flying training I found myself posted to the Vulcan force as a slightly reluctant co-pilot. I had wanted to go to the maritime world on the Shackleton. But, as there was only one posting slot available and we had an ex-Shackleton AEO on our course that was a bit of a lost cause. I wanted to fly something a bit more warlike than the C-130 Hercules and I definitely did not want to go to the Mk 1 Victor tanker. That bit about the curvature of the earth being included in their take-off performance calculation was quite unsettling. Thus, in 1970 I arrived to start a two-and-a-half-year tour on 101 Squadron at RAF Waddington.

Codeword – Sandwiches

The V Force exercised the activation of dispersal airfields on nearly a monthly basis. Although the exercise name changed at various times, they are probably best remembered as Kinsman or Candella. This was pre-planned and involved four aircraft from main base being tasked to land at a dispersal airfield following a training sortie. On arrival they were serviced and refuelled in preparation for a practice scramble the following day. The crews and dispersal staff would be accommodated overnight in the dispersal caravans and could be independent of the station facilities. The following morning the dispersal ops room would be manned and the crews and aircraft declared at readiness 15 (RS15). After a short time the bomber controller at High Wycombe would bring the crews to five minutes readiness (RS05) via the command broadcast system ('bomber box'). We would man our aircraft and await the RS02 call (start engines) via the telebrief and the subsequent scramble message. We would then launch off to complete another training sortie before recovering to main base. In this way both the personnel earmarked to man the dispersals and the host station personnel were exercised on a rotational basis.

Much less frequently, because of the cost and disruption involved, there would be a full-scale exercise of all the dispersal airfields as part of a force-wide generation exercise. This would commence with the early morning callout and progress with aircraft being despatched to their dispersal airfields as they were generated. Ground crew and dispersal operations staff would travel by road to the nearer airfields or be consigned by Hastings or C-130 to the more distant ones.

That was how, one day in 1971, I came to be in the group of huts that comprised the V Force dispersal at RAF Wyton. We had arrived the evening before as one of four Waddington crews allocated to the dispersal and were now on RS15, awaiting whatever the exercise controllers had in store for us. Facilities at Wyton were fairly basic. Although the sleeping caravans were located close to the station operations block and handy for the aircrew feeder, the dispersal buildings were located on the north side of the airfield, remote from the station itself. Apart from the inevitable bridge (or poker) school, there was little to distract us while we waited in the very basic hut that served as a crew room. Thus the main feature of life on RS15 became "When do we next eat?"

Mid-morning the routine was broken by the arrival of the dispersal commander; in this case it was the physical education officer (PEdO) who had drawn the short straw. He came to announce that the recently appointed AOC 1 Group, AVM Horsley was touring the dispersals and was expected later that morning. That meant that lunch might be delayed, news that was not well received. A little while later, the PEdO reappeared, this time bearing a large tray of sandwiches and pint bottles of milk along with some paper cups. "Too kind!" someone called as movement commenced towards the sandwiches (obviously recompense in advance in case lunch was delayed). The PEdO placed said sandwiches on the table in the centre of the room and declared, "This is for the AOC's lunch. Touch them at your peril!"

Shortly before noon, the AOC arrived. He came in to the crew room and chatted to us, explaining that he was intent on visiting as much of his command as possible to see the conditions under which we might have to operate. I must confess that it made a pleasant change to see an air officer out and about during an exercise and he made a good impression upon all of us. He ignored the sandwiches, prominent on the table throughout. He then left to visit the dispersal operations room next door and we presumed that he would return for lunch. Shortly afterwards he emerged from the operations hut and made his way to a waiting staff car making what was interpreted by the watching crews as 'goodbye gestures'. Clearly the AOC had other plans for lunch and the sandwiches and milk lasted little over a minute longer; they had to go round twenty of us after all. We now settled back into our routine, awaiting the call that transport to lunch in the feeder was available. Our reverie was broken, not by the call to lunch, but by our PEdO demanding to know what had happened to the sandwiches. "We've eaten them," he was told. "Come on stop messing about chaps, the AOC wants his lunch," got the same response. The enormity of his situation slowly dawned upon him, twenty apparently unrepentant aircrew and a hungry air vice-marshal. Maybe an extended posting to Stornoway might be the best he could hope for. As we couldn't do anything to replace the sandwiches there was a fairly collective shrug from the aircrew in the knowledge that we would either get away with it or not. In any case the matter was swiftly forgotten as lunch beckoned and as we waited to cross the runway we had to wait for the AOC's Hastings to depart on the next stage of his tour.

Early the next day we were roused from our sleep by the bomber controller as the force was brought up to RS05. After an hour or so strapped in to our aircraft the call came to advance to RS02. However there was one little variation to the standard broadcast. The RS05 message had been addressed to 'All Bomblists' but the RS02 call, although similarly addressed, contained the additional instruction 'Exempt Bedford'. Bedford being the dispersal airfield that was covered by crews from Scampton. The scramble message came very soon afterwards and we launched off to fly our pre-planned exercise sortie. If we thought any further about the "Exempt Bedford" instruction, we merely assumed that it was for deconfliction and timing purposes and that we would have been scrambled soon afterwards. We landed back at Waddington without incident, handed in our kit and it being a Friday afternoon were soon on our way to make the best of a weekend that we felt lucky had not been disrupted. The events of the previous forty-eight hours were soon forgotten.

Forgotten that is until I happened to be at the hatch in the Waddington operations room on the Monday morning when the bomber box gave its characteristic long tone that presaged a broadcast. The broadcast followed and it was for "Bedford only" bringing the dispersal up to RS05! I asked the ops staff what was going on and it was explained to me, "Yes, they were still there". Apparently our new AOC had read the war orders and lighted upon the paragraph that stated that dispersals had to be able to operate independent of station support for twenty-eight days. When he established that this had never been tried he ordered that it was about time we did it and hence four unfortunate Scampton crews were still on exercise and looked likely to be there a lot longer. But that was not the end of the matter, squadron leader ops recognised me and said, "You were at the Wyton dispersal, there's something you need to see". He then handed me a signal which went roughly as follows:

From AOC 1 Group

To: Station Commander Waddington

Pass to Wyton Dispersal Crews

Codeword – Sandwiches

Had time permitted Bedford would have read Wyton

Horsley

Yours truly shall leave it for others to tell the full tale of the 'Bedford Incident' and what happened there, but we had a lucky escape and were very fortunate that the AOC had a sense of humour.

Exercise Edith

Following the end of the requirement to have crews on QRA at the main bases, the Vulcan force still retained the ability to generate rapidly a QRA force in event of emergency. This was effected through Exercise Edith which required that a number of crews at each station, usually one per squadron, were to be available within one hour of being called out. This was no great imposition during the week but assumed significant proportions come the weekend. Remember, this was the late 1960s/early 1970s when mobile phones were still in the realms of science fiction and the only person you knew who had a pager (which was the size of a half brick) was the student district midwife you were seeing at the time. A straightforward trip into Lincoln on a Saturday afternoon required planning and a pocketful of change as you had to pop into a phone box every thirty minutes or so to check that you had not been called out.

One Saturday afternoon, someone at High Wycombe or Bawtry decided to exercise the system and the Edith crews were called out. The four crews reported to operations, drew their 'go bags' containing their allocated targets from the vault and settled down to wait whilst the aircraft were generated. As each aircraft became available a crew was despatched to carry out the combat checks and provided that the aircraft was serviceable they would then declare themselves on state at Readiness 15.

All was going smoothly to plan when our crew was called to go out and check an aircraft. We boarded the small and elderly Bedford crew coach and set off for the aircraft which was positioned on the far side of the airfield. All was going well until we took the bend in the taxiway just before the threshold of Runway 03 at Waddington. A slight sway developed and rapidly increased in amplitude. At this point the inevitability of what was about to happen struck me. The last couple of oscillations seemed to occur in slow motion followed by a quarter roll. Everything now speeded up and appeared to be going very fast as we slid across a combination of grass and concrete, with accompanying sound effects, before coming to rest just on the runway threshold.

Everything now was very quiet. I did a quick check and I seemed to be pretty much in one piece so decided to make for the nearest exit and then assess the situation. The nearest exit was where the windscreen used to be and on the way I collected the WRAF driver. As I helped her out of the vehicle she enquired of me "Do you think I'll get into trouble for this sir?" I was about to reply "probably" but stopped myself and said, "Let's not worry about that now". By this time the rest of the crew was emerging behind us and appeared in various states of disrepair, but thankfully no one appeared badly hurt. The nav radar was fine, having fallen on top of the plotter. However the plotter was a little worse for wear from this encounter. The AEO had now emerged and his training immediately kicked in; he went straight in to assess the casualties. This didn't last long. There was some blood around and he asked, "Where's the blood coming from?" The nav radar helpfully replied, "It's yours"; he had a nosebleed; and this was sufficient for him to lose interest in setting up a casualty clearing station. The captain now appeared and although physically all right, he was visibly shaken by the accident.

The fire service now appeared on the scene, followed closely by the crash ambulance and after a quick check over we were all taken to the station medical centre for further examination. Fortunately no one had suffered more than very minor injury. The AEO's nosebleed had quickly ceased, I had a graze to one knee and the nav radar was totally unscathed. The nav plotter was a bit sore and shaken from his colleague having landed upon him and the captain looked as though he was suffering from mild shock. The WRAF driver was also physically unhurt although still rather apprehensive about her fate. It was clear that we had had a lucky escape. So, three of us were judged fit to continue – the AEO, nav radar and I – but the captain and nav plotter were sent home. As we gathered up our bits of equipment, helmets and nav bags, someone enquired, "Where's the go bag?" For the second time that day it all went very quiet. The sealed nav bag that contained the top secret target material was nowhere to be found. There followed a succession of frantic phone calls to anyone who might have been in the vicinity of the overturned crew coach and could be able to cast some light upon its whereabouts. For the second time it was the fire service that came to the rescue. A fireman had noticed the unclaimed bag at the scene and put it in the cab of one of the fire engines so a quick detour was made to the fire section to reclaim it as we made our way back to operations.

Whilst all this was happening the clock was still ticking. The station had a limited time in which to achieve the aircraft and crew generation target and finding a replacement crew at this stage in the proceedings could prove challenging. The options were being reviewed when the station commander arrived to see how things were going. This resulted in a quick executive decision, he would take over as captain and the wing bombing and nav systems (BNS) officer, a nav plotter by profession, was collared to stand in for the other crew member. The station commander was in his Saturday afternoon civvies and the BNS officer in his blue uniform, but none of this mattered as we had to combat check the aircraft soonest and there would be time to change afterwards.

Combat checks complete, we declared ourselves on state at RS15 and returned to operations to await developments. No sooner had we arrived than the bomber box announced "Exercise Edith – Waddington crews only – Readiness State 05!" Having the station commander as captain meant an upgrade (of sorts) in crew transport. We all crammed in to his Austin 1800 staff car and set off for the aircraft, pennant fluttering on the bonnet. Very shortly after climbing into the aircraft we received a broadcast message to "start engines". This was an exercise in artificiality; rather than have the aircraft, which were positioned on dispersals around the airfield, start and taxi to the runway in response to a RS02 order we would start all four engines to prove serviceability and then shut down but remain locked in at RS05.

All went well and engines were duly started and shut down. We then did the thing we did best, we sat in the aircraft and waited for someone to make a decision. This arrived shortly in the form of another broadcast instructing us to revert to RS15. A short explanation is needed here, all reversions to a lower readiness state than the one in force had to be authenticated – shown to be correctly issued – and this was done by providing a codeword along with the reversion instruction. The authentication received would then be compared with a list of codewords in a sealed envelope held by the nav radar. The veracity of the message would then be confirmed by another crew member and the crew would comply with the instruction. This time however, the nav radar came up on the intercom and said, "it doesn't authenticate". Crew action in this situation was cast in tablets of stone – you stayed put until you received a correct authentication. We could see one of the other Edith aircraft and there was no movement there either, so it wasn't a case of us having the wrong envelope. It seemed that no one had the right one.

After a while air traffic control noticed that nothing was happening and helpfully re-broadcast the reversion message and authentication. They tried a couple more times before an anonymous voice replied, "it doesn't authenticate". Another delay followed and ATC came back with: "We've spoken to operations and that's the one they've received", followed by a re-broadcast of the incorrect codeword. Predictably, the crews stayed in the aircraft and the stalemate (quite correctly) continued.

In our aircraft there was now an unexpected development. The Wing BNS officer appeared on the ladder between the pilot seats and the following exchange occurred:

BNS: "Sir, I think I know what's happened."

Station commander: "Yes?"

BNS: "They've broadcast the exercise termination message instead of the reversion message."

Station commander: "Why would they do that?"

BNS: "When they receive the termination message they have to take it to the duty vault officer who authenticates it and issues the reversion codeword."

Station commander: "So why haven't they done that?"

There was now a short pause while the BNS officer took a deep breath.

BNS: "Well you see sir, I'm the duty vault officer and I've got the keys to the vault."

Station commander: "Well, the keys are in my car so you'd better get off and do what needs to be done and bring my car back ASAP. By the way, don't roll it, we don't want two MT accidents in one day."

The BNS officer departed and the necessary arrangements were made. A correct codeword was received and we all exited our aircraft, packed all the kit away and handed back the go bags. Following the scare with the temporary loss of our go bag it was decided that operational bags would no longer be issued on exercises. I don't know what was decided on the use of vault officers.

The WRAF driver did get into trouble and was charged and fined, albeit a modest amount. We bought her a big box of chocolates to show that there were no hard feelings.

Demijohns

It was the end of a squadron detachment to Akrotiri. We had spent an enjoyable ten days or so flying low level through Greece and were now preparing to return to Waddington. Ground crew and spare aircrew would go by VC10 and the lucky ones would fly our aircraft back. However, the day before we were due to depart it became apparent that one Vulcan would not be ready as it was unserviceable and awaiting spares from home base. It was our crew that drew the short(ish) straw to remain behind and ferry home the last jet.

The spare part arrived with the VC10 taking home the detachment and whilst everyone else departed our crew chief and a junior engineering officer set to work on the unserviceable aircraft. Rectification proceeded smoothly and they were soon able to declare that we would be able to plan our own return for the following morning, Sunday.

The next morning as the seven of us boarded the coach to take us to Air Movements for a pre-flight breakfast someone recalled the pre-detachment briefing we had attended at Waddington. In those days we used to have our own resident customs officer on the station who would normally live in the officers' mess. At the time the incumbent of the post was an affable and sociable Irishman called Jim. Jim had attended the pre-detachment briefing to advise on our customs allowances and had finished with the admonition:

"Now, it's my weekend off so Grimsby will be coming down to do you and as it's cup final day they won't be in too good a mood!"

Someone remembered this and had an idea. It went along the lines of:

"With just one aircraft coming back on a Sunday and it being Jim's weekend off, Grimsby won't want to come down to Waddington two days running so it'll be the station duty officer (SDO) who'll do the customs clearance."

The SDO would want a quick 'nothing to declare' on the customs form, for as we were all well aware anything at all declared under these circumstances would attract duty and mean unwelcome paperwork all round; not to mention payment.

We had all already purchased a demijohn[3] of Cyprus sherry. Even after paying some customs duty this would still be a good buy. However, by the time we reached Air Movements a plan had formed, we all went into the small duty-free shop there and each purchased a demijohn of brandy to supplement the sherry we had already acquired. Well it seemed too good an opportunity to miss, and what could possibly go wrong?

---

3. A wicker-covered thick glass bottle holding approximately 1 gallon.

The flight home was uneventful and we landed at Waddington in the early afternoon. As we turned into the dispersal I spied a little green Morris Minor at the far end. It was Jim the customs officer's car! My announcement of this sighting caused a flurry of activity in the cabin. Our quick thinking nav plotter dived into the nose section where the demijohns were stored and hurriedly tore the labels off, stuffing them into his flying suit pockets. This left us a short time to get our story straight which was basically "Don't say a word unless asked".

When the door opened, there was Jim at the bottom of the ladder:

"Hello Jim," I said "I thought it was your weekend off?" "It's no problem, I don't mind a bit of overtime for you chaps and it spares you from the clutches of Grimsby,[4]" he replied and added "just get everything on the coach and we'll be on our way."

As we unloaded our kit, a seemingly endless line of demijohns started to come down the ladder. Jim's eyes got wider, "How many more?" he asked. "...er quite a few" I said. He directed us to get them all on the coach "and we'll sort it out there".

Eventually we were fully unloaded and seated on the coach behind the serried ranks of unlabelled demijohns. Jim stood at the front with his book of duty tables and looked at them.

"How many have you got?"

"Fourteen, Jim."

"And how many of you are there?"

"Seven Jim."

"Oh dear, I don't know how we're going to work this out, how many did you say again?"

"Fourteen Jim, two each."

"Oh dear, oh dear."

Jim shuffled through his duty tables, made some notes and after extensive calculation said:

"If we call it two demijohns of fortified wine that will be £2.00 each. Will that be all right?"

We didn't haggle and paid up promptly.

Was it worth it though? Well no matter how hard you tried and what recipe you used brandy sours never tasted the same once away from Akrotiri. The illicit demijohn languished for a few years and eventually ended up in the punch at another squadron party elsewhere. In addition I have always felt a tinge of guilt at putting one over on Jim who was a really nice chap. So Jim, if you ever happen to read this, I'm sorry.

Epilogue

Shortly before the end of my tour I married the midwife referred to in the opening paragraph of the Edith tale. Even that was not without incident as a week before the

---

4.   The Grimsby rummage crew had an almost mythological and fearsome reputation.

wedding a no-notice exercise was called and with days to go I found myself in Karup, Denmark following an engine fire. I sent her a telegram saying: "Am in Denmark, hope to be back in time."

If she didn't know what she was letting herself in for already, that was a pretty big hint! Luckily I did make it back and we're still together over forty years later.

I finally made it to maritime following a tour instructing on the Jet Provost. The Nimrod lived up to my expectations and I spent fourteen years on the aircraft doing a whole range of interesting things. With the end of the Cold War I decided it was time to leave and departed for a new career in the airline industry. Whilst the flying was totally different that too was immensely satisfying and good fun. That lasted sixteen years and for a short period I was, at the age of 57, the oldest UK licence holder to do an Airbus conversion course. It was hard work, but the training I had received all those years before helped me through.

Bill Downs joined the RAF in 1954 and in 1960 was on 18 Squadron flying Valiants as a co-pilot on ECM support. In 1963 he joined 35 Squadron as a captain and remained on Vulcans until 1974 when he was on IX Squadron.

Bomb Hang-up

My crew was co-pilot Fg Off McKinley, nav radar Flt Lt Thomson, nav plotter Flt Lt Wilmshurst and AEO Fg Off Hannaford. Our training profile included 4 x 100-lb practice bombing on Jurby (Isle of Man) bombing range.

The procedure was to set up a racetrack pattern over the range, with the nav radar guiding the aircraft and releasing the bomb using, on this occasion, the H2S system. The nav plotter was positioned at the visual bomb aimer's position enabling him to confirm that the bomb had left the aircraft in a stable trajectory. The AEO also, by means of the periscope, visually checked that the bomb had left the bomb bay. Each of the four 100-lb bombs would be dropped one at a time and scored by the range operators.

In 1963/64 there had been within the Vulcan force a number of incidents involving practice bombing and as these 100 pounders were Second World War leftovers filled with high explosives, the hierarchy were a bit twitchy. All incidents were microscopically analysed and crews placed at fault where possible. Careers from air vice-marshals downwards were at risk! Consequently take-offs for practice bombing sorties were with fear and trepidation and the cockpits and nav bags stuffed with order books and SOP manuals. The atmosphere during the pre-flight steak and chips would be spoilt with apprehension.

We were on our third run in to the target having had two good results on the previous runs, when as the release point approached the bomb doors opened and the nav radar announced, "bomb gone". But it hadn't. Both the nav plotter and AEO said, "not observed". As with any release malfunction – 'you close the bomb doors' immediately, which I did. Whilst I was pondering what might have happened and the nav radar checked his equipment I checked that the bomb-door indicator doll's-eye showed black (closed) and at that very instant there was a thump and the doll's eye blinked white then back to black. I was as certain as my pending court martial, that we had a loose, and now armed, 100-lb bomb pointing forward and not far away from the bulkhead which could, under deceleration or pitch down, spoil our day. After discussion with the crew I decided the only solution was to carry out another racetrack pattern and open the bomb doors manually at the release point for the target. The range safety officer was happy especially as the range was the only clear area in the Irish Sea at that time. We checked every order and SOP relevant to our situation only to discover one had not yet been written. We were trail blazers! I thought I bet there will be one written before my court martial.

So, we carried out the run on target and at release point I opened the bomb doors. To our relief the nav plotter called bomb gone clean. As it had left the aircraft cleanly I hit at the R/T button and called "score it" which the range operators did. We did not attempt any more drops.

The Bill Downs crew 35 Squadron Cottesmore 1966. Anthony Wright, nav radar; Bill Downs, captain; Nigel Harding, AEO; Gordon Blackburn, nav plotter and Geof Delmege, co-pilot.

On our return to Coningsby I was immediately invited to the station commander's office. By the time I arrived he had covered his desk with a shed load of order books and SOPs. I felt I should advise him there was nothing in the order books that I had contravened but then decided I would be better off keeping quiet. During the 'interview' the ops officer entered the office and handed the station commander a piece of paper: on it was the score achieved by the last bomb. "Best score of the day", he said with some reluctance. The most significant thing I learnt that day was when engaged in a one-way discussion with a very senior officer you don't say "what would you have done sir?" They don't like it!

Hydraulic Failure

It was 17 September 1964. Our sortie was to drop sixteen 100-lb practice bombs on the El Adem range, operating from RAF Luqa. My crew this time was co-pilot Flt Lt Langdown, nav radar Flt Lt Thompson, nav plotter Flt Lt Wilmshurst and AEO Fg Off Hannaford.

Having dropped some of the sixteen bombs the main hydraulic pressure gauge indicated some unusual fluctuations. We ceased bombing and commenced recovery back to Luqa. Within minutes the main hydraulic pressure fell to zero. This meant we had no brakes, no nosewheel steering on landing: undercarriage lowering by nitrogen accumulator bottle gas only, a one-shot action. We still had some bombs in the bomb bay which we would have to jettison using the bomb door emergency hydraulic system.

The runway at Luqa was 7,500 ft long with a village close to touchdown on the eastern end and a quarry on the western end. Luqa was a no go! We raised a radio distress call with a request to land at USAF base Wheelus which had a 13,000 ft runway, clear skies and calm wind. Wheelus accepted our request. On route we overflew the Gulf of Sirte where we jettisoned the remaining bombs using the emergency bomb door system, which, thankfully, was electrically driven. After the doors had closed the system pressure also fell to zero. With plenty of fuel to burn off we had ample time to discuss my intentions on landing and informed ATC Wheelus. I reminded the crew of the implications of bale out with the undercarriage down and gave them the option of bale out under calm and controlled conditions before operating the undercarriage emergency blow down. Without dramatising, I remember thinking, everything should be straightforward providing the tail brake chute deployed and that I could maintain some directional control until a low ground speed. A call from crash/rescue asked what our threshold speed would be. I thought, USAF have everything but surely not 130 kt fire vehicles! Anyway the crew, bless 'em, decided to stay and not miss the fun.

On the final approach we blew the landing gear down and we got the three greens. Over the runway threshold was a helicopter with what turned out to be a bag of foam swinging underneath it. Comforting! Touchdown was good and with the combination of brake chute and aerodynamic braking, which always impresses the crowds, we tapered off the speed quite effectively but then, as expected, it took quite a distance to finally come to a halt. There was no problem keeping it straight.

Later on that evening we were in the bar at RAF Idris still in flying suits when a Hastings from Luqa arrived with our crew chief, various ground equipment and our personal baggage, plus a clutch of group captains of various trades and interrogatory skills. Before I knew it, I was nailed to the wall explaining our day's excitement. I remember a group captain engineer who in seriousness questioned my decision to go to Wheelus instead of Luqa. By now I was on a short fuse. I asked him if he was familiar with Luqa airfield, of course he was. He would know then that it had only 7,500 ft of runway with lots of nasty bits at both ends. I could see he was getting a bit narked and remember thinking to hell with my twelve-year direct commission career so I explained that my decision was based on Wheelus having 13,000 ft of runway with clear overrun at both ends and on this day it took 12,500 ft to stop. I don't think we paid for another drink that evening.

The Day I Nearly Died Twice

It was 16 March 1964. We were on Exercise Kinsman and my crew hadn't changed. Kinsman was a test in which a training sortie would be flown followed by a landing at a dispersal airfield. These were chosen for their remoteness from the home base and would be used in the event of increased alert states in times of political tension between NATO/UK countries and Russian/Eastern bloc countries. On this particular day we were to land at RAE Llanbedr (NW Wales) within the Snowdonia National Park. It is right on the coast and is bordered by a range of hills to the east.

On our descent to the runway 18 approach we were advised by ATC that due to the wind direction, from the east, severe turbulence was to be expected and they had ceased flying. After a brief discussion with ATC I took the option of continuing the approach to land at my discretion. All was well until at about 500 ft when all hell broke loose. With a very low wing loading the Vulcan could be a bit of a handful in turbulence and on this occasion was something I had never experienced before. I had obviously made the wrong decision to continue. Excess power at the low fuel weight saved the day and we climbed away and returned to Coningsby.

During the morning our wives went to the usual married quarters coffee gathering and were warned that a prowler was known to be in the area and seemed to know when their husbands were away. They should keep their doors and windows locked as a precaution. After landing back at Coningsby, it was early evening, and after all the excitement we decided a couple of pints in the mess would be nice before returning to our loved ones.

During the evening, the station duty officer informed us of the prowler problem and would we inform our wives. After another couple of pints we went home and this is when the real trouble started!

As usual, I went to the back door of our married quarter only to find it locked: I could also hear my wife shouting what sounded like "Bill, Bill, help!" What she was actually shouting, I later discovered was "Phil, Phil, our next door neighbour". Anyway my reaction was to get indoors quickly as the prowler was obviously in there. Fumbling with my keys in the pitch dark I finally entered through the front door, rushed through to the lounge/diner to be met by a deranged wife wielding a poker in a skull crushing manner. I managed to avoid head contact from the first swipe but she caught me with the second on my left shoulder. I managed to get my arms around her and stop the wielding motion. Any chance of a loving embrace at that moment was a bit out of the question. I was off flying for a week after that recovering from a damaged shoulder. They caught the prowler soon after that – we think he must have heard about my experience and gave himself up.

Bertie The 0.9 Mach Budgie
Early in my accompanied tour in Cyprus, 1972/74. I bought a cock budgie chick for the kids which they named Bertie. With no experience of caring for birds I sought advice and also purchased a book on the subject. One of the primary 'don'ts' repeatedly stressed was to protect the bird from stressful circumstances.

Bertie was a fascinating little pet who very quickly became one of the family and was quick to learn and mimic our speech. He was very sociable and was let out of his cage every day. On the many occasions we had post-flight beers, the crew would come round to our married quarter and Bertie would be let out of his cage and by popular demand allowed to socialise and share the beer. This he would do by perching on the rim of the glass and stick his beak in. He frequently fell in. Not to be put off, after rescue he would be off again onto someone else's glass and the process would be repeated. Brandy sour and beer were his favourites. He had many escapades that ornithologists would doubt he could survive – but he did.

Towards the end of our tour, September 1974, Sue and I and the kids could not face the thought of parting with Bertie so I decided to take him back to the UK on our final UK ranger. He was to be kept in his hooded cage with food and water under the care of Jim Herbert our nav radar and I included him on the crew manifest. I was a bit concerned as to how he would cope with all the noise and acceleration during take-off and as soon as we were established on the climb I asked Jim how Bertie was coping to be told he had fallen off his perch 'legs up' . After a blast of 100% oxygen he recovered and got back on his perch with no further incident. During the transit I increased the mach number to 0.9 in deference to the little fella – he must have had a world record.

At Waddington customs checked the manifest and queried the whereabouts of Wing Commander A Budgie. "Out there by the nosewheel," I said, "He's in a bird cage."

Bertie was cared for by a very good friend until we returned to the UK; he continued to live a very comfortable, and social life for some years after.

Monty Montgomery was the detachment commander in Ascension during the Falklands Campaign. Here he tells us what it was like when he was a junior co-pilot with Bill Downs as his captain.

SFOM Song

The Vulcan was built as a bomber, fact. However, for most of the public, the aircraft became something to be seen at air displays, its dramatic style and superb lines creating oohs and aahs all round. The fact that the aircraft was designed to go and level parts of what was then the Soviet Union was not widely signalled at the shows. For many of the aircrews (and not a few crew chiefs) the aircraft had a far better, and more ideal, role: the perfect configuration was with a large pannier in the bomb bay ready to be filled with goodies on a ranger at Offutt or wherever. But it was as a bomber she was built.

The SFOM view through the co-pilot's windscreen. *(Monty Montgomery)*

Crews were supposed to learn bombing skills on the OCU. This, of course, was a big fib. The course was in reality an aircraft conversion course – the 'operational' bit would come on the squadron. However, bombing was taught on the OCU – for the navigators. Well, bombing as they wanted it to be.

As a baby co-pilot, I was more than a little excited about what would be my first bombing trip on the said OCU. Like generations of my ilk before me, this wave of euphoria lasted for the first ten minutes of crossing middle England at 40,000 feet with the autopilot engaged. This thrill consisted of watching the dials on the flight director remaining crossed until some wise man at the rear remarked that the 'bomb' was gone. By the time we started on our tenth or so run, I was agog with a kind of indifference and a real interest in the ration box. Of course, all sort of gibberish emanated into the pilot's intercom from the back and, like countless idiots before me, I was talked into going down the ladder to have a look at what was actually going on. To see two grown men chortling away over blobs on a screen was not quite the stuff of *Enemy Coast Ahead*. I would soon learn that all they ever discussed was 'offsets' and the Bardney sugar beet factory or the corner of some hangar at Hemswell. Or was it Lindholme? Worse still, after trips, these fellas stood in the corner of the bar swopping bits of acetate marked with their favourite offsets – or at least that is what they told me. Let's face it – for the drivers, high level bombing was as exciting as trying to read Morse code but without the interest. And, of course, we never dropped anything more dramatic than a 'tone' which was measured by other navigators on the ground and they gave each other direct hits all the time. Russia, watch out!

For pilots, bombing only started when the aircraft got to low level. Now, this was a different ball game altogether. First of all, you had to *find* the target and no Bardney sugar beet factory in sight.

Any crew worth their salt picked targets for the annual training requirements that you could actually see – like dams, mountains or control towers. Unfortunately, the nebies who chose targets for bombing competitions tended to select slightly different targets: like farm gates; or huts in the middle of woods; or buildings on the reverse side of a hill. Now, as the Vulcan was designed as a nuclear bomber, I always thought farm gates were a bit unrepresentative of what we might be asked to do come 'the day'.

However, it was, of course, navigators who selected these targets. They wanted to keep the pilots out of it (except to the extent of doing – within their limited ability – what they were told).

This was back to the 'offset' stuff and 'let's keep Bardney in sight'. However, at low level, these offset things did not seem too obvious, as farmers did not tend to build sugar beet factories in the middle of Scotland – where most of the competition targets were. To compensate for this, some navigators, rather grumpily, let pilots in on a little bit of the act. This concession usually concerned asking the pilot to point at the target and to fly over it in a straight line. How the pilots found the target was another story but usually involved skilled map reading by the co-pilot or doing what the plotter told you until you saw (or thought you saw) the thing in the distance. The offset brigade in the back then looked after the ranging of the bombing run. This arrangement had the advantage that each could blame the other for the subsequent cock up. Really good pilot crews, of course, did the whole thing on their own and invariably scored great results – or missed by the size of Berwickshire. This technique, by the way, was the main reason for the fitting of the refuelling probe, which was really a visual bombing aid for pilots who needed something obvious to aim with. Other suggestions were made from time to time that would not be suitable for a family newspaper. Then came SFOM... SFOM is French for bombsight.

Someone, somewhere and at some time (it must have been 1 Group) decided that co-pilots should have a toy that they could play with to avoid them fiddling with the fuel tray. Amazingly, someone found an attic of these things (I suspect in Malta from Canberra BI8s when we were thrown out from that delightful place). To set up this device took about one full day. The bomber had to be put up on jacks (I'm not kidding) and an inclinometer fitted in the cockpit. After hours and hours, the device was declared calibrated to the airframe. If I recall, we first got these things in the blessed Bomber Wing in Cyprus (which was as close to heaven as a bomber crew could get) in 1973 and spent hours and hours boring each other to death on ground training days about how they might/could/should be used. If the bomber was flown absolutely straight and level at *exactly* 320 kts and 250 ft over a dead calm sea, it worked pretty well. Overland, with the aircraft pitching and the speed wandering by my usual half a knot, the thing was totally useless. Well, not quite. If the navigators really had to do some of that high level bombing boredom for the stats then the SFOM gave you something to play with ('aim at Crete') before you dropped the sight-glass down the side of the seat and spent the rest of the trip trying to recover it without admitting it to anyone else.

But... there are other ways to skin a cat. In these SFOM fun-filled days, I flew with a crew that had better remain nameless but the captain was Bill Downs. Now, a quieter, more steady, gentleman you could not meet. And, as he had taught the dreaded fuel system on the OCU, he did not particularly mind me screwing the fuel panel up. More importantly, I quite fancied my eye at the bombing bit. Those of you who recall balmy days on the Episkopi cliffs as 'bombing range safety officer' will remember having to code up scores when the dread twenty-eight pound terror weapon was dropped at the sea target.

If a crew had a good run, an amused RSO would transmit the code ONT-HER-AFT which saved a lot of fuss with codebooks and was worth a beer. Anyhow, sometime in 1973 an exercise loomed. These events (exercises) were quite secret (we could not let the Soviets know the secrets of SFOM) but you could always get the dates at Niazi's kebab house (and no, I did not make this bit up – ask Bill Downs).

The *good thing* about exercises was the control tower was usually a target – *and I could hit those kind of things*. However, the competition would be fierce and beer as much as honour would depend on it.

Aside from the top secret SFOM, the Vulcan had another clever device known in code as TDU – or time delay unit. This was most satisfying. The device was simply a timer that commenced when the tit was pressed and, at the end of the set delay – bingo – away went the 'bomb'. And the tit itself was highly satisfactory – not some electronic gizmo like the SFOM: this was a big piece of kit that would have been far more at home in a Lancaster. For those who don't know by the way, when the terror twenty-eight pounder (or something livelier) was not being dropped, then the impact point was calculated very accurately by a nose camera. Now, the view out of the front of the Vulcan is fairly limited but that out of the side window is really enormous – perfect for viewing sunny beaches and waving a fist at Lightning pilots. And ideal for identifying a cross track feature to start the TDU – to the nanosecond! *We* had a plan: all Bill had to do was line up on the Akrotiri tower; keep the height right and dead eye, Dick here (me) would release the TDU crossing the road to Bomber Wing HQ which conveniently crossed track at right angles – and which even I could spot. Of course, I was not allowed anything to do with the time calculations which were the province of the plotter (shades of Bardney). Best of all, no one else had thought of it. In the bag.

On the day selected by Niazi, sure enough off went the hooter. After two days of lumbering around pretending to defend the squadron against the enemy – a screen broken with surprising ease twice a day by the NAAfi wagon – the 'secret' scramble was on for the next day. Once away from the island, bombers became baddies and the whole place would be defended by the Bloodhound missiles and the Lightnings of 56 (F) Squadron. To allow the heroic Lightning defenders time to get up and put on their perfume and the like, we scrambled at about 0400 and wandered off toward Crete for an hour or two to allow the navs their high level fun; Bill to have a snooze; and me to screw up the fuel again. By 0700, we were at low level over the sea and heading for Akrotiri. As I said, in the bag. I told you that Bill was a quiet, mild mannered fellow. Well he was and is. *Until his dander was up* and, on this morning, up it was. One of the aforementioned Lightnings had almost got out of sight of land and was headed our way. Well, we could see the Akrotiri cliffs; indeed, I was looking up at the damn things as Bill shoved the throttles forward and pushed the aircraft lower. Not only *his* dander was up, the rest of us were behaving like madmen determined to win the prize. With a heave (from Bill) we shot over the top of the cliffs with this Lightning mate frantically trying to get a bead on us (it seems the rules said that you also lost if you were 'shot down') and suddenly there was a strange pinging noise in our ears. No time for that: with the TDU release now in my hand, I quickly spotted 'my' road and swivelled my head to get an exact line up – Bill would have to look after the line himself while still grunting about Lightning weenies. And there it was –exactly abeam– perfect NOW! Release – wait the calculated 4.5 secs and bingo and beer down the hatch. Bill pulled hard back and whoosh we went up like a rocket. Noise stopped too.

There were jets everywhere but, thankfully, looking and behaving like a homesick angel, (there is a hint here) we went clean through the lot. More grunting and a few back and forwards with the fuel transfer switches on my part (well the centre of gravity was a landing challenge) and mission over.

Three hours later out came the scores and we just knew that a DH was ours. Well, not quite – a slight overshoot of 500 yards. YARDS!

Well, as you have probably guessed, the fired up Bill in his determination to get rid of the Lightning Jock (which he did) had, well, sort of forgotten to close the throttles which kind of explains the pinging noise of the high speed warning device; the 415+ kts or so – and the 500-yard overshoot and the ability of the bomber to make for the stars like a spring chicken on heat. Never did find out how the Lightning missed the cliffs. Overall though, I thought we won the prize fair and square. Bingo!

CHAPTER 9

VULCAN TALES, AIR AND GROUND

Anthony Wright

Anthony Wright, navigator radar, who has co-authored this book has already written some of his V Force experiences in our books Vulcan Boys *and* Valiant Boys. *However, the space available in both books precluded him from including other stories involving his time on the squadrons and the aircraft. Here he has taken the opportunity to rectify the situation with some splendid new tales.*

I joined the RAF in 1960 with the sole intention of becoming a navigator. Thus after initial training at RAF South Cerney it was either to undergo navigation training at RAF Topcliffe, 1 Air Navigation School (ANS) or RAF Thorney Island 2 ANS. Although I had never heard of the latter I opted for somewhere by the sea and an island at that. However, towards the end of my course, during the flying phase, the school in its entirety split in two and moved inland both north and east. The piston-aircraft training on Valettas and Varsities was then carried out at RAF Hullavington and the final phase on jet aircraft was on Meteor NF14s, at RAF Stradishall. Needless to say with graduation accomplished the next hurdle to clear was an interesting posting to a good aircraft. Of course we weren't naive enough to believe that the RAF had our interests at heart. Therefore, the result was that the student who came top of the course, quite rightly, received the reward of the posting of his choice. The rest of us, so it seemed, got what 'the system' deemed suitable for it and certainly no account was taken of our preferences. Thus, as one of the front runners on the course I was told that I was one of the few 'lucky ones' selected for the V Force. Apparently this was both for my ability and my unflappable character. Clearly they knew me better than I did as I was unaware of the latter trait.

Holding Postings – Pre V Force

The operational conversion unit that I was destined for, could have been for any one of the three V bombers namely: Valiants, Vulcans or Victors. However, the timing of courses didn't always ensure a seamless change from one to another. Moreover, in my case I was told that as I was to be a navigator radar, a new name to me, I would have to undergo another course prior to the OCU. It was to learn the rudiments of the radar bombing system on the medium bomber force (MBF) course at the Bomber Command Bombing

School (BCBS), RAF Lindholme. Only after completion of the course was I to learn of my posting to a specific type of V bomber. In the end it turned out to be Valiants, on a squadron to be determined, within 3 Group, Bomber Command. Meanwhile, before and after that, just to fill in the time, I was sent on a couple of holding postings. Luckily for me I was to be the only one of my navigation course to secure two short postings that were actually involved in flying. The first was to Ansons on the Coastal Command Communications Flight (CCCF) at RAF Bovingdon, Herts and the second again on Ansons on the HQ 3 Group, Bomber Command, Communications Flight (BCCF) at RAF Mildenhall. On the BCCF I met the famous artist David Shepherd. As well as wildlife paintings he also undertook a number of military commissions, some of which included the V Force, hence the reason for the RAF flying him to the various stations. And it was on our first meeting that I flew him to RAF Manston and return. One of his famous paintings is of a Victor landing and streaming the brake chute. I last saw it hanging in the officers' mess ante room when I was stationed at RAF Wittering in 1998. His remark when I met him again years later, at one of his talks, was that he couldn't have painted it better and of the very large sum that the painting would fetch if it were ever to be sold.

Crew 7, 35 Squadron RAF Cottesmore, QRA Christmas Day 1967. Left to Right: Anthony Wright, nav radar; Gordon Blackburn, nav plotter; Bill Downs, captain; Geof Delmege, co-pilot and Jim Patterson, AEO. *(Anthony Wright Collection)*

Although I didn't know it at the time I was also, by chance, to be introduced to well-known V bomber men. The AOC, with whom I flew in the Anson from time to time, later to be Air Chief Marshal Sir Brian Burnett, had dropped the first bombs from a Valiant as OC 148 Squadron during the Suez debacle. Many years later I was also to serve under him at HQ Far East Command, HQFEC, Singapore, during my ground tour as an intelligence officer, when he was C-in-C Far East (CINCFE). His deputy at HQ 3 Group was none other than the WWII fighter ace Gp Capt 'Johnnie' Johnson with whom I also had the pleasure of navigating as second pilot. One day one of our BCCF pilots, Flt Lt Larry Donnelly, and I were tasked to take Johnnie on a visit to Woodford. Johnnie, who, quite naturally, always wanted to pilot the aircraft, was at the controls and on our approach Larry had asked him if he was happy to land it. To which he replied in the affirmative. Unfortunately, the weather on that day provided some extremely bumpy conditions and I was standing behind the two pilots watching the runway and hanging on to the backs of their seats as the Anson was being buffeted about. Just as I was wondering if it was going to be a missed approach Johnnie decided that landing the Anson was a bit different to a Spitfire. Clearly it was a little too much for him and, to give him his due, he was man enough to hand over to the captain. On another occasion, again with just the three of us on board, we had to land at Lympne to collect a package. Larry stayed with the aircraft with engines running while we reported to the operations building. The first person that we met was a girl in reception who wanted to know the weight of the aircraft. The question was not unusual as the normal practice was for airport authorities to charge visitors the appropriate landing fee worked out on the weight of each type of aircraft. As Larry was still in the aircraft Johnnie asked me. Needless to say I did not have a clue. I had not undergone any official course on the Anson and I assumed that the weight of the aircraft was in a pilot's terms of reference. However, I was able to tell him that he didn't actually have to pay there and then, which he clearly thought he was being asked to do, as the Queen would pay. With the weight found from the receptionist's manual and the money problem resolved a visible look of relief and a grin appeared on his face. Later, still as a group captain, he was to become station commander of RAF Cottesmore with its Victor bombers. That was prior to the Vulcans from RAF Coningsby replacing them and the Victors moving to RAF Marham to fill the gap left there by the scrapping of the Valiants.

HQ 3 Group were responsible for the Valiants and Victors and so many of the senior officer pilots currently 'flying a desk' wanted to 'keep their hand in' so to speak. Any aircraft was a bonus and so they often arrived at the Comms Flight to fly a sortie. The Anson was their temporary means of escape and so I ended up flying with a number of different pilots. Most of the time it was just me and the pilot on freight runs without passengers. Sometimes it was with the AOC on his station inspections. Although it sounds strange it didn't occur to me at the time that any of the pilots might have previously flown a V bomber. One didn't ask those sorts of questions, or any other, of senior officers in those days. At my lowly rank it was purely a matter of responding, if he asked a question or made a comment, not to initiate conversation. However, one of pilots stands out in particular. It was a Sqn Ldr Coventry who, unknown to me, had been a captain on Valiants. I only discovered this years later in *Valiant Boys,* when a pilot, Graeme Kerr, who earlier was on 148 Squadron Valiants with me, related a story concerning Sqn Ldr Pete Coventry. Apparently he was known for leading a Valiant tail chase around Malta and Gozo with run-ins and breaks at Takali airfield while rehearsing for a three-ship scramble for their air show. On top of that some illegal close formation was also carried out away from prying eyes. To me a sharp, so I thought of myself, twenty-one year old he was just a squadron leader, old enough to be my father, who wanted to get out of the office. Little did I know.

After meeting Sqn Ldr Coventry for the first time everything followed the normal pattern. We got in the aircraft, started up, taxied and took off. After getting to the top of climb and whilst flying along the first leg he got out a packet of cigarettes and asked me if I wanted one. In those days I did smoke a bit, not a lot, but carried cigarettes from time to time. However, I was now in a dilemma and especially with a senior officer. It was the policy that before each sortie, crews had to sign as having read air staff instructions (ASIs), group air staff orders (GASOs), and that month's flying orders in the flying order book. Not to do so was an offence. Likewise, contravening any of the instructions, or orders, after having read them also resulted in a formal interview, or in the event of an aircraft accident or incident, could even result in a court martial.

Now I knew that as crew it was contravening the orders and instructions to smoke in the Anson. Having wondered how I could get round this question, I decided that I couldn't afford to ruin my career early on by digressing from the party line. And I thought that it may have been that he didn't know that it was against orders and he ought to be alerted to the fact. Therefore, I replied, quite correctly, that we weren't allowed to smoke in the aircraft. His quick response was "I know that, do you want a cigarette?" Clearly I had to make another decision as I didn't want to incur his displeasure. I decided that he knew the rules, he'd been told them by me anyway, and as he was much senior to me he could take 'the can' if we got found out. I replied that I'd like a cigarette and he gave me a light. Of course I enjoyed the cigarette even more because it was against the rules.

Flying along, and after a few puffs, the ash on the end of the cigarette got longer. Clearly I couldn't let it drop on the floor as that would be evidence that we'd been smoking. I looked around and couldn't see what I could do. I knew that he'd have the answer so I asked him and he replied, quite nonchalantly, that I could flick the ash out of the window. Clearly that was it. The side cockpit windows of the Anson were designed to slide open, just like some makes of car, and so I slid my cockpit window open. Without a thought I put my wrist and part of my arm out of the window to flick off the ash and nearly broke my arm when the slipstream threw it against the side of the window strut!

I hadn't twigged about the slipstream. Clearly Sqn Ldr Coventry had, and thought he'd get me back for being a know-all regarding the orders and instructions. I pulled my arm in, slid the window shut, looked across at him who, at this point with a straight face, was staring ahead flying the aircraft. I didn't say a word. Nor did he until we'd both nearly finished our cigarettes and he pointed to the small honey-combed container, that I had never noticed, and was positioned on both his side and mine that was designed to take the ash and to put cigarettes in to extinguish them. I'd been had. It has always stuck in my memory as a good example of a junior officer, namely me, getting a lesson on knowing when to keep his mouth shut.

While at the HQ I got friendly with one of the flight lieutenant secretarial officers who was in charge of postings. Chatting in his office one day I enquired whether he knew where I was posted to. He showed me my name literally pencilled in arbitrarily against a Valiant squadron. As I saw someone else's name pencilled in against 543 Squadron the Valiant PR squadron, a much better bet so I believed, I asked to have his name rubbed out and swapped with mine. This was done. In due course I went off to 232 OCU, RAF Gaydon on 97 Valiant course, to train, so I thought, for 543 Squadron. Unfortunately, unknown to me another student, John Mammon, from my BCBS course at Lindholme had, while I was at HQ 3 Group, got his holding posting to HQ Bomber Command at High Wycombe. This was the highest level in the command structure and therefore above HQ 3 Group. He had also befriended a 'poster' there, saw my name against 543 Squadron, did my trick, had my name deleted and his put in. I still haven't forgiven him!

Valiants to Vulcans

My first tour in the V Force on Valiants on 148 Squadron, RAF Marham ended abruptly, whilst I was on QRA at the time, by their unfortunate withdrawal from service through metal fatigue. I next found myself on 230 OCU at RAF Finningley on 58 Mk 2 Vulcan course. From there, both my nav plotter, Gordon Blackburn, and I were posted, as a team, to RAF Scampton on Blue Steel. However, we considered that it was not a good move as we had heard that the Blue Steel crews rarely left the UK. Therefore, before we left the OCU we successfully talked our way out of it and swapped it for a posting to RAF Cottesmore and the freefall squadrons which we knew were more likely to travel abroad. We were posted to IX (B) Squadron at RAF Cottesmore.

IX (B) Squadron Detachment to RAF Tengah, Singapore

After a somewhat rapid induction to the squadron our crew were quickly declared operational. Thus in November 1965, now fully prepared, we flew out to join the other half of the squadron detachment already based at RAF Tengah, Singapore as part of the RAF's contribution to defending Malaysia in the conflict formally known as the Indonesian Confrontation.

During that period Tengah accommodated a large number of different types of aircraft with commensurate aircrew either stationed there or on detachment. Added to that the ground crew, plus the normal administrative back-up that goes with every airfield, clearly made it an interesting and busy station.

Resident squadron aircrew gave us all the information that we needed as to where to go in Singapore city. This meant that from time to time we all went, in small groups, into the city at night especially to visit the famous Bugis Street to eat and drink at the tables of the makan (food) stalls watching the antics of the transsexuals. We were also bullied into playing noughts and crosses with the small children who would come up to our tables and challenge us to a game for ten cents. As our judgement was often impaired by Tiger beer the children invariably won! Other favourite japes were to buy special fireworks that would, by pulling a string, fire missiles with a large bang into the various upstairs windows on the street. The response was the sound of clattering windows hastily being shut, one after another, as the residents realised what was going on. I also watched one drunken seaman, sitting alone at a table, in evening dress oblivious to the explosions of a string of crackers which one of my colleagues had quietly tied to the bottom of his chair legs and lit. The street itself was effectively taken as the demarcation line beyond which there was a 'no-go' area and as servicemen we were forbidden to go into this very small part of the city. It was patrolled by military police, of all services, whose job it was to ensure that we didn't 'stray' into the off-limits area.

At Tengah we were accommodated in the officers' mess. Not, I may add, in the 'new' accommodation, with air-conditioned sealed rooms, tailor-made specifically for the V Force and people like us on detachment. Those rooms had been purloined by the non-detachment bachelor officers serving on the station. Our rooms, on the other hand, had open slatted doors and were clearly designed to allow the mosquitoes to feast on us. Our protection from the irritating insects was from a mosquito net over each bed. As to temperature control we were only barely cooled by means of a ceiling fan.

Outside the entrance to the mess and next to the porch, one on each side, stood two Japanese field artillery guns, painted black, and acquired after World War II. These were often put to great use by us, during raucous boozy parties. They were wheeled through the doors of the mess into the downstairs Pigs Bar, stuffed with gunpowder from numerous Chinese firecrackers whereupon projectiles were fired from one of the guns at one end of the bar at the dart board on the wall at other end.

The Pigs Bar was a 'one off' that I have never met in any of the multitude of RAF messes that I have either visited or been a member. It was a long narrow room, entered by a door at the reception end, the only air-conditioned public room in the mess, with a bar that extended down most of one side of one of the longest walls. There was another door that led out onto a patio area. A dart board, already mentioned, was on a shorter wall at the far end of the room. It was exclusively a male only environment. No female was allowed in the bar at any time and so it was a marvellous male retreat. This meant that those in the bar could behave as raucously as they wanted. They could sing loud, bawdy RAF songs, lie drunk on the floor or swear to their heart's content. Normal mess rules just didn't seem to apply. It was a brilliant place to let your hair down where 'anything went' with no comebacks. One of the real wags who loved that particular bar was a Canberra navigator on 45 Squadron. I'll omit his name to save him embarrassment. He was a real live wire and used to have everyone in fits of laughter with all his antics. I met him, years later, and he was a much changed man. So much so, I heard, that he'd become a vicar!

While on the subject of high jinks in the mess one of the favourite party tricks of some, with a few Singapore Tiger beers under the belt, was first to switch the ante-room ceiling fans to a reasonably fast speed. Most of the squadrons had representatives, who were either foolhardy or brave, and who would stand on a chair and then proceed to gradually raise his head nearer and nearer to the rotating blades until his head was touching them. At this point there would be the constant thud as each blade hit his head and his head juddered up and down. Continuing to raise his head further into the fan meant that the thuds were greater, his head moved up and down faster, and that the fan started to swing on its suspension and gradually the objective was achieved. His head had stopped the fan from rotating. Others were out to better this act and so the speed of the fan was increased and the position of the head was moved inwards or outwards of the rotating blades for maximum impressive performance. Luckily I never saw any blood spilt.

Another good party piece was one that was taught to us all from visiting American aircrew. It was their homemade version of the bazooka (tubular rocket launcher). It consisted of a minimum of four empty Tiger beer cans. Three had their tops and ends removed while the fourth only had its top removed. All were placed end to end where each can was mated to the other by bodge tape which was wound round to join the cans together to make one complete tube comprising the four cans with one open end. The closed end was subsequently punctured to make a small hole in the middle. The bazooka was then ready for action. One chap placed the bazooka on his shoulder while another squirted Ronson lighter fuel through the small hole into its 'barrel'. The 'ammunition', now loaded, was a tennis ball that fitted exactly down the tube. All was ready to fire. Whilst the operator aimed at the target in the ante room, normally wicker waste paper baskets piled on top of each other or a rotating fan, his assistant would hold a cigarette lighter against the tube hole where all the lighter fuel fumes were escaping and flick the lighter on. The flame would ignite the fuel inside the tube, a long jet of flame would emanate out of the back of the bazooka and the tennis ball would be shot out of the tube at a great rate of knots and fly across the room to hit the target amidst great cheers. A non-shoulder position for the bazooka, fired from between the legs, favoured by one particular aircrew member, was also tried and found effective. Later light bulbs and whisky glasses were also used as missiles. However, the latter two objects of armament

Depiction by Eric Day of IX (B) Squadron, Indonesian Confrontation, 15 December 1965.

Co-author Anthony Wright on Atkinson crew, low level, west coast of Malaysia. (Anthony Wright)

were discontinued because of the shattered glass that landed on the ante-room floor and the chance of injury to mess members.

Apart from the social life all IX (B) Squadron personnel worked extremely hard during our four-month detachment. From the aircrew point of view we covered a multitude of our tasks which included: flying low level routes up and down the Malay Peninsular and across to Labuan and Kuching, dropping conventional bombs on Song Song range and on China Rock, taking part in a jungle survival course, undergoing sea drills in the South China Sea, maintaining QRA with a Vulcan loaded with twenty-one 1,000-lb conventional bombs at RAAF Butterworth, Malaysia and flying to RAAF Darwin and RAAF Amberley in Australia for exercises with the RAAF air defence squadrons.

And so on return to the UK it was back from an enjoyable time in the sun to the not so enjoyable weather and, among other things, approximately six weeks a year back on nuclear QRA.

HQ 1 Group Dining-in Night at RAF Waddington

Not long after our crew returned from the Far East it was to be split up. This was due to the fact that the three others in the crew had come to the end of their tour on IX (B) Squadron whilst the nav team, Gordon and I, were only a few months into our current tour. Although we didn't want to move it was decided that we were needed on 35 Squadron, also at Cottesmore, as part of Crew 7 on Bill Downs' crew. Despite our reluctance to change it turned out to be a very good combination of personalities and expertise. It led to us taking part in the Strategic Air Command (SAC) Bombing and Navigation competition, entitled 'Big Flight' in 1966, selected again in 1967 and re-named as 'Giant Voice', although cancelled due to the Vietnam war, completing a Pacific ranger to the Far East and undertaking many more rangers and detachments abroad. Apart from a change of AEO early on we stayed together as a crew for my entire tour.

We hadn't been there long before we were to take part in the infamous HQ 1 Group dining-in night. This was an occasion that the powers that be at HQ 1 Group, in hindsight, wished had never happened and so little is documented of the event. To set the scene, Bill had earlier, in 1966, been on a round-the-world trip, as captain of the backup Vulcan to the other aircraft which carried the AOC 1 Group. The two Vulcans were followed by a Britannia carrying the ground crew and spare equipment. The AOC was a very social person and loved parties. During the trip, on one such occasion, while talking to the aide-de-camp (ADC), Bill was told that the AOC had been thinking of having a 1 Group party for the V Force. The ADC went on to say that he'd remind the AOC on their return. Not long after the idea turned into reality but not in the way that it was originally intended. Unfortunately, the AOC's good intentions were hi-jacked by those further down the line with the result that it all got out of hand.

Morale in the V Force was not particularly good at that time. Low pay, constant detachments, QRA and limited leave if you could get it, the latter being a concession not a right, the thought of at least six years in the force with little chance of an overseas tour, along with many other duties were taking their toll. Dining-in nights were parades which one had to attend and this was accepted as a duty. However, on this occasion HQ 1 Group had decided to hold a mega dining-in night to which all available 1 Group aircrew from the various stations, not on QRA, detachment or on leave, plus other officers were ordered to attend without question. This would take place at RAF Waddington. The event was to be on top of our regular dining-in nights and would involve a much larger bill that we normally had to pay. Furthermore, to add insult to injury, we had heard that Air Marshal Sir Harry Broadhurst, Air Officer Commanding-in-Chief (AOC-in-C) Bomber Command, who was involved in the crash of the Vulcan at London Heathrow Airport was to be in attendance.

Our anger revolved around the 'mixed' escape system in the V bombers. The two pilots were supplied with ejection seats while the rear crew had to make do with only a parachute each to escape from the aircraft. It was a very emotive subject. The case in question, promoting our ire, involved Sir Harry, who was occupying the co-pilot's seat at the time, and the crash came during an attempt to land, in bad weather and which went disastrously wrong. The result was that he and the other pilot at the controls ejected while the rear crew, including another pilot who had been the co-pilot during most of the Australia and New Zealand trip, all without ejection seats, died. Rear crew throughout the V Force, and especially us on Vulcans, to say the least, never forgot this particular accident. The full story of the circumstances leading up to the crash along with the subsequent enquiry have been well documented and should give an indication as to why this particular accident is to this day still etched in all the minds of ex-Vulcan aircrew.

There was clearly an operational order of some kind for the 1 Group dining-in night, which we at grass roots level did not see. If anything it was to ensure that the planning of an event involving rival squadrons went smoothly. Aircrew from all ten Vulcan squadrons and the OCU based at the three stations namely, Cottesmore, Scampton and Waddington itself, along with some other officers including, I recall, females of the Princess Mary's Royal Air Force Nursing Service from RAF Nocton Hall attended.

On the night in question all of us who were detailed at Cottesmore were summoned, in mess kit, to the officers' mess ante room at a specified time for a briefing. Our transport, the thirty-two-seater coaches, were already positioned outside the mess. We were told that each coach would have a squadron leader in charge, and a navigator at that. He in turn was issued with a one-inch scale Ordnance Survey map of the forty-four-mile route to Waddington. Why I'll never know. We were also given a time check with our watches and then ushered onto the RAF coaches lined up outside the mess. We were to arrive at the gates of Waddington as per the normal Bomber Command timing on any target, i.e. plus or minus two minutes. Sqn Ldr George Podger, a navigator from Operations Wing, was in charge of our coach. The first error was that the planned departure time was much too early. This was only discovered going up the A1. Despite George's demands for the coach driver to 'throttle back' and thus drive as slow as possible we all knew that it wouldn't work. If we had been airborne then an orbit or dog leg would have sufficed to lose time. However, as this was not possible our orbit consisted of stopping our coach outside of The King's Head public house in Navenby village high street just a few miles short of Waddington. Already in rebellious mood we decided that we certainly weren't going to just sit in the coach and wait patiently for the minutes to disappear. Therefore, we all piled out of the coach for a quick beer and then got back on board just before it was time to move off again.

We arrived on time at the Waddington gates, our coaches from Cottesmore in the south, just as the Scampton coaches were also arriving from the north. Needless to say now in visual and sound contact aircrew 'pleasantries' were exchanged by means of shouting and gesticulation between us and the opposition. We heard later that the Scampton guys had been smart enough to arm themselves with beer on board their coaches and so were already a few beers ahead of us.

Because of the large number of us 'press-ganged' officers involved at the dinner, the Waddington hierarchy had decided not to use the officers' mess dining room but had erected a huge marquee with the complete normal dining-in night set-up of tables, chairs, place settings with our names, cutlery, napkins, candlesticks, squadron and station silver, along with squadron standards in position behind the top table. A RAF band was also inside the marquee playing music. The officers' mess ante room for the usual pre-dinner drinks was also not used but instead a further smaller marquee leading into the first was employed for the purpose. This first marquee was also furnished with soft armchairs and sofas plus the odd side table all taken from the officers' mess.

Now that we were inside the ante-room marquee the second major error in the planning was discovered. This time to our advantage of which we made maximum use. On a normal dining-in night pre-dinner drinks of sherry in small glasses were initially served, during the small talk, with possibly just one other before dinner was announced and we trooped in to take our places at the table. In this instance, to cater for such numbers, the mess staff decided that if after the initial drink was consumed we needed another, instead of us having to replace it ourselves with another new full glass from a tray they would be helpful and just wander among us with large jugs of sherry and pour us another refill whenever we wanted. The 'green light' was definitely on now as many were having another drink poured from the jugs, or taking command of a jug from a poor mess steward, downing a glass of sherry in one and having another followed by another. The chatter and laughter was getting louder with the aid of the lubrication, the female company also joining in the merriment to the full and things got more hilarious. At one point an officer climbed on top of a table waving a bra around his head shouting "it's still warm and she's here tonight". It was also said that some extra male and female shenanigans were going on behind one of the sofas. Whilst I witnessed the former, the latter I did not and therefore cannot verify the rumours that were rife after the event.

Eventually, above the din, the gong for dinner was sounded and we were asked to go through to the other marquee to take our place at the tables. Most of us who were still standing, and not too inebriated, did as we were told. However, I heard the odd remark from some others who were already 'well oiled' that they wouldn't bother with the dinner and that they would continue to drink where they were.

To avoid any rivalry or disturbances between squadron members the organisers thought that splitting us up would solve any problems. This was a pointless exercise as most of us knew each other anyway whether it be during training, courses, OCUs, or from serving on the former Valiant squadrons and now posted to Vulcans. Being re-acquainted with old mates, stories were told and it was a situation where all of us, as a large disgruntled body, were against those of senior rank that had forced us to be there.

Awaiting the meal to be served I noticed another navigator near me brandishing a large carving knife. On questioning the reason for the implement he told me that he was expecting trouble and if the marquee went up in flames he'd be in a position to cut his way out! As dinner was being served, with the background music from the band, the first of the bread rolls started to get thrown between all the tables, to the merriment of us lower beings, but much to the annoyance of the dignitaries overlooking the spectacle from their top table. This was pretty tame considering what was to follow.

Dining-in night etiquette decrees that if one needs to leave the table at any time before the end the person requiring to take leave of absence must walk to the top table and ask permission from the president. Here the rule was totally ignored and people were drifting in and out to visit the mobile toilets outside the marquees. Before coffee I too decided to nip out and was amazed to see an officer holding onto a toilet door handle keeping it shut from the outside as he declared that he had pushed a senior officer in at the same time as having lit and thrown in a thunderflash. Things were definitely hotting up quite literally. On my return it was time for coffee, port, madeira and the liqueurs to be served. However, with the tables now cleared of plates people started playing skittles by sliding, at great speed, the remaining heavy salt and pepper pots along the shiny surface of the tables that were placed end to end, to see if they could smash the bowls of sugar along the way. One drunken member crawled underneath the tables with a lighted candelabra and offered the presiding officer of the evening, normally entitled the president of the mess committee and other dignitaries on the top table a light for their cigars. That 'courtesy' certainly wasn't welcomed.

It was now time for speeches and the president of the mess committee started the address and introduced Sir Harry to make a speech. When Sir Harry started to utter a few words this incensed us all. Among the boos and jeers that greeted him there were also shouts to 'shut up, sit down and resign'. What the invited Lord Lieutenant of Lincolnshire, a brigadier I understand, thought of our behaviour I can only surmise. Despite the protestations of the president and shouting of orders for us to stop he and the diners at the top table had no control. Speeches were stopped, the formal dinner cut short and the normal social gathering afterwards was cancelled. We were all ushered outside the marquee to await our coaches back to our stations. Of course that didn't happen immediately as the official cars had to take the air officers away first. The vehicles had to line up in order and subsequently tailed back along the road and round the corner of the main marquee. This gave an opportunity for some wags who, regardless of the drivers' protests, got into the rear seats of the cars and gave royal waves to us all as the drivers drove round the corner up to receive the real passengers. There was also talk of some guy ropes of the marquees being cut and the latter's partial collapse but I didn't witness that as I was far too busy watching the other antics of my colleagues outside on the grass.

The possibility of a fire engulfing the marquees was considered. Therefore, the fire section had already attached fire hoses to fire hydrants and so the hoses were left unwound on the grass. My nav plotter spotting this decided to hose down the official cars and shouted to another nav plotter to turn on the fire hydrant, as it already had its large key inserted, and he would aim the particular hose at the cars. As the jet of water shot out of the nozzle a small airman steward, rather unwisely, rushed up towards my plotter shouting for him to stop. He immediately got the steward in his sights and aimed the jet of water at him with a direct hit. The force of the water striking him in the chest bowled him over completely. His unwarranted interference produced zero sympathy and so he disappeared out of sight.

Eventually, the fire section arrived to take charge and the car jackings also ceased. We all then staggered on to our coaches. As our coach started off it wasn't long before

trouble broke out at the rear. I hadn't realised, until I turned round to see what the noise was all about, that apart from carrying a purloined road sign we had also kidnapped an RAF Regiment officer who was supposed to be going home north to Scampton and not south to Cottesmore.

Things didn't get any better when going down the A1 as most of us, apart from our officer in charge of the coach, and another squadron leader, decided that we were now hungry. The MT driver had to ignore the latter's command for the coach to turn off the A1 for Cottesmore as the mob shouted for the driver to continue south to The Bloody Oaks petrol station. Which he duly did and we disembarked. In those days to be served anything more than petrol, oil and water was usually a bonus and so packets of crisps had to suffice which quietened everyone down.

However, just before our arrival at Cottesmore officers' mess entrance the argument at the back of the coach erupted again. A nav plotter and the kidnapped officer had a set to and the squadron leader who decided to break it up got too close and accidentally, we believe, got punched in the eye for his trouble.

When the coach stopped the first two to get off at the run was the nav plotter hotly pursued by the enraged squadron leader, while the rest of us repaired to the Gents. While we all stood in a long line at the numerous 'stand ups' the plotter chased by the squadron leader entered by one door, rushed past us all and they both exited out of another door at the end.

The next day all the station commanders of those personnel attending were summoned to HQ Bomber Command for a major dressing down. The result was that on their return they were all expected to administer the same to us. Therefore, the next morning, a Saturday I believe, we were all summoned to be in the Operations Wing briefing room for the official bollocking. This was carried out by OC Operations Wing whilst trying to keep a straight face, just like the rest of us, and concluded by saying that the station commander believed that none of us were to blame. The fact that the huge RAF Waddington crest in flowers and a neatly rolled up fire hose, both liberated from Waddington, were strategically positioned on the front steps of the officers' mess at Cottesmore clearly was dismissed as irrelevant.

At the time none of us wanted to attend the fiasco. Moreover, after the dust had settled I for one, and echoed by many attendees, said that HQ 1 Group would never have another – and they didn't. Since that day it has been quietly airbrushed out of history although many have heard about it second or third hand. With hindsight, this was an experience not to be missed.

A Fishy Tale

A regular haunt, particularly for the Valiants and Vulcans, was to visit Royal Canadian Air Force (RCAF) Goose Bay, Labrador. The main aim was to fly low level across the remote and vast areas of pines and lakes as far as Hudson Bay and return. In 1964, on 148 Squadron, I had been one of the two Valiant crews from RAF Marham selected to initially test the first low level routes in such a desolate area. The routes had been designed by the Joint Air Reconnaissance Intelligence Centre (JARIC) at RAF Brampton. The routes were to emulate the low level terrain that we would expect to encounter en route to our targets in Russia if we were called upon to execute a nuclear strike in defence of our country. Later as everyone down the years flying Valiants and Vulcan bombers and then Tornados flew them it was quite something. Especially as I had been the first to pioneer two of them. Indeed, having flown my two Bomber Command routes at the start in a Valiant I was still flying them, plus other low level routes, on Vulcans right up until February 1982. This was when practising night terrain following radar sorties for the Red Flag exercise in Nellis AFB, Nevada which, by chance, was both prior to the Falklands War and the start of the run-down of the Vulcan force before its eventual cessation on 31 March 1984.

In 1968 on Crew 7, the Downs' crew, 35 Squadron, Vulcans at RAF Cottesmore our normal Goose Bay ranger was raised to VIP status when we were selected to take Marshal of the Royal Air Force Sir Charles Elworthy, then the Chief of Defence Staff (CDS) out to Goose Bay. It was a well-known pattern whereupon once a year the current CDS

Depiction by Eric Day of 148 Squadron flying the first low level route trials from Goose Bay, Labrador, 15 April 1964. Co-author Anthony Wright on Foreman crew. *(Anthony Wright)*

Anthony Wright at home in the Nevada Palace Casino, Red Flag, Nellis 1982. *(Anthony Wright)*

would be flown to Goose by Vulcan and then he would transfer to a smaller aircraft to be flown to another remote venue up country to Eagle River for salmon fishing and for a meeting with his service counterpart from the United States. Meanwhile, during his time away we as a crew would fly the low level routes out of Goose and on his return a few days later fly him back to the UK.

Our aircrew preparations for the flight were standard. The only difference was that we would only be taking one crew chief in the seventh seat whilst the CDS would occupy the sixth seat and, once airborne, either relax lying in the visual bomb aimer's area or occupy the co-pilot's seat. The 'VIP fit', as it was called, of an angle poise lamp and a minuscule table to enable him to work on his papers or read, if he so desired, was incorporated as an added extra by the ground crew for such occasions.

Having changed into our flying kit we went to the aircrew buffet, also known as the 'feeder' or 'greasy spoon', for our usual pre-flight meal. It must be said that the cooks and staff always provided us aircrew with excellent meals. Indeed the V Force was so well catered for with pre-flight meals, after-flight meals and in-flight rations that aircrew from other commands termed us being in 'Eating Command'. This time though we were really impressed. Much to our surprise on this occasion we were joined, along with the CDS, by both the station commander and OC Operations. A long table was set up with table cloth, linen napkins, silver service and wine glasses. Clearly the station commander was looking after his annual report. The mess waiters in their white uniforms served us an excellent meal of fillet steak and poured out a good red wine to accompany it. My nav plotter, Gordon Blackburn, and I felt it our duty to drink the wine so as not to offend. It was a really pleasant way to start a flight.

Arriving at Goose we bade farewell to the CDS and he was whisked off on his next part of the journey. Over the next few days we completed our low level sorties and awaited the return of the CDS. When he did arrive it was just a matter of the usual flight planning back to the UK. However, just before departure it was quite normal for all the V Force crews visiting Goose to purchase the excellent, non-farmed, wild salmon that the RAF Detachment operations staff sold to the crews. The wild salmon, not always easy to get in the UK, were always plentiful in Goose and were deep frozen ready to be transported. The ops staff were always, up to then, very helpful and only too pleased to sell salmon as a sideline that brought in the dollars. However, on this occasion their attitude had changed and we were told that there would be no salmon for us. We were to transport the CDS's salmon and also to take salmon ordered by other senior staff back in the UK. The latter weren't even anything to do with our station. Despite our protestations we got nowhere. As it was one of the few perks that we got in those days our crew was decidedly miffed.

The conversation regarding our feelings and annoyance, to put it mildly, continued out to the aircraft. Although the CDS hadn't arrived his packed frozen salmon and a pack for those of the others had. We found the CDS to be a charming officer and clearly it wasn't his fault that we were to be deprived of our salmon. However, to transport salmon for others, with us denied the perk, was to rub salt into a sore wound. Therefore, it was decided to load the CDS's salmon in the normal place, to keep it frozen, but that it would be a good idea to load the other package in the bomb bay that always had to be kept warm.

We had an uneventful five-and-a-half-hour flight back to the UK. However, it was common practice for us to deviate from track just before we were due to land. This was to alert Sue Downs, Bill's wife, who would send the children to play outside their house in Bourne. As soon as the Vulcan was sighted by the children Sue was able to get into the car to go and collect Bill from Cottesmore. So no salmon for the crew but salmon for the CDS. For the others? Well they had a 'fishful' experience.

The Libyan Incident

This incident and the sequence of events that followed mainly involved my co-pilot and myself. Therefore, I decided that we should both relate parts of our own side of the story. To set the scene one of the regular V Force detachments or rangers abroad was to RAF Luqa, Malta. The detachment was called Exercise Sunspot where the whole squadron, personnel, aircraft and equipment, were involved. During the stay, normally over two weeks, the aircrew flew across to Libya to drop conventional practice bombs on the bombing range situated at RAF El Adem. The ranger was different in that it was not termed an exercise as such but known as a conventional bombing lone ranger (CBLR). This was normally one crew flying either to RAF Luqa or to RAF El Adem, staying at the squadron programmed base for a few days, but still bombing on the El Adem range. Needless to say the Luqa option was preferable as it offered more entertainment during off-duty hours. However, on 18 November 1968 my crew of 35 Squadron RAF Cottesmore were detailed for a CBLR to El Adem. Unfortunately, Bill Downs, our former captain, had been posted and so the rest of us had been flying with other squadron captains. On this occasion, Rusty Russell, with whom we had flown twice earlier in the month stepped in to make another 'guest appearance' with Geof Delmege our co-pilot, myself as nav radar, Gordon Blackburn as nav plotter and Jim Patterson as the AEO. The normal detachment at El Adem lasted four days. It consisted of flight out followed by a couple of days flying at medium level, or the Libyan low level routes, with conventional bombs that varied in size and could be 25 lb, 100 lb or 1,000 lb and dropped as singletons. Dependent on the bomber training requirements, either the nav plotter dropped the bombs visually lying in the visual bomb aimer's position in the nose using the T4 bombsight or the nav radar dropped them by radar using the H2S. The normal pattern of a CBLR was to return on the fourth day. We departed Cottesmore, in XJ825, on 18 November 1968 for an uneventful four-and-a-half-hour flight to El Adem loaded up with the requisite number of 1,000-lb bombs.

Geof Delmege recalls:

The next day we set off on a low level navex planned to finish with some practice bombing runs on the El Adem range. The captain, Rusty Russell, was in the right seat. I was flying as first pilot in the left seat.

The navex completed, we joined the range. The bombing runs were to be carried out by Tony on the radar. On what I recall the first run, at the bomb release point nothing happened. I quickly looked down to the left-side panel, just to make sure that I had selected, 'bomb doors auto'. I had done so and on looking round the instrument panel saw that the hydraulic pressure had dropped to zero, which explained the lack of bomb doors opening.

It was clear that without hydraulics and, among other things, the inability to use the brakes we would probably need to find a longer runway than we were used to. As we all discussed the situation I recalled being told, by Bill Downs some time weeks before, that faced with a similar failure whilst in the wastes of the Libyan desert his crew at that time had diverted to the long runway at Wheelus AFB. Therefore, the decision was made not to land back at El Adem but to divert to the American air force base at Wheelus, near to Tripoli, the extreme western end of Libya as akin to us currently at the eastern end.

35 Squadron Vulcan line-up for Exercise Sunspot, Luqa.

(Anthony Wright Collection)

On the way to Wheelus, with permission granted, some of our time en route was spent deliberating on the ways of helping the aircraft to stop. One idea of the two navs was to open the door as we were rolling down the runway at Wheelus and slide the six extra individual desert survival packs, that were stowed in the visual bomb aimer's position, down the door in front of the two nosewheels. However, that idea was abandoned as we knew that the brake chute could be deployed and should solve the problem. However, we then decided not to stream the brake chute, as was 'recommended' in the operations manuals, as I for one wasn't enthusiastic about re-packing the chute as it entailed the co-pilot climbing perilously on the back end of the aeroplane and I was frightened of heights.

On landing at Wheelus judicious use of aerodynamic braking and the emergency brake switch to top up the brake pressure brought the aeroplane to a stop in about 6,000 ft of the 11,000 ft runway and without deploying the brake chute. We subsequently learned from base operations that a firefighting helicopter had been hovering above us to take any action needed and emergency vehicles and a film crew had positioned themselves at the 9,000 ft point expecting to see us go sailing past them still trying to stop the aircraft.

As the bomb release signal had happened as advertised on the bomb run there was some concern by Tony that a bomb or bombs might fall off the carriers if the bomb doors were subsequently opened. I recall that Tony and Gordon climbed into the bomb bay and tied the bombs to the carriers with lashing tape, just in case. In order to repair our Vulcan, which still contained the bombs in the bomb bay, our friendly American hosts then towed it into a hangar.

It was now time for a bit of serious thinking. All we were wearing was our flying clothing as all our other clothes were back in our rooms at El Adem. Also missing was a very important member, our crew chief who was also back there. Meanwhile, after a telephone call to El Adem to try to sort things out we went off to the officers' club. Events then became amusing as we were obviously going to find purchasing drinks nigh on impossible. We only had UK money and Libyan pounds with us and the only currency on use on the base at Wheelus was American scrip dollars, a financial measure designed to stop the unregulated flow of dollars into the local economy. This caused us some problems with little things, like having no scrip or dollars with which to purchase food! Luckily we arrived in time for 'Happy Hour'. However, without any US dollars we were obviously going to find life a bit difficult. The first hurdle was crossed as the Americans were so delighted to meet us that they generously kept on treating us to jugs of beer. However, the currency problem had to be resolved. The prime minister at that time was Harold Wilson and one of the rules brought in by his Labour government was to limit the amount of foreign currency to £50 that people could take out of the country. Moreover, the V-Form rule was that it was even entered on the inside back page of your passport. In Libya we were unable to get any US dollars sent to us from the UK to finance our unplanned stay as our government refused to budge. In our case we were told to tell the American who took the money at the till for any meals that we had in the club to send the bill to the UK. In retrospect another fine example of the government's concern for servicemen and a complete lack of understanding about anything outside the Westminster bubble.

We spent some time in the officers' club playing the fruit machines in order to win a little money so as to be able to purchase the odd burger. I recall us meeting 'Texas Johnny' in the club, the F-4 pilot who had pushed another F-4, which had leaked all its fuel away after being hit by North Vietnamese fire, out over the sea so that the crew could safely eject over water. In spite of the Texas label he was quite a small self-effacing chap. He got the disabled F-4 to lower its arrester hook and then manoeuvred his F-4 such that he positioned the hook at the top of his windscreen arch and applying a lot of power he managed to push the other aeroplane.

Meanwhile, we had contacted the British Mission to the Military Forces in Tripoli for some help and the next day I was taken there by car, which proved interesting, as it was the first time that I had ever been delayed by getting caught up in a camel jam. Unfortunately, I only managed to get some more Libyan pounds to put into the crew imprest. These were, as I've already said, useless to us on base.

Anthony Wright again:

It was obvious to me that having heard of Geof's abortive sortie to get US dollars it was only a matter of time when our luck would run out playing the fruit machines in order to eat. However, help was at hand when I was offered some dollars, in exchange for a British cheque, by a British travelling troupe who befriended us and were at Wheelus to entertain the US servicemen and women. As I always carried my chequebook everywhere with me it proved to be our saviour. Meanwhile, we heard that back in the UK our currency plight had gone right to the top and to Harold Wilson. At that point they relented and said that they would send us some dollars via American Express. They never did arrive and we could only conclude that they were sent by Pony Express.

As to the crew chief and kit situation that was also solved as he arrived next day by civil air. He also told us that he had heard of our involvement in a near miss, the fault of a Canberra, earlier on the range. Therefore, because we had not carried it any further the Canberra crew would return the favour and pack up our belongings, abandoned and still in our rooms, and fly our suitcases to us at Wheelus which they duly did.

After the crew chief's assessment of what spares were required we signalled Cottesmore for some hydraulic pumps and a hydraulic test rig. While we were waiting, as we had nothing to do on the base, the Americans kindly offered to take us in a small plane to their air-to-ground firing and bombing range at El Uotia. The range was managed by Wheelus and the range safety officer was flown up there daily. I think that I was the only one to go to see the action. In fact watching from the safety of an observation tower I was fascinated by the USAF Phantoms and to hear the sound of their gatling guns firing away at the target just before they pulled out of a steep dive.

Back at base we couldn't understand why the spares that had been ordered hadn't arrived on a particular British Airways flight. It transpired that someone had sent them to South America and so another set of pumps and rig were on their way. This time hopefully to the civilian airport of Idris in Tripoli. Once we heard of the BA flight arrival Geof was sent to Tripoli again. This time it was to collect three hydraulic pumps and the test rig from the bonded store at Idris after they had been delivered there by the BA staff. Eventually Geof arrived back with our precious cargo declaring that a little greasing of palms had been necessary to expedite releasing it from customs into our care. However, the second test rig sent had arrived with its single spark plug broken. As American spark plugs differed in size to British spark plugs that was another setback. Fortunately, we espied an American-owned 1959 British Ford Prefect in one of the huge car parks on the base and tracked down the owner. He kindly removed one of his spark plugs and loaned it to us for a short while.

I was still worried about the state of the bombs as I feared that because a release plus may have gone down to the electromechanical release unit (EMRU) on the carrier of the bomb, or bombs, then it was just possible for a bomb to drop off when the bomb door operating cycle was checked on the jacks in the hangar. I'd already experienced a bomb hang-up in the bomb bay of a Vulcan on the El Adem range before and a 'spinner' dropping outside of the danger area when the bomb doors were opened again. I didn't want a repeat performance on the floor of the American hangar.

After the hydraulic system was repaired our crew assembled in the hangar to watch the retraction tests and the bomb doors being opened. The jacks were at the limit of their extension, being used normally to service USAF fighters, and as the undercarriage retracted and extended the whole aircraft wobbled and moved alarmingly and nobody relaxed until it was back on its wheels. Meanwhile, with the movement of the bomb doors opening I was praying for the bombs to stay on the carriers. Luckily, for all our sakes everything was completed satisfactorily.

Come the day that we were to depart our 'new' friends of the entertainment troupe arrived to see us off. As a thank you for their help we took them for the promised look inside and conducted tour around the aircraft. It was at this point that I was taken aside by one and asked if I wouldn't mind taking a small brown paper package back to England and post it to his aunt. With alarm bells ringing in my head putting together the elements of North Africa, drugs, small packages and entertainers in the equation I diplomatically said that we were grateful for their help but were not allowed to carry mail in a service aircraft. Thankfully, we all parted amicably. Now with our aircraft serviceable we took off on 28 November on the tenth day from our unscheduled landing at Wheelus. At air traffic's request we flew a low pass over the airfield before climbing away and as we did so a flight of F-100s, returning from the local El Uotia range, formated on us. Unfortunately, the one on our starboard wing tip appeared to get involved with the wingtip vortex, so Geof reckoned, and rolled rapidly away.

On our return the story didn't end there. The weather was too bad to land at Cottesmore and we were diverted to RAF Marham for the night. Air traffic control clearly directed us to the wrong parking area as the station commander, of a station full of Victor tankers, was not happy with a Vulcan aircraft still

Exercise Tapestry – oil rig patrols carried out by 27 Squadron, 230 OCU and towards the end, as well as tanking, by 50 Squadron. *(Anthony Wright Collection)*

loaded with bombs being left in that particular spot and wanted it moved elsewhere. The station did not have the correct towing arm and so the junior engineering officer (JEngO) told us that he would sort it out by tannoying for some extra airmen who would push it. Despite our protestations that it couldn't be done as the leading edge of the wings was too high he still insisted. At that point we gave up and left him and went to the officers' mess. In the mess we met a Victor crew that was departing to the USA the next day and over a few beers Geof exchanged some of the dollars from our imprest for some British notes so that they had a few more dollars in theirs. This caused some consternation when we arrived back at Cottesmore and handed the imprest back to accounts as it now had Libyan pounds, English pounds, American dollars and a few scrip dollars. Shortly after our return our station commander was due to speak at a bankers' dinner and we understood that he was going to relate our plight and the currency difficulty that we encountered.

In March 1984, the last month of the Vulcan's operational service on 50 Squadron, I flew XJ825, not as a bomber but as a K2 tanker. It was on Operation Tansor at 65 degrees north in the Faeroes Gap to refuel Phantoms following two Russian Bears. Clearly our crew chief back in Libya in 1968 had done a grand job on the hydraulics.

Return to the Far East

Unbeknown to me it was not the last time that I was to be re-united with RAF Tengah. At the end of my tour at Cottesmore in 1969 I was posted on to a ground tour. Luckily, although I was not flying, it was to involve most of the time working with the envy of my colleagues as it was at Tengah. This time I was to be the station intelligence officer (SIntO). Now established in the Far East Air Force (FEAF) having left the V Force, I

Squadron display crew at RAF Waddington Open Day 1980. *(Anthony Wright Collection)*

thought that my time associated with Vulcans had come to an end. However, in January 1970 a detachment of Vulcans from 101 Squadron, RAF Waddington arrived at Tengah to take part in Exercise Castor Oil. It was to be held at RAAF Darwin, Northern Territory, Australia. The exercise, held regularly by the Australians, was designed to test the defence facilities of Darwin. It was the same exercise that I had taken part in during the Indonesian Confrontation on IX (B) Squadron in 1965 and then called Exercise High Rigel. On this occasion 101 Squadron Vulcans were to be flown from Tengah to take part. The scenario was that Darwin was to be subjected to simulated attacks by air and ground, carried out by both RAAF aircraft based at Tindal and by our RAF Vulcans detached to Darwin.

At that time the majority of British forces were gradually being withdrawn from Singapore and Malaysia to be replaced, on 1 November 1971, by the new Australia, New Zealand and United Kingdom (ANZUK) tri-national force. Meanwhile, Tengah was already running down in preparation for the Singapore Armed Forces (SAF) to take over the real estate. This meant that over the next few months some squadron aircraft were flown back and equipment returned to the UK. At the same time a flood of postings were being issued. Needless to say, in the interim, those personnel remaining had to take on the jobs that others had now vacated. The result for me was that while I, as SIntO, was painstakingly destroying the contents of the intelligence library and classified documents in the station vault, Sqn Ldr Plans, 'volunteered' me for the extra posts, of station operations officer (SOpsO) and station navigation officer (SNavO).

With any one of my three posts I was the designated station liaison officer with the aircrew of 101 Squadron Detachment. Therefore, as I was in regular contact I decided to record the final line-up of Vulcans at Tengah as I thought that they were the last that I would see in such number. I was wrong. I eventually got posted back to the V Force and Vulcans some years later.

Three Vulcans of 50 Squadron, RAF
Waddington passing overhead the
Mansion House. Lead Vulcan XL426 Roger
Dunsford – captain, Anthony Wright – nav
radar. *(Anthony Wright Collection)*

Falklands Victory Parade Fly-past
12 October 1982

I have already related my part during Operation Corporate during the Falklands War, in *Vulcan Boys*, as Vulcan adviser at the War Headquarters, RAF Northwood for the Black Buck raids and later in the Black Buck cell at RAF Waddington.

Almost four months to the day, after the seventy-four-day conflict and Argentine surrender on 14 June 1982, the Falklands Victory Parade in London took place. At the same time as the parade marched past the reviewing platform outside the Mansion House, in the City, aircraft representing those that took part in the war flew overhead.

I was one of the minority of the personnel at RAF Waddington who were actually involved in Operation Corporate and so fortunately flew in the lead Vulcan. All three of our aircraft were from 50 Squadron, the last remaining operational Vulcan squadron in the RAF. The captain of my Vulcan B2 XL426 was Roger Dunsford, one of the flight commanders, leading the Vulcan element in the long stream of different aircraft types.

Before the flying rehearsals began, because of the complexity of joining and keeping together such a large number of aircraft with different performances, there was a mass briefing for the leaders of each element of the formation at RAF Marham. There was a second mass briefing prior to the final rehearsal. It was apparent to all that poor weather, particularly low cloud, would be a showstopper. On each occasion, Roger queried what the procedure would be if we all got together in good weather, began our run-in under London's heavily congested airspace and then ran into low cloud. The thought of a dozen or more aircraft being forced to climb to safety, in cloud, into the air traffic around Heathrow and Gatwick, was less than appealing. It was also too difficult for the authorities to come up with a solution, so the consistent answer was that the formation would take place under visual flight rules (i.e. not in cloud), or not at all.

We started rehearsing formation practice on 28 September, call sign Stanley One. However, on our next flight the call sign was changed to Ascension One. I believe that we kept that same call sign throughout the total of five practice runs, and the day itself. On the fly-past day the formation of aircraft was led by a small number of helicopters followed by three Victors accompanied by four Harriers, three Vulcans, three Nimrods, one VC10 and finally three Hercules. The Met Office was forecasting a weather front approaching from the west but that the cloud base over London should be "...no problem for the fly-past..." Dodging the increasing clouds over East Anglia made for a pretty fraught join up but was achieved successfully. As we began our run-in, flying at 1,000 ft, Roger was acutely aware of the cloud base decreasing and everything getting darker as the rain started to fall. There was no turning back now, however, and the lack of a plan if we ran into cloud and instrument flight rules (IFR) was becoming increasingly alarming. Twenty minutes later and it would have been a different story but, as luck would have it, we were just under the cloud base when we successfully overflew the parade and the estimated 300,000 people who lined the mile-long route, of those marching, from Armoury House to the Guildhall. The Lord Mayor of London, Christopher Leaver took the salute on the steps of Mansion House, along with Prime Minister Margaret Thatcher and Admiral Sir Terence Lewin, the Chief of the Defence Staff (CDS).

While this was all happening I was running the F95 camera in the bomb aimer's position in the nose of the Vulcan. It was standard operating procedure (SOP) for the nav radar to load film into the F95 camera in order that a record of the run-in to a target and the release of either a simulated bomb or otherwise, at low level, can be assessed after the flight. Clearly, there was no need for film on this particular day as we were not going to either bomb the prime minister or fly low level. However, I decided to load a film purely to commemorate this special occasion.

On our final track, for the flight across London, I switched the camera on early and kept it running continuously until we broke off, turned starboard just before Buckingham Palace, and headed back to Waddington. At that point we were indeed, as Roger predicted, in IFR. The crowds had been lucky. As to the aerial shots I wrote on the photographic reconnaissance report 'aperture dull'. That said it all.

Author's note: I have not heard of, or seen, another aerial record of the event since and so it must be a unique piece of photographic history.

Aerial view of the Mansion House and crowds from Vulcan XL426 at 1,000 ft. (Anthony Wright Collection)

After Anthony's flying days were over he was posted to the Nuclear Directorate in the Ministry of Defence in Whitehall and then to Royal Air Force Armament Support Unit, RAF Wittering where, as both second-in-command of the unit and OC Training Squadron, he was responsible for the training and standardisation of all RAF aircrew and engineers specialising in the nuclear role.

On leaving the RAF in 1998 he joined the Air Cadet Organisation at Headquarters Air Cadets, RAF Cranwell which was responsible for both the Air Training Corps and the Combined Cadet Force RAF in the Royal Air Force Reserve as squadron leader corporate business. He decided to finally retire on 1 January 2003 – his 61st birthday.

OC RAF Armament Support Unit, RAF Wittering, Phil Woolford and OC Training Squadron Anthony Wright with the unit's first piece of silverware, the Blue Danube, subscribed by the officers. *(Anthony Wright Collection)*

CHAPTER 10

NAVIGATING ALL THREE V BOMBERS

Spike Milligan

*Following on from Norman Bonnor's chapter on navigating the V bombers it is very relevant to read '**Spike' Milligan's** account of his air force career starting as a navigator plotter in the RAF since he had the distinction of flying operationally on all three V bombers. The story that he relates is particularly interesting since he got steadily promoted while he was in the V Force and thus he is able to give the reader different perspectives as he climbs from flying officer to air commodore.*

My involvement with the V Force had its origins at RAF Topcliffe in 1958 when I was undergoing navigator training. It was made clear that any aspirations to progress to fighters would be detrimental to career prospects. The bomber route was recommended, with the much vaunted medium bomber force as the leading contender for ambitious young officers. But in those days, no first tourist navigator plotters were allowed, so a tour on Canberras was a must, and this is what happened to me. The Canberras were described as the light bomber force.

During my Canberra tour in the bomber role at Binbrook and Coningsby, I decided it would be a good idea to investigate at firsthand what the MBF, alias V Force, was all about. I had no difficulty in arranging a familiarisation trip in a 207 Squadron Valiant B1 at Marham. On 2 June 1960 I got airborne in the sixth seat of WP219, captained by the burly red-headed and moustached Sqn Ldr 'Dan' Daniel, a much bemedalled veteran from the world of single-seat, single-engined fighters. His co-pilot was the equally large Flt Lt Tony Alder, complete with black moustache. He was also an experienced fighter pilot, ex-RAF Germany, and together they made an interesting adversarial combination of flying a large four-engined bomber using traditional fighter techniques. The sortie did not go smoothly, as the Green Satin Doppler overheated and filled the cockpit with noxious smoke. The nav plotter, Flt Lt Colin Bell, assisted by the redoubtable nav radar, Flt Sgt George Foster, removed the offending black box from its mounting and consigned it to the visual bomb aimer's position down below. Much to my surprise the 3 hours and 30 minutes sortie continued and fighter procedures in the circuit were something to beheld! None of this put me off – not that I had any choice.

Aircraft flown by No.69 Valiant course and below from back row, left to right:

Flt Lt Cottingham, Flt Lt Hill, Flt Lt Butterworth, Plt Off Trigg. Front, left to right:

Fg Off Arnold, Fg Off Milligan, Plt Off Charlton, Plt Off MacDonald (Spike Milligan)

And so to the end of my Canberra tour on a 1 Group station and a posting to 232 OCU Gaydon in 3 Group to do the Valiant conversion course; in those days HQ 1 Group Bawtry had nothing to do with HQ 3 Group Mildenhall and there appeared to me to be more than just a north/south geographical divide between the two rival groups.

My first Valiant trip on the course was on 12 May 1961 in WZ361, captained by Flt Lt Tiff O'Connor, a highly experienced Valiant man who had taken part in the nuclear bomb trials in the South Pacific with 49 Squadron on Operation Grapple in 1957/58. Other 49 Squadron 232 OCU instructors of the same background included pilot Sqn Ldr Barney Millett and nav radar Flt Lt Alan Washbrook who was in the crew of Wg Cdr Ken Hubbard which dropped the first thermo-nuclear weapon at Malden Island on 15 May 1957 from Valiant XD818. All five members of the crew received AFCs.

The other Valiants employed on my OCU course were WZ360, WZ364, WZ369 and WZ374. During my time at Gaydon I remember routine visits from Vulcan B1As on dispersal exercises. I was surprised that 1 Group permitted their aircraft to use a 3 Group airfield.

Having completed my conversion course of thirty-six hours, I was posted on 7 June 1961 to 49 Squadron at Wittering. Serving on the squadron were two more of the Hubbard crew, viz nav plotter Flt Lt Toddy Hood, and pilot Flt Lt Bob Beeson. My time at Wittering was short lived – the squadron was earmarked to relocate to Marham on 27 June and Bob Beeson and I were the advance party to make sure Marham was ready to receive its new unit (later sadly, Bob was killed in a Hunter at Boscombe Down).

Under 49 Squadron Wg Cdr Alan Chamberlain the move went smoothly and my first sortie from Marham was on 30 June 1961 in XD824. All squadron members quickly settled in at 'El Adem with grass'.

Social life at Marham was lively with four Valiant squadrons, crewed by a large proportion of high-spirited young single officers who lived-in in the large officers' mess. Happy Hour at 1700 hours on a Friday was always well attended. Two of the other three Valiant squadrons were bombers, viz 148 and 207 Squadrons and the fourth was 214 Squadron in the air-to-air refuelling role. Wg Cdr Peter Hill took over command of 214 Squadron from Wg Cdr (later Marshal of the Royal Air Force) Michael Beetham who had done much of the pioneering work on air-to-air refuelling. The co-pilot to these two distinguished aviators was Flt Lt Eric Macey, who went on to make his considerable mark on Vulcans, as well as playing many lively tunes on the piano.

On 8 September 1961 we performed at the SBAC Air Show Farnborough as part of a mass formation flyover which was highly unspectacular being at 37,000 feet.

Before switching to the low level role most sorties were of high level navigation and simulated radar bombing using the NBS/H2S systems against mobile radar bomb score units located at various points around the UK. In these radar bombing sorties the nav radar was king. However, the nav plotter was responsible for all the visual bombing, normally 8 x 100-lb practice bombs dropped from 25,000 or 35,000 ft featuring the visual T4 bombsight on El Adem range in Libya. This involved a three-night deployment to Luqa in Malta. The eyes of a couple of nav plotters had become so accustomed to close range chart work that their visual bomb scores were somewhat excessive leading to eye test and the issue of spectacles.

All the bomber squadrons spent an inordinate amount of time on target study and were poised to react to any threat whilst on QRA, sleeping in caravans on the far side of Marham airfield adjacent to the strictly controlled wire fence which surrounded the nuclear-armed Valiants. A contingent of USAF personnel guarded the access to the compound (the weapons were American).

Also adjacent to the caravans was a little-used public road separated only by a hedge. To relieve the boredom at weekends some enterprising souls would arrange to meet their girlfriends on the other side of the hedge. I know of no assignation to have been interrupted by an alert.

Feeding arrangements were less than satisfactory in that the food was cooked

The only bachelor crew in the whole of V Force on QRA RAF Marham 1961. From left to right: Fg Off (later wing commander) Taff Morris (AEO), Flt Lt Bob Weeks (nav radar), Sqn Ldr John Cheesbrough (captain later wing commander), Fg Off Spike Milligan (nav plotter later air commodore) and Fg Off John Ford (co-pilot). *(Spike Milligan)*

in the mess in the main part of the station and towed to the far side in a supposedly heated trolley attached to a Land Rover. To alleviate this situation some enterprising folks visited Swaffham market and bought a second-hand cooker which worked very well until the powers-that-be discovered it and banished it from the QRA premises.

Overseas flights – lone rangers and western rangers – were a welcome distraction from the mundane training routine and QRA. A popular route was from Marham to Idris or El Adem and thence to Nairobi and Salisbury, Southern Rhodesia (now Harare, Zimbabwe). On one such trip the aforementioned Tony Alder, now a squadron leader and a flight commander on 49 Squadron, met up with the British Lions rugby squad who had encountered a problem getting their baggage and kit back from South Africa to the UK. The gallant Alder undertook to load it into the Valiant bomb bay pannier as illegal freight. On staging back to the UK via El Adem with a load of contraband liquor in boxes stowed in the cockpit, the take-off was not successful in that Alder's fighter technique replicated the one he had used on Venoms in Germany – get the nose up early. On a shortish runway on a hot day and with a fully laden aircraft, this did not work. The take-off was not achieved until he had ploughed through the upwind and approach lights, demolishing them. Undeterred, the flight continued, with uncomplimentary signals flashing from station commander El Adem to his opposite number at Marham.

After eventually landing at Marham, Alder espied a group of senior officers accompanied by a posse of customs personnel awaiting his arrival at dispersal. He decided to taxi the long way around the airfield peri-track, unloading en route the boxes of hard stuff. He was not popular.

On the subject of customs and excise (Waterguard) a privileged insider knowledge of customs procedure revealed that the best time to avoid official scrutiny when returning from overseas flights was at high tide in King's Lynn, the local port, when the Waterguard's priority was ships not aircraft. This meant that the station duty officer or a RAF Police corporal would greet the incoming aircraft, with the certain knowledge that any refreshment on board was destined for a squadron party or the Summer Ball, and never for resale. This explains why a certain crew always carried King's Lynn tide tables as part of their nav kit.

Western rangers were also popular. These would depart on a Thursday on the first leg to Goose Bay, Labrador, and if a westerly jet stream was blowing this could take over 6 hours and 30 minutes. The Friday would be spent flying to Offutt AFB, Nebraska the home of USAF's Strategic Air Command (motto 'Peace is our Profession') aiming to arrive in time for Happy Hour at the vast oval bar in the officers' club. The weekend was free before starting to retrace the route for the homeward journey, this time with a following wind. About twenty-two hours would be the average for the whole trip.

A notable western ranger which did not go according to plan involved an experienced crew from 148 Squadron who did not pay enough attention to transatlantic navigation. Once Rockall (known as Rockall, Cock All and all points West) had been reached on the first leg, the captain, Harvey Hilliard, left his seat to make up a bridge four down the back with the nav radar Tony Willson-Pepper, the nav plotter Tony Norman and the FSgt air electronics operator. This left the co-pilot Chris Welles in sole charge up front; it did not occur to this young man (an international hockey player) that he should have to shield his eyes from a strong sun whilst flying on a westerly heading at noon local. There had been a compass malfunction which was undetected by the nav plotter's couple of perfunctory heading checks which had revealed about the right difference between true and magnetic headings but in the wrong direction. This seemingly was a problem with the automatic variation setting unit (AVSU) which should have done the job automatically without any prompting. All this resulted in the aircraft flying more south than west, only noticed when a routine radio check failed to raise the expected Western Atlantic weather ship and enlisted only a faint response from the Azores weather ship. This certainly set alarm bells ringing and the abandonment of the card school; rapid fuel checks were carried out which left only marginal amounts of fuel available for achieving the intended destination of Goose Bay. If only to save face, a correct heading was adopted and they pressed on with fingers firmly crossed, and made it with only fumes to spare.

I happened to be on the next western ranger after this epic flight and as the 49 Squadron navigation leader I made sure that everything was on top line assisted by my talented nav radar Bob Weeks. I think I spent half the flight standing on the plotter's table doing heading sun checks using the telescopic astro sextant and when I was not doing that carrying out innumerable compass comparisons, comparing the G4B and E2A, and monitoring the AVSU. On return to Marham we were met by the 3 Group navigation officer who impounded my log and chart for analysis to assist him in his inquiry. I am sure he must have been impressed by my industry and level of activity.

The appointment of nav leader was interesting as I was the most junior of the nav plotters and only recently promoted to flight lieutenant. The nav leaders on the other squadrons were all about ten years older than I was. The over-riding qualification was to be in possession of a gold-plated general list permanent commission (PCGL) rather than the lesser supplementary list commission. There was a noticeable lack of PCGL nav plotters on the squadron so I got the job. From my perspective it was not ideal to have a nav plotter as OC 49 Squadron, in the shape of the highly experienced Wg Cdr John Langston whose previous service included a tour on 617 Squadron Lancasters. My nav leader duties entailed crawling over his log and charts for assessment purposes; I was very conscious that this activity did not appeal to him at all.

A memorable incident concerning the Valiant's electrical system occurred during a routine high level sortie when the tranquility was shattered by seven red warning lights appearing simultaneously above the head of the AEO, Flt Lt Taff Morris. This signified that all four generators and the three rotary transformers had tripped off-line – a very serious state of affairs. I have never seen an AEO react more speedily and expertly to sort out the situation.

On another sortie another worthy AEO, Flt Lt Murray Duff, had cause to be concerned when he smelt smoke in the cockpit. He instantly reported this to the captain, Tony Alder (him again!), and was told there was no problem and to belt up. The smoke persisted so Murray seized a fire extinguisher and climbed the steps to find Alder puffing away on a cigarette, despite being surrounded by oxygen equipment. Without further ado, the extinguisher was activated and the fire put out. The captain had to convince the ground crew that the extinguisher had been somehow discharged accidentally. The incorrigible Alder did not have a leg to stand on and did not succumb again to his desire for a quick airborne infusion of nicotine. Score AEO 1 – Alder 0.

Another well-known AEO at Wittering and Marham was the charming and eccentric David 'Woobs' Wooberry, an electrical engineering officer who had done AEO training and one tour on 49 Squadron Valiants. He had acquired a grey parrot on a trip to Africa and en route back to the UK, air traffic gave instructions to strangle the parrot, meaning of course switch off the identification, friend or foe (IFF) (codeword 'parrot'). Woobs feigned righteous indignation at this cruel command!

I remember two of the trials that took place during my time on 49 Squadron. First was the prototype to replace the air-ventilated suit which was worn next to the skin under the flying suit. This new model was water cooled through a myriad of narrow bore capillary tubes leading to and from a water reservoir located somewhere in the bowels of the aircraft. It would have worked fine but for the fact it leaked profusely. It did not come into service. The second trial was the moving map which appeared to me, even in the far off days of the 1960s, as baroque technology. It was not at all accurate. I well remember one of the trial low level sorties in the UK when I was expected to give the pilots a running commentary on the terrain ahead. Unbeknown to them I had left my seat and was standing on the steps behind them giving a highly accurate and precise account of what lay ahead. They were suitably impressed until I threw in the comment that they should expect to see a herd of black and white cows one mile ahead. At that point they turned their heads.

The structure of the flying stations in those days meant that OC Administrative Wing (OC Admin Wg) was always a general duties wing commander and the station adjutant a general duties flight lieutenant. The OC Admin Wing at Marham was the redoubtable Wg Cdr Ken Rees, whose World War II career was mostly spent in POW camps having been shot down in a Wellington in 1940. He was in Stalag Luft III at the time of the ill-fated Great Escape. Ken was a charismatic Welshman who was a former captain of London Welsh rugby team, and who had been a trialist for the Welsh International XV. He was a tough nut of short but burly physique which he used to great effect when a 49 Squadron member misbehaved at a station function when Ken was the president of the officers' mess committee. He invited the miscreant to take the night air on the front steps of the mess. Ken stood on the top step with the 6ft 5ins offender at ground level – but not for long; he was rendered horizontal by a procedure not unknown in Welsh rugby scrums.

Ken's posting was announced shortly after – from flying a desk in Admin Wing, he made a quantum leap to command an operational V Force squadron in the shape of 148 Squadron at Marham. In the meantime the young co-pilot on the infamous Atlantic crossing had succeeded with his piloting skills and had been promoted and made captain of a Valiant. Very sadly he and his crew were killed in WZ363 on 6 May 1964 in north Lincolnshire, near Binbrook, in an accident which was largely unexplained. It was thought to be caused by a tailplane trim runaway; in later years, another possible cause was postulated – that of metal fatigue of the main spar leading to structural failure.

This accident reminded me of the early days of the Canberra when a particularly alert pilot experienced a 'runaway down' tail trim. He quickly inverted the aircraft causing it to do a negative-G outside half loop to a safe height from whence they successfully carried out a Martin-Baker descent – despite the red eyes. The evidence for the Board of Inquiry was invaluable.

After finishing my tour on 49 Squadron at Marham on 26 March 1964 I attended the staff navigation course at the College of Air Warfare at Manby. The boss of all post-graduate navigation training was the expert and highly knowledgeable Wg Cdr Pinky Grocott.

On graduating I was posted to the staff of 232 OCU at Gaydon which involved doing an in-house conversion on to the Victor I as my instructional duties involved both the Valiant and Victor. The chief instructor at 232 OCU was Wg Cdr Arthur Steele a fine pilot with a double AFC and an eye for precision in all aspects of flying with a 49 Squadron background of the nuclear drops during Operation Grapple. Also at Gaydon was Des Hall, a well-known bomber man, and OC of the Valiant and Victor simulator section.

My duties on the OCU were twofold viz first as a ground school lecturer on many subjects including astro-navigation, Green Satin Doppler and radio compass, and secondly as an airborne instructor/screen navigator. For this role, the nav plotter instructors acquired a good knowledge of the NBS/H2S, and

Wg Cdr Spike Milligan, detachment commander, at the then USAF-operated Sculthorpe 1978. *(Spike Milligan)*

frequently flew in the nav radar position. The ground school element included a steady stream of familiar faces from the front-line Valiant and Victor squadrons on refresher courses, plus periodic courses from Transport Command who used our facilities to save setting up their own. In these olden days blackboards were in use and all us instructors wore white coats when in the 'chalk and talk' mode.

The metal fatigue problem with the alloy used in the construction of the Valiant is now well known – but it was not then. We all knew about non-destructive testing (NDT) carried out by the engineers and assumed it was all going ahead routinely without any cause for concern across the aircraft inventory in the RAF.

It came as a nasty shock when the 232 OCU QFI, Flt Lt Taff Foreman experienced a problem whilst flying an instructional sortie in Valiant WP217 over his native Wales on 6 August 1964. The way I remember it happening was when the flaps were selected down in the Gaydon circuit an unexpected roll occurred. He de-selected flaps and initiated an overshoot and later wished he hadn't when he found out it was the main spar breaking. As he taxied in the crew chief could not believe his eyes when he saw the huge droop on one wing. An urgent evaluation then took place to ascertain the size and scale of this 'happening'. One outcome was the decision to alter the conversion course of OC designate 207 Squadron, nav plotter Wg Cdr Jimmy Stewart – we switched him on to the Victor I course and he duly graduated taking over command of his Valiant squadron without ever been in one. Once the grounding of the Valiant fleet had been slightly relaxed with the aircraft subject to limited IAS and radius of action, I was given the job of flying from Gaydon to Marham in the station flight Anson to check out OC 207 Squadron on his first-ever trip in a Valiant. This was successfully achieved on 9 October 1964 which turned out to be my last trip in a Valiant. My notes record that all Valiants were grounded on 9 December 1964 'except for National Emergency' (we were nuclear-armed and assigned to SACEUR). The final decision to scrap the Valiants was announced on 26 January 1965, effective the next day.

232 OCU at Gaydon continued to operate with the Victor 1 until June 1965 when the ground school element moved to Finningley and the flying side, which was christened Tanker Training Flight (TTF) redeployed to Marham on 22 June 1965. TTF could not be called Victor Training Flight (VTF) as that was the title already in use by the Victor IIs at Wittering. TTF was a misnomer as we were purely a conversion-to-type unit, with the tanker training carried out by the air-to-air refuelling instructors on the squadrons.

TTF was a small and harmonious unit with our own aircraft with TTF emblazoned on the tail fin – two B1s XA933 and XA940, plus five B1As XH589, XH592, XH593, XH594 and XH614. TTF was commanded by the multi-talented Sqn Ldr Tony Fraser who later became the OC of the Buccaneer OCU. The flight commander was Sqn Ldr Denys Mobberley who had achieved the seemingly ancient age of forty, at least to those of us in our twenties. Denys' pilot instructors were Dick Russell, later of Black Buck Falklands fame, Bill Gallienne, Les Ketcher, Bill Cox and Mike Hastings. The nav radars

Top left: Loading bomb bay to come home after
Indonesian Confrontation. *(Nigel Baldwin)*
Bottom left: 35 Squadron at RAAF Darwin. *(Nigel Baldwin)*
Top: Approach to Gan. *(Nigel Baldwin)*
Bottom: Refuelling at Nicosia on return from RAF Tengah,
Singapore *(Nigel Baldwin)*

Top: Welcome home from Singapore. 35 Squadron, RAF Cottesmore. *(Nigel Baldwin)*

Bottom: 101 Squadron Detachment RAF Tengah, Singapore, 1970. *(Anthony Wright)*

Top right: Vulcan XM647 over Akrotiri Hospital. *(Spike Milligan)*

Bottom right: Vulcans at Akrotiri. *(Spike Milligan)*

Top: Red Flag 82-2, Waddington Vulcans, Nellis
preparing for the night take-off. *(Anthony Wright)*
Bottom: Vulcans at Nellis preparing for night
take-off. *(Anthony Wright)*

Top: United States base on Ascension. *(Alan Bruyn)*

Bottom: The post box that residents had erected on the way to
the summit where passports could be stamped. On the far right is Badger
Brooks – a notorious tanker pilot who recovered an aircraft after
a horrendous equipment failure and fire (see *Victor Boys*). *(Alan Bruyn)*

Right: Two ship from RAF Waddington. *(Anthony Wright collection)*

Top: Accommodation bungalows on US base until
the 'inferior' concertina huts arrived. *(Alan Bruyn)*
Bottom: Avro Vulcan at home. Flying over Lincoln

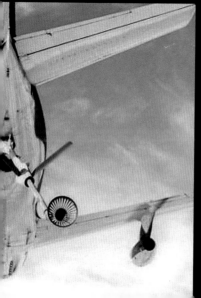

Top: XH649, a 57 Squadron aircraft, landing at Gan during Exercise Magic Palm, to the Far East Air Force in November 1968. *(Stewart Waring)*

Bottom left: Operation Desert Storm. French Mirages waiting to refuel. *(Adrian Richardson)*

Bottom right: Operation Desert Storm. Refuelling from a USAF KC-135. *(Adrian Richardson)*

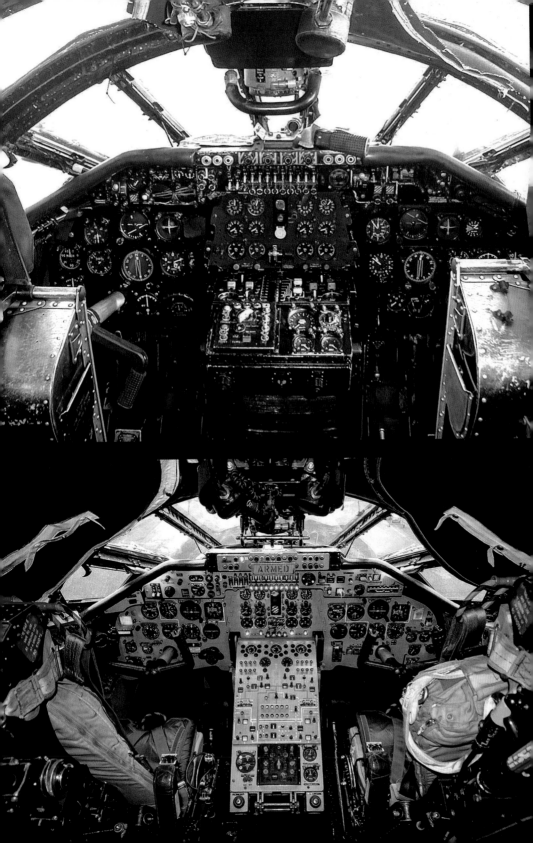

Top left: Victor B2 on arrival at Woodford. *(Charles Masefield)*

Bottom left: Victor K2 after conversion. *(Charles Masefield)*

Top: Vulcan XM603 on its final flight to Woodford flown by Charles Masefield. Photo taken from Avro's Dove G-ARHW by Paul Cullerne. XM603 is now next to the Avro Heritage Museum. *(Charles Masefield)*

1

2-3

6-7

4-5

8-9

10-11

12-13

1. 148 Squadron Valiants RAF Marham. *(Anthony Wright)*

2-3. 230 OCU Vulcans RAF Scampton. *(Anthony Wright)*

4-5. 50 Squadron Red Flag 82-2 at Nellis AFB 1982. *(Anthony Wright)*

6-7. 50 Squadron Vulcan tankers and bombers, RAF Waddington 1982-1984. *(Anthony Wright)*

8-9. Lincoln and 25th anniversary of the Vulcan at RAF Scampton 1981. *(Anthony Wright)*

10-11. The RAF detachment at RCAF Goose Bay Labrador. *(Anthony Wright)*

12-13. Vulcans Operation Corporate RAF Waddington 1982. *(Anthony Wright)* were Tony Young, Dave Young and Eric Burroughs. The nav plotters were Tony McCreery, Mick Somers-Joce and myself. Completing this bunch of instructors were the hugely experienced ex-WW2 trio of AEOs viz Ernie Butcher, Dick Waddell and Greg Peck. We were a very social crowd encouraged by Tony Fraser who was very partial to gin and Noilly Prat! The unofficial motto of TTF was 'We Put a Tiger in Your Tanker' – an allusion to the well-known petrol advert at the time.

Despite the demise of the Valiant the total allocated number of lone and western rangers remained unchanged. Because of the 'use it or lose it' rule, the aircrew, crew chiefs and ground crew worked hard to ensure nothing was lost, using all-instructor crews, sometimes with an imported co-pilot from the squadrons, to fulfil this onerous commitment.

One notable trip was planned to fly to Malta for the weekend and appropriate beachwear was packed for the sunny climate. On arrival at operations, we found our destination had been changed to Offutt AFB in chilly Nebraska with no time to repack. This sudden change of plan was to take spares to AVM Splinters Smallwood of 3 Group who was stranded in another Victor 1 with a fuel tray snag which rendered it aircraft on ground (AOG). This sortie was achieved with no difficulty and we were extremely well looked after by Gerry Moss, an ex-49 Squadron Valiant SNCO who had retired to the Omaha vicinity after a tour on the RAF Detachment at Offutt. He and his wife Billie ran a rather good motel, the Balti Hi, and would lend us one of his cars.

A memorable and hardworking trip was the proving flight to the Far East of the two-point tanker, Victor B1A(K) XH647, in January 1967 with Dick Russell in charge, assisted by the Marham station commander Gp Capt Pat Kennedy. It was a strenuous outing, via Akrotiri, Muharraq and Gan, where we received a warm welcome from the station commander, the well-known and afore-mentioned Wg Cdr Ken Rees.

Our sleep patterns were disturbed by the famous Battle of Britain ace, AVM Johnnie Johnson, who happened to be there at the same time and insisted on conducting a late-night poker session which he was normally expected to win.

From Gan we flew to Tengah, Singapore on 27 January 1967 where we were greeted by Gp Capt Phil Lagesen and Wg Cdr Knight. The return trip was no picnic with a double-stage via Gan to Muharraq. At Gan there was no ground crew available as they were fully occupied with their number one priority of Transport Command aircraft. In extremely hot and humid conditions we had to turn round the aircraft, including the tail chute, before departing to Bahrain arriving suitably tired after nine hours flying that day. On arrival at Akrotiri the next day we had a chance to re-hydrate with copious quantities of Keo and Kokinelli.

One of my students on TTF was the navigation guru of Manby, Pinky Grocott, who was converting on to the Victor before taking over as OC Operations Wing at Marham. As you would expect he sailed through his conversion and I was amazed at his work rate and accuracy.

Whilst on TTF I thought it would be interesting to see what happened at VTF at Wittering. I duly managed a sortie with Flt Lt Tim Taylor in Victor B2 XL513 and was highly impressed by the mighty performance of the B2 especially on take-off – quite unlike the B1.

I had already mentioned from my squadron Valiant days at Marham that mess life was lively and this extended to dining-in nights. On one such occasion a grey horse belonging to Mavis, the wife of the spirited and popular OC 57 Squadron, Wg Cdr Des Hall was imported into the foyer of the mess without her permission and knowledge, much to her chagrin. It was not unknown for a motorbike or Mini to be driven at high speed along the extensive main east/west corridor of the mess, with the sound (and fumes) reverberating in the confined space.

Another wheeze was to ascend the tall and very slim fireplace at the west end of the ante room. One athletic young officer, Martin Todd, managed to perform the difficult task of turning through 180° on the narrow mantelpiece. As he held out his arms to receive the acclaim and applause of the admiring congregation the whole fireplace detached itself from the wall and collapsed into the room in a cloud of dust and debris. Martin was happily unhurt but I am not sure who paid for the barrack damages.

My last flight in a Victor B1A XH593 was on 28 November 1967 with Bill Gallienne, a 3 hours and 30 minutes sortie, day into night. That was the end of my happy association with TTF, and I then was promoted to squadron leader, with no flying job to go to.

A ground tour was selected for me which came as an unpleasant surprise to someone who wanted to continue flying. I was posted to a weapons appointment at HQ Bomber Command on 22 April 1968; on 30 April it was retitled HQ Strike Command with the distinguished Australian, ACM Digger Kyle, remaining as C-in-C. I was very lucky with my boss, Gp Capt George Bastard (pronounced as it is spelt!) who had commanded IX (B)Squadron at Binbrook on Canberras as a squadron leader. His A Flight commander was Des Hall. George went on to be station commander Cottesmore. A truly splendid officer and very much a V Force exponent.

I shared an office at High Wycombe with three other V Force boys, all good friends of mine, Frank Mason, Frank Guard and Pete Yeo. It was certainly a convivial working environment. One of my tasks was to oversee all the bombing/weapon ranges in the UK and to harmonise weapons procedures on these ranges which included Wainfleet, Holbeach, Donna Nook, Cowden and Jerby IoM. This involved a great deal of liaison with the USAF HQ 3 Air Force at Ruislip to agree range patterns, procedures and RT calls. As part of devising protocols I flew with the USAF in the F-4C and F-4D from Bentwaters and the F-100 from Lakenheath with detachments to Wheelus AFB, Libya, to evaluate procedures at the El Uotia range near the Tunisian border. Although I was well versed with LABS manoeuvres from my Canberra days, some of the profiles I found exciting, particularly the 45° dive bombing with an 8 g recovery. The end result was a jointly produced set of range orders entitled USAFE 55-1 for the Americans and Strike

Command air weapons range orders (STCAWROs) for the British. There were lots of pretty diagrams and acceptable procedure for all USAF, RAF and RN aircraft plus visitors from other NATO nations.

Almost coincident with the publication Gaddafi came to power in Libya and we were kicked out of our two RAF bases at Idris and El Adem with the loss of ranges at Tarhuna and El Adem. The USAF was similarly disenfranchised. This was a great pity as I had my eyes on the excellent El Uotia range and hoped to get a slice of the action for the V Force. At this time the Canadians had decided to give up their quarter share of Decimomannu in Sardinia and I moved quickly to secure it and the Capo Frasca range for the RAF. This entailed some flights in the F-104 which I remember vividly – 540 knots at 50 ft dropping laydown bombs.

The new range orders publication was designed, inter alia, to resolve conflictions between aircraft transitting to and from the ranges. Sadly just before it was published an horrendous night mid-air collision took place on 19 August 1969. A TTF Victor Mk 1, XH646, flown as a four-man crew captained by Bill Gallienne was climbing north out of Marham on an ICC sortie with Fg Off Roger Morton in the left-hand seat. At the same time a Canberra was climbing out of Wainfleet range on its way to Germany. The eastern radar unit at Watton was plagued that night with heavy clutter including cumulonimbus cloud which heavily obscured the radar picture. The two aircraft met nose-to-nose and all six blameless aircrew were killed instantly.

My weapons job at High Wycombe was certainly full of variety; I was approached by the Fleet Air Arm at Yeovilton about some proposed bombing trials using their newly acquired Phantom F-4K, a pure air defence aircraft with no capability of dropping 1,000-lb bombs on anti-shipping strikes. After much discussion I agreed that the ship target at Wainfleet range could be used providing I was involved to ensure no undue liberties were taken. The sorties were flown using the Mk 1 eyeball and chinagraph marks on the cockpit Perspex. Our results left a lot to be desired and luckily the RN work-up squadron (700P which became 892 Squadron) lost interest because the Transatlantic Air Race became top priority. I continued to fly with them on the lead-in to the race cruising down the English Channel and Cornwall at 1.6 M at 46,000 ft to establish the best fuel consumption figures. As my uniform was the wrong shade of blue it was decided I was not required for the actual event.

Another fascinating part of my job involved the 1969 Battle of Britain film. The film company requested permission from MoD to drop bombs from Heinkel 111s which were on loan from the Spanish air force, suitably badged with Luftwaffe markings. As the bombs were to be dropped on a bombing range there was a certain sensitivity of bombs landing off range – the dreaded ODA, outside danger area. There had been a recent spate of ODAs (always USAF!) which had provoked parliamentary questions in which I was highly involved. I got the job as a project officer and MoD sent a letter and signal appointing me as captain of the lead Heinkel for the bombing sequence so if anything went wrong

Flt Lt Maurice Stocks (AEO), Wg Cdr Ron Dick (captain), Sqn Ldr Spike Milligan
(nav plotter), Flt Lt Steve Stevenson (nav radar), and Flt Lt Adrian Sumner (co-pilot),
RAF Masirah 1971.*(Spike Milligan)*

they had a fall guy all lined up. For the record I dropped four 500-lb and sixteen 100-lb bombs at Wainfleet, every one definitely within the danger area, despite the German calibration on the bomb sight and the inability of the Spaniards to speak English.

Having never had an overseas tour my ambition was to secure one, preferably an exchange flying tour with the USAF in somewhere like Florida, Texas or California. I kept putting this in the 'choice of next posting' in the annual confidential report, Form 1369, in the hope it would succeed. Towards the end of my tour a supernumerary squadron leader was posted-in to my office to kill time before a posting to IX (B)Squadron Vulcans at Akrotiri. He confided to me that he was not going as he had decided to PVR –premature voluntary retire. I saw the 'overseas tour' lights flashing, albeit not in the USA. Whilst he was writing his decision letter to the Air Secretary, I was writing mine to the same man, requesting under the relevant Queens Regulations a posting back to my old squadron, IX. Both letters went in the same envelope. It worked. Following Vulcan conversion at RAF Scampton I was posted to IX Squadron Vulcan B2s in the low level bombing role at RAF Akrotiri in Cyprus 1970.

Flying in Cyprus was somewhat restricted in many ways, with the high altitude sorties being confined to east/west tracks to Crete and back. Apart from exercises low flying was carried out around the single low flying route (LFR) around the island, ending up with dropping four or six 28-lb practice bombs on Episcopi range. To relieve the familiarity with the Cyprus LFR we frequently flew in the reverse direction. To add a bit of variety (and bad weather) we would regularly return to the UK to fly the UK LFRs from Waddington. On the Cyprus LFR I remember one pilot adding his own little bit of variety by returning to base with sand and sea shells embedded in a wing tip.

At this time I wondered what had become of my ex-Victor Mk 1 friend Pete Yeo from High Wycombe. I found out to my alarm that he had been posted to an exchange flying tour with the USAF – the job I wanted. I felt a lot better when I was told he was now resident at Elmendorf, Alaska enjoying the snow.

Some exercises in the Mediterranean were interesting, particularly low flying in Italy and Greece often against US Navy fighters launched from carriers. I had the fortune of being selected as an observer for one of the exercises and was collected from Akrotiri by a US Navy C-2 Greyhound (twin piston) known as a COD, carrier on-board delivery. We landed using the arrester hook on board the USS *Franklin D Roosevelt*. That was quite a different experience, surpassed only by a catapult launch and recovery next day in an A-6 Intruder.

The UK was a member of the now defunct Central Treaty Organisation (CENTO) of which Iran was a signatory. I led a detachment of six Vulcans to Mehrabad near Tehran, and flew hi-lo profiles against the F-4s of the Royal Iranian Air Force. Many of the ex-NEAF Bomber Wing personnel will remember the untimely end of XJ781 which terminated its days in Shiraz due to a complicated hydraulic fault. The pilot, Flt Lt Eddie Baker of IX (B) Squadron was a former Vulcan hydraulics instructor on 230 OCU and, of course, he was totally without blame for converting the Vulcan B2 into a load of saucepans. This spectacular Cat 5 had a supreme cleansing effect on various inventories some of which were worryingly deficient and needed mega write-offs to put that right. I know a certain crew chief, Tony Regan, was seen smiling for weeks afterwards.

Popular flights were the lone rangers to Nairobi via Bahrain, Ankara and Malta. One especially enjoyable interlude was to Asmara in Eritrea with Ron Dick. The whole Vulcan experience in Cyprus was a joy, but a rather different sort of lifestyle awaited me – a one-year course at the Army Staff College, Camberley and a posting to Hong Kong as PSO to an army general.

Having survived the rigours of the mystic Orient, and getting promoted in-post to wing commander, it was deemed possible that I would return to the Vulcan force. This thought was overtaken by the fact that I was the only wing commander available in the timescale required with a Canberra and Victor background to take the appointment of OC

RAF Luqa, 1971. *(Spike Milligan)*

55 Squadron XL513, Marham, September 1976.

(Spike Milligan)

Operations at Marham, where both types were based. The Victor 1 was shortly to be replaced by the Victor 2 so I embarked on my fourth V Force conversion on 232 OCU at Marham and a Canberra refresher with 231 OCU, also at Marham.

Whilst on the 232 OCU course a serious incident involving 55 Squadron's Victor 2 XL513 occurred during take-off, when a bird strike was suspected. The take-off was aborted well above decision speed and the aircraft ran off the end of the runway; it was Cat 5. The captain was used to flying the Victor 1 and he could not cope with the huge amount of extra power of the Victor Mk 2 and it simply ran away from him. I believe he did not fly again.

The Marham station commander, the highly intelligent Gp Capt (later Air Chief Marshal) Benny Jackson was a former OC 13 Squadron on Canberra PR9s in Malta and a recognised expert on the Victor 2 at Wittering. When flying as a co-pilot in Victor 2 XM714 on 2 March 1962 the aircraft captain misdiagnosed juddering after take-off as possible structural damage caused by an engine fire, and then undoubtedly misread his airspeed indicator by 100 knots. Benny correctly diagnosed the juddering as the onset of a severe stall and ejected. All the other crew members perished.

On a more pleasant note we did some flying together with a preferred crew of co-pilot Sqn Ldr Hurrell, nav radar Flt Lt Pancho Painting and AEO Mike Beer. Our favourite sortie was a western ranger or western tanker to Offutt.

HM the Queen was appointed an honorary air commodore of Marham and her inaugural visit was highly organised as you would expect. As OC Operations Wing I had to brief our distinguished visitor on the operational role of the station. As a secondary duty I was the president of the mess committee of the officers' mess and responsible for hosting a very smart luncheon with HM on my right and the station commander on the other side. Unexpectedly halfway through the proceedings the mess manager, Tony McQuarrie, entered the dining room and made his way to the top table to whisper a message in my left ear, to which I made a brief reply. The lady-in-waiting sitting on my left was fascinated by this performance and gently enquired the reason. After I secured a promise that she would not tell HM until the Rolls-Royce had exited the station, I explained that the first item on the programme after lunch was a visit to a highly bulled-up airman's barrack block. The whispered message was to tell me that a disgruntled airman had set fire to it and it was burning nicely. My response was "get another quick" and resolved to slow down the lunch as much as possible. The visit to barrack block Mk 2 was a complete success.

The top priority task at Marham was the air-to-air refuelling of the UK's air defence aircraft engaged in intercepting Russian incursions into airspace close to the UK. These aircraft would fly over the top of Norway aiming for the GRIUK gap (Greenland, Iceland, UK) to test the effectiveness of our defence.

Another task was to be the airhead for royal flights carrying members of the royal family during their winter residence at Sandringham. This commitment was complicated by the resurfacing of the main runway, which entailed the deployment of all the Victors and Canberras to the bolthole airfield at Sculthorpe which was under care and maintenance for the USAF. I was appointed detachment commander for the lengthy duration which coincided with the worst winter weather in living memory, with abundant snow. I had elected to live on base, which was just as well bearing in mind some of the country roads were often blocked with deep snow. We had major problems keeping the runway clear for the air defence scrambles as well as for the royal flights. The Duke of Edinburgh was the most frequent user with his long-standing regular crew of pilot Geoff Williams and navigator Iain Anderson, who was ex-148 Squadron Valiants and shared an office with me at 232 OCU Gaydon. I was not too popular with the duke when a North Sea 'haar' fog bank was steadily approaching, being driven inland by a northerly wind. We would be the last to succumb as Sculthorpe was located in the Norfolk alps, with an elevation of 214 ft. Having recalled all the airborne jets I had to assess the situation when the final Canberra was unable to clear the runway because of zero visibility. My radio transmission to the inbound Andover, call sign Rainbow, informing it of a Grade 1 mandatory diversion to Mildenhall was unenthusiastically received. When we next met I declared my involvement and he was very good humoured and relaxed.

With my previous experience with the USAF, I had a very good relationship with the Sculthorpe base commander, Major Greg Paterson, which ensured there were no difficulties with our temporary occupation of his base.

From time to time we had visiting USAF aircraft, including a deployment of an Air National Guard Squadron (ANG) of F-105 Thunderchiefs from Tinker AFB Oklahoma. These were flown by highly experienced veterans from the Vietnam War, who had retired from the USAF into a variety of professions such as

HM Queen at Marham in January 1978 with Wg Cdr Milligan. (Spike Milligan)

airlines, medicine, dentistry and accountancy. They were very professional aviators but regarded the ANG as a super flying club, and were out to enjoy themselves. On their flying programme was bombing and air-to-ground gunnery and I was well pleased to give them advice on this. We got airborne as a pair to pay a visit to Donna Nook range, near Theddlethorpe, where some enthusiastic strafing took place. On the recovery from some of these strafing runs I found myself looking up at the strafe panels. It was decided to do a practice diversion to Marham, and the low pass certainly woke up the station.

Unbeknown to me a surprise had been plotted for me on return to Sculthorpe, where a left-hand circuit was in force. As we ran for a 420 knots run-and-break with me in the No. 2 aircraft, I was mightily surprised when the leader broke right! I got a full faceful of the upper surface of a Thud – a heart-stopping moment, and which was a source of much amusement to the perpetrators.

One day the base commander told me that two full colonels would be visiting to have sensitive discussions with me. They duly arrived and stated that they were planning to bring a Blackbird into Sculthorpe for a highly classified mission. I greeted this news with great pleasure and told them of my admiration of the Blackbird and how much I would welcome the opportunity to see one at close quarters. They assured me that this would be entirely possible. To my amazement they asked me if I would like a ride in the Blackbird. I expressed my surprise, especially when one considered the semi-astronaut clothing which had to be worn with all the attendant specialist briefings. Again, this apparently would be no problem. However, it quickly became apparent that we were talking about different things – the colonels were special forces commanders and were bringing an all-black-painted C-130, known to them as a 'black bird'. I found several good reasons why I did not wish to have a ride in a C-130.

My last ever flight in a V Force aircraft was in a Victor K2 XH671 from Sculthorpe with Sqn Ldr Dick Lumb on 9 March 1979 doing AAR with Phantoms, Lightnings and Buccaneers, thereby ending a long and happy association with V aircraft (all except the Vulcan 1, which somehow could not be fitted in!)

Sculthorpe 1978. *(Spike Milligan)*

I am frequently asked which aircraft I preferred. All were good, with the Valiant being a nice-looking machine, the Vulcan an eye-catching and spectacular shape, and the Victor an aesthetically pleasing design. The Mark 2 versions were a huge leap in performance from the Mark 1s and were potent aircraft. On balance the crew accommodation in the Victor 2 was far superior to the Vulcan 2 so the Victor is my vote.

Talking of Mk 2 aircraft, I think it was fortunate that the Valiant 2 did not go into production as undoubtedly the same alloy as the Valiant 1 would have been used. I believe it is scandalous the same management of Vickers, the engineers and the metallurgists did not communicate their misgivings about the known flaws in the alloys to the RAF hierarchy who would have taken a robust view. The switch of the Valiant 1 from high level to low level operations was obviously the wrong decision bearing in mind the much higher factor on airframe life. By keeping silent, certain senior people have a case to answer for the way they let political and commercial pressures stand in the way of common sense.[5] Moreover, the number of V Force aircrew lives lost due to the non-provision of ejection seats for the rear crew is another scandal. I am sure the Martin-Baker designs would have worked perfectly well, saving many lives.

Having left the esteemed V Force boys club I proceeded on my career path to the National Defence College, Latimer, and thence to the Royal College of Defence Studies, Belgrave Square, London. From 1982 to 1986 I was in the Ministry of Defence, back on PSO duties to the same army general I served in Hong Kong 1974 to 1976, although he was now a field marshal and chief of the Defence Staff. We got to know each other quite well.

From that rather splendid job, I was posted to be commander RAF Hong Kong, which suited me very well, especially as I got promoted in-post to air commodore. Instead of being posted back to MoD I was deployed to the RAF College, Cranwell, as assistant commandant. Three group captain close colleagues at Cranwell were ex-Vulcan B2s, Ed Jarron (pilot), Al Ferguson (nav, director DIOT, and ex-OC IX Squadron Tornado) and Ben Laite (nav, director DAW, and ex-CO 208 Sqn Buccaneer).

My final tour was to be NATO air commander in Gibraltar, and the deputy commander British Forces in HQ British Forces. The NATO job was mainly a maritime one, and my two bosses were located in Lisbon and Naples. To prepare for the two NATO hats (the other was air defence) I did three senior officer acquaint courses on the Nimrod, Buccaneer and Tornado F3. These three types would be chopped to me in times of hostilities. It all made for fascinating pre-employment training.

It is interesting to note that some of my illustrious Gibraltar predecessors in this predominantly maritime environment were V Force boys John Langston (Valiants, nav plotter), John Pack (Vulcans, pilot) and Ken Lovett (Valiants and Victors, pilot). It just goes to prove that V Force boys are omnipresent!

---

5. See *Valiant Boys* Chapter 19 by same authors.

CHAPTER 11

VULCAN LONE RANGERS

Tony Thornthwaite

Tony Thornthwaite joined the RAF at age nineteen after being in the Air Training Corp and getting his glider wings. He left the Vulcans when 617 disbanded and finished his service on Tornados. He then entered theological training at St Andrew's university; his churches were widely spread in Scotland going from Morningside in Edinburgh, Bettyhill near Cape Wrath and currently he is in Dundee approaching retirement but still riding motorbikes. Surely a splendid example of how the RAF prepares people for varied careers in later life.

My first trip as a trainee navigator was on 3 March 1971 in a Varsity T Mk 4 on 147 course from RAF Finningley (now Robin Hood Airport Doncaster). After 75 hours on the Varsity, 12 hours on the Jet Provost T Mk 4, and 73 hours on the Dominie (RAF version of the HS 125) I graduated in January 1972 and was posted to NBS on the Avro Vulcan. This meant six months ground training at RAF Lindholme (now a prison) near Doncaster.

Here we learnt in fiendish detail, and for no reason I can think of, exactly how the navigation and bombing system of the Avro Vulcan Mk 2 actually worked. The intricacies of analogue, often WW2 technology, were explained and examined. The triangle solver, H2S Lancaster vintage radar, square rooting pin wheel and emergency scanner erection were instilled into our young brains and for the most part are still there in this old brain, I can't get rid of them. Outside the Bombing School at Lindholme was a WW2 leftover. A giant 22,000-lb Grand Slam bomb on a plinth that we all had our photos taken in front of. I was told that when Lindholme shut to be made a prison they tried to move the bomb but the crane could not lift it. That was because it still had ten tons of high explosive in it, enough to flatten the whole camp.

My first flight as navigator radar in a Vulcan was on 21 August 1972 on 230 OCU RAF Scampton which my logbook states was the first of ten 'radar trial' sorties which I think replaced training on radar-equipped Hasting aircraft which really did resemble the last war. I met my crew and we began training together in November 1972 finishing in December.

My first squadron was 101 based at RAF Waddington. I was to learn over the next ten years of Vulcan flying the truism that one of my instructors told me. "On Vulcans

WRIGHT BROTHERS
TONY
MIKE
BARRY
T3
MCK
BILL
MIKE
JIM
ROBBIE
MARTYN

No 1 VULCAN COURSE

The nav radar squadron instructors, a nav plotter instructor and two staff pilots alongside a 230 OCU Hastings used for student nav radar training. *(Tony Thornthwaite)*

my boy," he said, "a normal posting is you stay on the same squadron, a big posting is you change squadrons and a huge posting is when you go from Scampton to Waddington or vice versa." How true!

It was an exciting time for a brand-new navigator, twenty-two years old and still very wet behind the ears. Looking at my first few months they included strange exercises like Black Eagle, Reno Roulette and the more mundane exercise Co-op. We dropped practice bombs on Tain range in Scotland and Jurby in the Isle of Man. There was also fighter Affil where as I remember Lightnings from neighbouring Binbrook would try to get on our tail. The Vulcan had a great way of escaping the clutches of a Lightning. We would go as high as we were allowed – 45,000 ft or if no one was watching a bit higher – and dare the Lightning to try and catch us. Struggling for breath the fighter would climb as high as he could and then we would use the Vulcan's big wing that worked really well at high altitude and simply turn round in tight circles. The poor Lightning would run out of lift, airspeed and ideas all at the same time and plunge earthwards while we made off in the other direction.

The next excitement was a lone ranger to RCAF Goose Bay in Labrador, Canada. A remote place in the back of beyond where our low level flights would not annoy anyone except the odd moose. Some of the routes involved a two-hour high level trip north before descending to 300 ft for our low level. I remember coming out of cloud at about

2,000 ft over the Arctic tundra well above the tree line with the ground covered in many feet of snow and thinking, if anything goes wrong and we have to jump out we are very poorly placed as there was absolutely no search and rescue cover for days.

My other memory of Goose Bay was flying at low level up a steep valley leading to the coast. Above the valley was nothing but tundra, but inside was like a lost world, green trees and grass, waterfalls crashing down the sheer sides, a blue river at the bottom, staggeringly beautiful.

Our next excitement was a return to Waddington and a load of seven 1,000-lb bombs to drop on Garvie Island off the north coast of Scotland. It was my job as nav radar to go up into the bomb bay and check that the armourers (always known as plumbers I don't know why) had put all the arming wires etc. in the right place. I had never seen a real bomb before so how I was meant to check I don't know. I climbed into the little access hatches at the front of the bomb bay and crawled along the bomb doors to the carrier with its seven live 1,000-lb bombs hanging there. To get to the back of the bombs to check the fuses I had to squirm between the bombs and the bomb bay doors, just and only just enough room, and of course it was dark in there apart from my torch. Good job I am not claustrophobic. After checking then it was the same route back. I was so glad to get out of there.

We were only to drop four bombs for some reason. I had never been to Garvie before and there was no run through, no practice we were dropping live on the first pass. Farad's head showed clear on the radar and I deleted the offset and aimed at Garvie Island itself. It was very close and things were happening very fast. The Vulcan rumbled as the bomb doors opened and then the 90-way bomb selector on my left began to click 1, 2, 3, and 4. I think, I hope I was aiming at the right place. We heard the four dull crumps behind as the bombs exploded and then nothing, the range officer's radio simply went totally silent. Suddenly the captain starts shouting. We have total hydraulic failure. I was still worried that I had just bombed the range safety officer but we had a more direct problem. No one fancied landing the Vulcan with no hydraulics and possibly no brakes at the best of times but we still had three 1,000-lb bombs with us. Eventually we jettisoned the bombs in the North Sea and returned to base. The brakes did work enough for us to stop and be towed back to the hangar. The attack on Garvie Island was a success with a direct hit; the range radio just happened to fail at the same time. Phew!

The next month saw us on a trip to Cyprus and then Offutt AFB, Omaha in Nebraska USA. In Cyprus we dropped practice bombs on Episkopi range and I was introduced into the delights of kebabs, Commandaria red wine (so cheap they did not charge extra no matter how much you drank) and the rowing club on Lady's Mile beach, which had a bar but no boats.

Offutt was the headquarters of the American Strategic Air Command and for some reason we went there to fly American low level routes that were called 'oil burners' quickly changed to 'olive branches' after the Yom Kippur war in Israel a couple of months later. In Omaha I loved the American life staying in a nice hotel off base, eating more steak than I knew what to do with and discovering I really did not like American beer but I would drink it anyway.

The three-year tour progressed in the same way. More exercises with strange names, Blue Moon in Denmark, Jareval in France and Exercise Index where we dispersed to operational readiness platforms that were four hard standings at the end of a runway 'somewhere in England'. We were on fifteen minutes readiness so a scramble from sleeping was a busy event. On one occasion as we were all trying to get out of the bus and into our Vulcan it suddenly seemed a bit crowded. I realised that we had two AEOs instead of one. More to the point another Vulcan did not have one at all. Fortunately the guy got out before we took off.

To start the engines in a hurry the pilot would often use high pressure air to start one engine and then put that one up to full power and use bleed air to start the other three engines. Unfortunately no one had told the young WRAF crew bus driver this. She thought she would park 100 yards behind the four Vulcans and watch the scramble. The power of the Vulcan's Olympus jet engines blew every window out of her bus, fortunately apart from a very bad hair day she was ok.

We finished the tour watching the rest of the squadron take off on a round-the-world jolly. I can't remember what this was called but it looked great fun. We stayed at home because we had been selected for Giant Voice, the annual American bomber competition that four Vulcans were allowed to take part in. It was my bad luck to take some form of virus and miss the whole affair but my crew won the navigation part of the competition.

This was the end of the tour and we all went our different ways. I was posted to Cyprus on a ground tour but the Turks invaded the island and the Vulcans were brought home. Instead I went to Scampton as an OCU instructor. Here we mainly flew the plane I had missed in training, a Handley Page Hastings fitted with a Vulcan H2S radar in a fairing underneath. Strangely we did not train Vulcan navigators on this ancient relic but Buccaneer and Phantom ones instead.

The Hastings had a secondary role as transport for senior officers on a jolly. This was how we ended up taking a bunch of retired old duffers to a party in Brussels NATO headquarters. Left to our own devices I was led astray by the antique Hastings pilot Jacko Jackson and his engineer who told everyone in the bar that the last time he was in Brussels he had been shot down and was hiding from the Gestapo. They really were that old. Jacko could easily drink me under the table and I staggered back to our hotel still in my best number one RAF uniform only to be caught up in a riot. The shop next to the hotel was Iberia the Spanish airline and a whole group of folk were chucking petrol bombs through the window protesting about General Franco. I was in the middle when the Belgian riot police arrived and was lucky not to see the inside of a Belgian gaol.

Later in 1975 the Icelandic nation decided to stop British trawlers catching their fish and the Cod War began. The navy were deployed and the RAF decided to send its Vulcan radar-equipped Hastings to frighten the opposition. It took the best part of four hours to get to Iceland from RAF Kinloss in Scotland and four hours back. This gave us around two hours to do something useful. The navy's idea of something useful was to deliver their mail so we would fly as low and slow as possible, cut the big piston propeller engine on the left side, open the door and chuck the sack of letters out close to the ship. For this we awarded ourselves a day-glow cut out of a cod and an envelope with wings on the outside of the fuselage placed under the pilot's cockpit window.

Eventually this tour too came to an end and I made the big trip of ten miles down to Waddington to begin with another crew on 44 (Rhodesia) Squadron. Life as a nav radar continued. We discovered that if you put two drum tanks in the bomb bay we had enough fuel to fly from Waddington to north Italy, descend to low level along the River Po valley for forty minutes and return to Waddington without refuelling. What Italians must have thought of a low level Vulcan flying up and down the river still makes me wonder. Another discovery was that if you followed the NATO United Kingdom low level route it ran down the M6 motorway just outside the Lake District. There is one steep pass where the motorway winds through the hills. By judicious use of lots of bank and throttle, if you got it just right, you could fly the Vulcan through the pass. Again what motorists thought is beyond me; I hope we did not cause any accidents.

In June 1978, three months after I was married we set off to land at Chièvres airfield just outside Brussels in Belgium. I am sure we had a number of genuine tasks to do but the real reason was that the squadron commander had been posted to Supreme Head-quarters Allied Powers in Europe (SHAPE). He wanted to meet his boss and we had his washing machine in the bomb bay. All was uneventful until we tried to take off on our return. It was a very hot day and the runway was much shorter than we normally used. Just as we reached decision point, about 145 knots, there was a huge bang followed by another and the Vulcan slewed across the runway. We had hit a pigeon that was ingested by the engine and it blew up. A design flaw of the Vulcan was that if this happened the engine spat the blades out of both the front and back. The turbine blades coming out the front are ingested by the other engine which also blows up.

We aborted take-off and shut down and pressed the fire extinguishers on the two engines. We also streamed the brake parachute. However, it did not seem enough. From the rear-crew position there was no way to see outside the aircraft, we had to rely on the gauges to know what was happening. I knew we were in real trouble when the pilots started praying: "Oh stop, please stop, Oh God please stop!" We were going too slowly for their ejection seats to work; of course the rear crew did not have ejection seats. Eventually after what seemed an age and amid more and more frantic prayers we juddered to a halt. I opened the door and we all ran away. The aircraft was on fire from the two engines and one of the wheels. In a fit of bravery and adrenalin the captain ran back to the Vulcan, got in, released the fire extinguisher and fought the brake fire until the airfield fire appliances arrived. It was at this point that I realised we had stopped just a few feet from a deep drainage ditch that ran along the airfield boundary. The prayers certainly worked.

The aircraft was very badly damaged and eventually after a double engine change and all the wheels changed it was flown back to Waddington with its gear stuck down. It disappeared into a hangar and we thought it would never come out. However, the aircraft number was XM607 which went on to fly on the Black Buck missions to the Falkland Islands and drop its bomb on the Port Stanley runway.

Broken XM607 Chièvres, Belgium 1978. Before Black Buck 1! From left to right: Jon Tye, Tony Benstead, Vince Hobbs, Wg Cdr Mears, John Barnard and Tony Thornthwaite. *(Tony Thornthwaite)*

In August 1978 we set off for the Abbotsford air show in western Canada. As we stopped in Goose Bay overnight we chatted to the other air show Vulcan that was on its way to a show in Chicago. With a bit of good-natured ribbing we agreed that while our show was good theirs was probably better. We were not to know that they would all be killed two days later in a crash during practice.

Many people know it is possible to roll a Vulcan and it was done in the early days during Farnborough shows. To my surprise our pilot decided to do the same at Abbotsford. Our display finished with a high speed run along the runway followed by a steep climb. As we were very light on fuel the old girl could really perform and we liked to think we imitated a homesick angel. However the pilot decided to wow the crowds by rolling during the climb. Except it all went wrong. I was standing jammed between the ejection seats looking out when we turned upside down and then for some reason stopped turning. The only way out was to complete a half-loop and I did not think we were high enough. I will never forget pointing vertically at Canada, the pilot pulling to the g limit and turning the air blue with expletives. We made it, not by much, and he did not do that again.

When the news of the crashed Chicago Vulcan got back to Waddington there was much confusion over which aircraft it was. My new wife had a phone call from her uncle in Scotland who had seen in the press that a Vulcan had crashed in North America killing the crew. He passed on his sympathy to my wife as he thought she was a young widow. We were very fortunate that day.

Giant Voice, Barksdale 1980. From left to right:
(back row) Tony Thornthwaite, Vince Hobbs, Tony
Benstead; (front row) unknown, Malcom Pluck,
John Barnard and unknown *(Tony Thornthwaite)*

In December that year we flew to RAF Luqa in Malta for more Italian low level. I was standing idly by as the Vulcan was being refuelled and watched a Canberra take off; except he didn't. I saw him set off down the runway and get up to speed but suddenly two little parachutes appeared and a few seconds later there was a huge pall of smoke. I never knew what went wrong but they aborted take-off and the pilot and navigator successfully ejected. Tragically they had a young pilot hitching a ride on the jump seat which had no ejection facility. He died in the crash at the end of the runway. We were called to take off on the other runway and photograph the crash with our F95 vertical camera. When we landed the operations officer came up to us with this cheerful news. "Well," he said, "the Canberra crash was not due to fuel contamination, we know that because you were refuelled by the same bowser; did not think about that until you were airborne."

One of the better trips was to the Italian base at Istrana in northern Italy. From here we would fly early morning low level exercises over the stunning Italian countryside. The advantage was that afternoons were off and it was a very short train ride to Venice. I still remember a very 'happy' crew chief falling off the Vaporetto (water bus) into the Grand Canal. Fortunately he was fished out and made a soggy journey back to base with us.

We finished the tour with the American bombing competition Giant Voice. Two months at Barksdale AFB in Louisiana. Here I managed to snatch defeat from the jaws of victory with what is known in the trade as a 'switch pigs'. But these things happen; after this we were posted to different crews and I finished my Vulcan time up the road in Scampton again, this time on 617 Squadron. After nine months on 617 my logbook reads, 'December 10, 1981, XL425 captain Flt Lt Lebrun my last Vulcan sortie total hours Vulcan 1786.40'.

CHAPTER 12

VICTOR EARLY YEARS

Dick Russell, Gary West, Peter Sharp

Dick Russell and Gary West have memories of early Victor flying and Peter Sharp tells what it was really like putting out brake fires on a Victor.

Dick Russell *was probably the most experienced Victor tanker pilot and QFI starting with the underpowered Mk 1 tanker and then transferring to the very capable Mk 2, later flying with Martin Withers in a Vulcan at the front of Black Buck 1. Here he describes his early Victor flying plus a later trip to Australia in a Victor K2.*

The year is 1961, I was a QFI and flight commander on the piston and Jet Provosts at Linton-on-Ouse. A posting arrived for me to join 82 Valiant Course at Gaydon as a co-pilot. Somehow that did not thrill me. A year or two before, new arrivals to the V Force were interviewed to assess their suitability, but the force was getting larger and I got the impression that anyone would do.

It was February 1962 and I went on leave ready for the change but whilst away and with ten days to go I got a phone call at home telling me that all had changed. Now the posting read 41 Victor course as a captain and squadron QFI; it was like going from the third division to the premier league.

I rang a friend at Honington, a Victor station, who said that he felt it would not be long before the Victors would all be painted blue to match the ground equipment. This was his polite way of telling me that the Victor was having reliability problems and that the four-month course was likely to last a great deal longer. Because of this and because we were living in our own house in York we decided to let our house, buy a caravan and live on the station so that we would get removal expenses if we were at Gaydon a day over six months which was possible.

During the lead up to the posting a Victor was lost climbing out of Honington and then during the course another crashed on take-off at Akrotiri. As the course finished another crashed on the approach to Cottesmore, and three months later yet another crashed at Gaydon all from different problems.

So in March 1962 the Russell family complete with caravan arrived at Gaydon and the course started a week later. One thing we had to be particularly careful about was the landing and take-off because the tail chute was electrically operated and it was very unreliable. There were several failures whilst I was on the course and since the brakes were of non-ceramic material it was not unusual to have a brake fire if the chute failed; in fact I had one when the parachute just dumped on the runway, I have a feeling that a fire tender was always nearby when a Victor was making a final landing. We understood that work was in progress to convert the chute operation to hydraulic power and to change the brake pad material to ceramic for the MK 1A but we knew that those changes would be on the squadron and not for us on the OCU. So on the OCU we were told not to rely on the parachute when calculating our stop and go speeds for take-off. This meant that the stop speed often was less than the go speed, not by much since the MK 1 was a lightweight on the OCU as it was without electronic counter measures equipment. It was just something that we accepted and fuel loads were relatively light.

Mid July and the course was complete. Every sortie went as planned with the only blemish being that I had no dual night take-off, and no final handling; in fact I did fly the final handling but it was for the nav plotter not for me because the chief flying instructor was out in Akrotiri doing a Board of Inquiry on an accident out there.

On our arrival at Honington 55 Squadron was in the middle of a royal visit by Princess Marina, so as a new crew we took a back seat. Although it was not a new crew just a new captain and co-pilot, my rear crew had to go through training at Cottesmore so Rick my co-pilot and I took over a crew whose captain had been posted. At the time the big changes being carried out were the introduction to the Victor 1A and the duty of QRA.

The conversion at Gaydon had been to the Mk 1 Victor. Now 55 Squadron had the Mk 1A with a probe for flight refuelling, new UHF radios, and cabin pressure limited to 8,000 ft – all very welcome improvements. QRA could only be carried out by combat-ready crews so, as a new captain, my crew had to go through the process of getting combat ready all over again.

QRA meant that each of the two Victor squadrons at Honington provided one crew, normally for forty-eight hours. Both squadrons were not up to full strength having only six or at the most seven crews so that the duty came round every ten days or so.

Dick Russell crew. From left to right: Dick, Flt lt Bendall, Fg Off Payne, Fg Off Morris, Fg Off Elwig, Flt Lt Walters. Elwig was the 55 Squadron engineering officer. *(Dick Russell)*

QRA crews were on a continuous fifteen-minute alert and were provided with a Standard Ensign car day and night and stayed with the crew at all times. At night the car was garaged with the doors open and plugged in to a water heater and battery charger, essential during the winter, next to the crew sleeping quarters. Each crew, from the sounding of the siren, had to get to the nuclear-armed aircraft, start the engines and make the take-off point within fifteen minutes; the crews were exercised every day at any time but were never required to take off. Failure to make the time meant a report to the station commander. There were very few failures.

At night and in bed in the special hut allocated to the QRA crews it became normal to wake before the Tannoy actually sounded; the noise of the switch turning the Tannoy on was enough and I certainly would be out of bed putting my flying boots on before the announcement came.

Life on a V Force squadron was built around the QRA. Normal training continued with each crew flying about six times a month and to keep each squadron commander happy each sortie was to be of not less than five-and-a-half hours, six if possible. This was because squadron efficiency was measured by the number of hours flown. Early after my arrival my crew were tasked with the dropping of thirty-five 1,000-lb bombs in one stick. We did this with three sorties, dropping fourteen, then twenty-eight and then the final thirty-five all on Jurby range on the Isle of Man.

The final sortie needed careful planning because the Victor 1A had a maximum take-off weight of 180,000 lb. The basic weight of the aeroplane was around 96,000 lb and the maximum normal landing weight was 125,000 lb with the minimum fuel for landing depending on the diversions available around 12,000 lb. So for this operation with the aircraft weighing 96,000 lb and the bomb load weighing 35,000 lb the maximum fuel load could only be 49,000 lb and we had to be back on the ground with 12,000 lb which meant that only 37,000 lb of fuel could be used on the sortie. Start taxi and take-off took 3,000 lb and the climb to a useful height about another 8,000 lb. This meant only about 26,000 lb was available at altitude which equated to about a total of two hours and forty-five minutes flying time. In addition the centre of gravity with an empty aircraft with the bomb load was outside normal limits so the fuel had to be put in the appropriate tanks to compensate. Once in the air, the fuel had to be managed by the co-pilot so that on the release of thirty-five bombs at once, the centre of gravity still remained within limits. Careful planning was needed. The last sortie to drop the thirty-five 1,000-lb bombs meant a climb, transit to roughly Newcastle, from there the run-in was to Jurby just off the Isle of Man and a transit back to Honington to land with minimums. The odd thing was that on release there was no discernible change in the trim of the aircraft.

The winter of 1963 was bad and the airfield had some six inches of snow. Since we had to maintain QRA it was necessary to clear the 9,000 ft runway which was 200 ft wide. The station did not have proper snow ploughs and a tractor with a plough fixed to the front was the norm, so the station commander got all available aircrew (not ground crew) out on the runway each with a shovel. This was soon realised as an impossible task so the next step was to taxi two Victors out to the runway and try to blow the snow off. This proved even worse because the eight engines of both Victors merely melted the snow which promptly froze as soon as the aircraft moved on. Removing the ice was impossible and the airfield was out of use for far longer than would have been the case. I, along with Denys Mobberly, did try one sortie on the ice when the wind was directly down the runway; we took off with just 30,000 lb and spent the next forty-five minutes wishing we hadn't. However a tail chute made the landing and the stopping not using the brakes uneventful but three of the sixteen tyres had to be changed, they apparently did not like ice.

It is a wonder that V Force crews in the 1960s were not overweight. We flew about twice a week and since each sortie was planned to make the most of flying time it was thought that normal meal times could well be compromised; this was mainly because our targets were managed by about four or five radar bomb plots. All practice bombing runs were tracked on radar and the drop was plotted by the unit and the theoretical hit was scored. Since targets had to be booked, sorties had to be planned when the bomb plots were available and the result was that take-offs could be almost any time of the day or night; this meant that meals at home or in the mess might well be missed. To this end, an aircrew buffet was established at each V Force station. It was open all the time flying took place. Each crew if they wished could have a pre-flight and an after-flight meal and since sorties were never less than five-and-a-half hours, six being the aim, crews always planned to have the pre-flight meal and in addition they always took in-flight rations which would normally include a tin of soup and sandwiches. The after-flight was a rarity but was available.

In 1964 feeling rather rich I ordered and took delivery of a Vauxhall Viva. It was delivered on my birthday and the first day going to work at Honington I drove the car. On the station outside each hangar was a little notice which said 'STOP' aircraft ahead. There was nothing there, the hangar doors were shut; if I saw the notice I ignored it. Drawing up outside the squadron a Mini parked alongside. A wing commander got out and said, "You are banned from driving on the station because you ignored the stop sign". I admitted I had and a long chat with him elucidated the fact that I could drive to my quarter (house) since it was on the station but not to the mess and that the ban would last for three months. The next day I was programmed to be on QRA and I was the only one on my crew with a service driving licence. We turned up the next day to assume the duty of QRA from the outgoing crew only for me to announce that we could not because we could not drive the QRA car. I don't need to tell you the result; we did QRA.

In the spring of 1964 Exercise Chamfrom was declared, the reinforcement of Singapore by the V Force because of the increasing belligerent tone coming from President Sukarno of Indonesia; as a result it was decided to commence air-to-air refuelling training.

Whether the command had ideas in that direction was not known. Compared with the training for air-to-air refuelling years later one can only speculate that it was half-hearted. Denys Mobberley was the designated air-to-air refuelling instructor for our squadron probably because we were to be the first squadron to go to Malaya on Chamfrom.

The sortie always included a nav stage and or bombing and on one occasion it was combined with an intermediate co-pilots course prior to the rendezvous for the air-to-air refuelling. I took part in two of these sorties and had as my partners for training Flt Lts Farlam and Bissell.

Compared with the later training it was a half-hearted affair and none of the trainees became proficient. It came to a halt when Denys in XH594 with Nobby Clarke as a student had plugged in and the main fuel pipe which ran from the probe through the roof inside the cabin burst. Denys broke contact to find that the cabin was flooded with fuel with a real danger of fire. They returned to Honington and landed and when the crew door opened fuel cascaded out. I haven't the date of that flight but some six weeks later I took XH594 out to Malaya. I think that a complete cabin change had been made. Our transit to Butterworth was uneventful.

Before finishing I remember a memorable trip to Australia in a K2 in 1986. With the closure of 232 OCU and the amalgamation into 55 Squadron, somehow 1 Group thought that the Australians might purchase refuelling equipment from us and decided that a Victor and a VC10 would go to Australia ostensibly to show them the hose and drogue that we were using. However, I have a feeling that the trip was also a reward to 232 OCU on closure.

Be that as it may, in February a Victor and a VC10 with a spare Victor crew on board aiming to fly alternate legs on what was to be a round-the-world sortie set off for Williamstown in Victoria on the coast of Australia. The captains of the Victor were myself and Paul Millikin.

I flew the initial leg Marham to Wright Patterson AFB (WP) planned to be 8 hours and 40 minutes, which was at the extreme limit of the Victor's range because during the Falklands the Victor had operated at the maximum design weight of 238,000 lb almost for every sortie, and had consumed an immense amount of fatigue and on return to normality to spin out the fatigue that remained, had been limited to 223,000 lb maximum auw; luckily the VC10 had no such problem. The weather forecast at WP was some twelve hours old and was uncertain. Crossing the Atlantic the forecast went from indifferent to poor and then got steadily worse. The planned fuel on approach to WP was on minimums so passing Griffiss AFB I decided to divert and refuel. This we did, and virtually the whole station came out to see an old ex-V Force bomber. The problem lay in the refuelling method which was finally overcome when the Americans unearthed a bowser with the correct connections. Two hours later we were airborne again and landed at WP in 300 ft and 1,000 yds, but with enough fuel to divert to the nearest diversion airfield. Paul and his crew took the next leg to McClellan AFB. The following day was our leg to Hickham AFB, Honolulu, while Paul took the next leg to Pago Pago part of the American Samoas. Our leg next was to Williamstown, near Melbourne. The forecast was good, and we were cruising at 34,000 ft and ran into light cirrus cloud which became thicker and a shade turbulent. As we progressed the cloud produced rain and suddenly we lost all of our air driven instruments, the airspeed indicator, the machmeter and the climb and descent indicator, although initially the co-pilot's seemed ok, but within a few minutes they went too. Navigation relied on Omega and reception, for us at least, was poor in that part of the Pacific. We had the H2S radar but being 500 miles from nowhere with a range of some 100 miles that was useless.

We did have from the Green Satin a radar speed and drift readout so I decided to divert to the nearest land which was Fiji about 300/400 miles away. A descent was commenced some fifteen minutes later and we made a radio call to Nadi international airport. The descent was awkward without airspeed indicator, machmeter or vertical speed indicator but the Green Satin in the back gave a ground speed read out and the electric artificial horizon gave attitude. We were lucky and broke out of cloud at about 10,000 ft and at 2,000 ft the ice in the pitot-statics thawed and back came our air driven instruments. We were lucky that it was daylight, had it been dark it would have made things a little more difficult. An elevator-powered flying control unit (PFCU) failed during the descent which whilst not a problem made a simple repair after landing rather more of a problem. RAF Hercules travel the world, even so it was a surprise to see one parked at Nadi as we taxied in and this one had a line of washing strung up across the open tailgate.

Once parked the crew chief and AEO quickly drained the pitot static, the new PFCU took two days to arrive and twenty-four hours to install by the same pair, something of a miracle we thought. We landed at Williamstown after being escorted by two Aussie Hornets for the last 100 miles.

The return trip was planned to be Williamstown, Darwin, Butterworth, Colombo, Bahrain and Marham but 1 Group screwed up the diplomatic clearances over Indonesia. Rather than wait for the necessary seven days clearance it was decided that we would stage to Ceylon via Christmas Island and that the VC10 would go direct from Darwin to Ceylon.

Paul flew the aircraft to Christmas Island; this was the first and only occasion a Victor visited there and refuelling was a problem. However, it was managed and it arrived in Ceylon some hours after the VC10. I flew the next leg to Bahrain where the nosewheel oleo collapsed. Luckily Paul was doing the last leg so I and my crew flew straight home in the VC10 while the Victor was stuck waiting for a replacement.

Unfortunately, the Australians appeared to be little interested in our refuelling gear, which seemed to bear out my original thought that the trip was a thank you to 232 OCU.

Gary West was flying Victors as a co-pilot about the same time as Dick Russell. Like others before and after him he had trouble with bombs coming off the bomb racks.

A Bit of a Trial – a Story of '494'

In early 1965, I was stand-in co-pilot with an experienced Victor B1A crew. We were tasked with taking part in a trial – Trial 494 – to drop 1,000-lb bombs which were fitted with experimental radar fuses, on West Freugh range in the Solway Firth. Six of these weapons were loaded on to the Victor, XH590, and were to be dropped singly from medium level, so that observers on the range could assess the performance of the fuses which were set to explode the bombs at 50 ft above the surface.

We made radio contact with the range and were cleared, having made one dummy run over the range, to make our first 'live' drop. With the aircraft lined up on the run, the bomb doors were opened, the navigator radar/bomb aimer was issuing instructions to the captain with an increasingly anticipatory tone, up to the point when it was expected he would announce a triumphant "bomb gone!", like they always do in the war films, but no such announcement came.

Now the bombs were mounted on a rack in the Victor's capacious bomb bay, by means of the notoriously unreliable electromechanical release units (EMRUs). At the operation of the bomb release switch in the crew cabin, an electrical signal was designed to open the large claws of the EMRU, allowing the weapon to drop. A lanyard, fixed to the aircraft and attached to the bomb, would arm the fuse as the weapon fell about nine inches off the EMRU. In this case, the EMRU did not open.

The captain said (expletive deleted – roughly translated as "Oh dear"), then selected bomb doors to 'close' before informing the range controller of the problem and turning the aircraft left to position for another attempt at dropping the bomb, but during the turn the crew heard a muffled thump from behind the cockpit, accompanied by a slight shudder of the aircraft. Someone asked "What (expletive deleted – roughly translated as 'on earth') was that?" It was agreed that the EMRU of the selected bomb had operated at last and allowed the bomb to drop on to the bomb doors. There followed a detailed discussion between the crew and with the range controller. It was agreed that we would fly over the range again, open the bomb doors and allow the bomb to drop safely into the sea. So, once again, the aircraft was lined up for this, now unconventional, bomb run, and when we were safely over the range, the captain selected bomb doors to 'open'. Immediately, the bomb doors emergency light illuminated.

The bomb doors on the Victor were operated by hydraulic power. Because the aircraft's raison d'etre in event of nuclear war, was to drop the atomic weapon on its target at any cost, a device was incorporated in the bomb-door operating system to allow opening of the doors, should the normal hydraulic system fail, to do so. This was indicated to the crew by the illumination of a red warning light on the instrument panel in front of the captain (and, if I recall correctly, replicated on the nav radar's panel at the rear of the cabin), and this was precisely what had now happened. I cannot remember (yes, yes, I know, but it was nearly fifty years ago!) what the further consequences were of using the emergency system to open the bomb doors, but I think it might have been that the whole hydraulic system would be switched to 'emergency', thereby limiting some hydraulic operations – undercarriage, flaps, airbrakes, brakes and nosewheel steering were all hydraulically operated. In any case, at this stage it was decided that the trial would be postponed and we would return to base.

At this time, I was still a young and very inexperienced co-pilot. It wasn't quite the situation where the lowly co-pilot was told to "sit there, say nothing and don't touch anything", but I was certainly in awe of these generally older and undoubtedly very experienced crew members. Nevertheless, on the way back to base, I was giving some thought to our situation. It struck me, inter alia, that if this bomb had been selected to be dropped, and fused to explode at 50 ft above ground by extending the lanyard when dropping off the bomb carrier, it could be 'live' to explode as we passed 50 ft on the approach to landing. I agonised over this for much of our flight south. Surely these experienced chaps would know all about these things and would dismiss my thoughts as being ridiculous. But maybe they had *not* thought about it. I really didn't want to die, however gallantly, at this time of life, but equally I didn't want to be made to look like a fool.

At about the time we arrived at the radar entry point to start our descent to base, I decided that the desire to stay alive, even if I was looked upon as a fool for the rest of my precious life, was the preferable outcome, so I hesitantly and very nervously broached the subject over the intercom. This prompted a short silence (while I cringed in fear of ridicule) followed by assorted expletives from some or all of the crew, and a discussion on the feasibility of my observations and the action to be taken. Much to my relief, the captain decided that, despite the fact that the possibility of the bomb exploding at 50 ft height was remote, the AEO was to contact base and get an expert opinion on the subject. While this was being progressed, a discussion was held on the subject of the rear crew baling out – they, of course, did not have the luxury of ejection seats. In the event and after some time, the message arrived from the armaments officer at base, who confirmed that the bomb was 'safe', and that we should continue to landing. I continued, and I suspect some of the other crew members did too, to feel rather nervous as we flew down the final approach.

The landing, in the expert hands of the captain, was smooth and uneventful. We taxied slowly round the taxiway until we had sight of the marshaller and turned into the parking bay. I noticed that our marshaller looked distinctly distracted as he waved us in for the final few feet, and his arm actions seemed to slow to an unusual pace. As we went through the closing-down drills, there seemed to be a dearth of ground crew in front of the aircraft, but the crew chief reported on the external intercom as usual. He did, however, report that "something appeared to be hanging down from the bomb doors". The crew disembarked rather more quickly than my limited experience would have considered normal – I think I was last out of the aircraft.

Once on the apron, we could see what had been causing the consternation. Our selected bomb had dropped on to the bomb doors as diagnosed earlier, but the bomb doors had failed to open because the nose of the bomb had penetrated one door (and was now hanging perilously close to the ground) while the tail of the bomb had penetrated the other door, thus locking the doors together.

I never did find out why the weapon was not primed to explode at 50 ft, but the event did nothing to endear me to the bombing role, and I was happy eventually, to continue to fly the Victor when it was converted to the air-to-air refuelling role.

Addendum

Recently, I was told by Dick Russell, probably the most informed man alive on the subject of the Victor, that the likely reason for the bomb's fuse to be 'safe' was that it had to be activated by the rotation of a small propeller on the nose of the bomb as the weapon fell earthwards. I assume this would build up a charge in a capacitor which, on the operation of, in this case, a radar-operated switch at 50 ft, would cause the fuse to do its work. Damage to the propeller when the nose of the bomb penetrated the bomb door would have prevented this happening.

Dick Russell at the beginning of this chapter referred to the Victor brake fires. **Peter Sharp** *tells us what it was like dealing with brake fires on the receiving end. He was ground crew at Marham in the early 1960s waiting for his aircraft to taxi in.*

Practical Fire Fighting, RAF-style

I was at Marham on 49 Squadron in the early 1960s awaiting my aircraft to taxi in. It was intended to be an early finish for the night shift that evening. The last kite was due down just before dark, on what could only be described as an end to a wonderful summer's day. ATC must have warned the dispersal of her imminent arrival, as we got the call for the 'seeing in crew' to man the dispersal. I cannot recall now what year it was, but the events as they unfolded will never be forgotten. As dusk approached, the eyes in the skies appeared as she approached slowly descending to join the approach. She majestically swept across the airfield boundary and touched down on the runway. About one third down the runway, the engines suddenly protested as they responded to the full throttle command and roared along the runway for her to execute a roller. A groan went up from a few of those on the reception party as we waited for her to complete the circuit. The question was how many rollers was she going to make before landing on and coming back to the dispersal. We waited as another aborted landing was carried out. The light was fading as she once again took to the skies and many eyes followed

The Valiant taxies in on a beautiful evening. An instant later peace and serenity was changed to chaos as a mass of flames suddenly erupted, from wing tip to undercarriage strut. *(Peter Sharp)*

her maliciously around the circuit as she made yet another approach. This time the subdued engines didn't suddenly erupt into a defiant roar. Instead the engine noise decreased and she slowly rolled along the runway to the hockey stick.

There were periodic changes to the engine noise as she turned along the lazy way towards the perimeter track, then with a sudden blind flashing of light her landing lights briefly flashed across the dispersal as she turned towards us. Slowly she inched her way towards the dispersal where we awaited her arrival. Up the slight incline she travelled as she trundled towards us, past the SSA and then on to the peri-track towards her parking place. One of the marshallers stepped out onto the peri-track to intercept her and guide her into the waiting arms of the servicing crews. She slowly made her way along the peri track, her engines howling as the pilot revved the engines against the gently rising slope of the track. The peri-track marshal's wands suddenly moved to the horizontal position fully pointing to his right and she swung towards us. The daylight was slowly fading as she turned and the dispersal marshaller started to wave his illuminated wands beckoning her to her designated parking area.

Suddenly the twilight sky was illuminated by a brilliant orange flame, which blossomed from the port undercarriage wheels and flared instantly up the tall oleo leg. It rapidly spread along the underside of the port wing and the engines faltered. I stood mesmerised to the spot at this sudden development. I decided there and then that I was the one who would summon the fire section and started to make tracks towards the dispersal telephone. I had travelled only a few yards when a stentorian voice thundered out, "get that fire extinguisher". I looked to see the crew chief a few yards behind me, running in the same direction. I passed the extinguisher on my way to the telephone to be abruptly guided by a vice-like grip on my shoulder. My headlong rush was suddenly arrested under the powerful influence that grabbed my shoulder. "Over there," came the command. I paused briefly, considered my options and went to continue my flight.

The hand tightened upon my shoulder and I was pulled forcibly across the dispersal towards the fire extinguishers. I turned and protested that I was going for the telephone to call the emergency services. It fell on deaf ears as I was guided towards the large red CO2 extinguishers nearby. I struggled weakly and then gave in to the superior authority commanding me to glory. Once again I shouted that I was going to call the fire section, to no avail. The grip on the shoulder strengthened and pulled me towards the huge red painted fire appliance. I hesitated and then finally succumbed to this authoritarian grip upon my shoulder.

Grabbing the extinguisher, which consisted of two small CO2 bottles attached to a two-wheeled trolley I turned to face the conflagration that was taking place a few yards from me. The aircrew were already out of the aircraft and running clear as the engines slowly clattered to in their dying throes. I really wanted to make that phone call or console the frightened aircrew who now cowered amongst the blades of grass besides the parking area. Why couldn't I join them? I had never before had occasion to call the fire section for help and really wished to now. The authoritarian bellow in my ears commanded that I approach the burning aircraft and operate the extinguisher as instructed. I protested, and then submitted to the crew chief's urging command. Pushing the trolley ahead of me, I approached the blazing aircraft. To get things into perspective, the Valiant undercarriage was some ten feet high and at half wing's span was all of fifty feet. The wing towered some ten feet above me and was alight from undercarriage to wing tip. Once again I faltered as the urgent pushing continued as the crew chief shoved me to my impending doom. Why was I here? Why couldn't I be the one phoning for help as the aircraft blazed away to its doom? The pushing and urging continued as I approached the inferno. I found myself in something of a daze as I automatically followed the incessant instructions still emanating from behind me.

I pulled the operating handle and there was a sharp crack as the CO2 bottles fired. Somewhat startled, I watched the 'steam' issuing from the end of the long nozzle, which further startled me as the boom suddenly shot out to double its length. It was on a telescopic pole and it was now all of ten feet in length. I was pushed once again towards the inferno and guided towards the enormous wheels and undercarriage legs that supported the aircraft. Safety guide lines suddenly entered my frightened brain. When fighting a tyre fire, stand to the side because when the tyre explodes, most of the debris is thrown directly forwards. Then, when fighting an aircraft brake fires stand to the front as the hot metal shards explode out of the wheel apertures and will kill anyone standing alongside of them! Where was I standing and what the f*** was I doing here? All I wanted to do was call the fire section. A quick frightened glance around me did nothing to instill courage. All five aircrew had abandoned the aircraft and were standing safely some distance away. Other members of the seeing in crew were frozen in various poses of action, some towards safety others towards their doom. The hand strengthened upon my shoulder and urged me to spray the emitting gasses onto the flames. My brain complied whilst trying to work out the best place to be, behind or alongside, or preferably on the phone in the crew room.

Meantime, the hell-bent hero behind me shouted to carry out his bidding. It was either unuttered or unheard and the urging to extinguish the flames became the objective. I was urged onwards walking into the flames of doom. The fire seemed to be everywhere. It was a beautiful orange reddish colour which lit up the suddenly darkened sky. Suddenly the flames that I had been spraying with the CO_2 gas started to subside. The hero in me urged me on to glory as I guided the extinguisher up the undercarriage leg towards the wing. I was winning ... the flames were actually less now in intensity that they had been a short while ago. I advanced towards the conflagration spraying CO_2 gas everywhere. My heart stopped its frantic activity as my courage returned with an almighty rush. We were winning. What a feeling of elation! The flames started to subside considerably and I thought that my troubles were over. Wrong. At this point the small two-bottled handcart of a fire extinguisher that I had been forced to push before me, rapidly diminished to a little fizzle as the gasses ran out. My fear and doubt returned. Here I was under a burning aircraft and all my means of fighting the conflagration had suddenly ceased. My courage faltered as the flames started once again to descend down the enormous undercarriage leg. It was time that Sharpy got out of here and called for the fire service.

Suddenly another white spray of CO_2 mist erupted from behind me, and I turned to see that two other courageous members of the seeing in crew had brought up one of the huge CO_2 extinguishers and that they were hosing down the area. My courage returned as I now surrendered my position to their superior firefighting power. I watched the flames diminish and then rapidly get snuffed out. The incident was over. My heart was still in overdrive forcing the blood through my body at a terrifying rate. It was extreme relief as I slowly realised that it was all over. I gathered up my expended fire appliance as the fire section rolled up spewing foam towards the aircraft. The crew chief leapt forwards in an effort to prevent the foam from contaminating the airframe. Slowly normality returned and the pace of life resumed its pre-emergency pace. I could hardly believe what had just occurred. It was too surreal to be true... was it a nightmare or was it a dream? Well it certainly happened and everyone who witnessed it and took active part in it agreed that it was mind blowing.

It turned out that the aircraft had developed a leak in the port outboard fuel tank and that fuel had run along the undersurface of the wing. All was well until the aircraft turned and the wind had blown the leaking fuel onto the undercarriage strut, and onto the hot brakes. Our prompt action saved the loss of the aircraft and a massive fire. As things returned to normality, the MT section arrived with an aircraft tug to tow the aircraft into the dispersal. The seeing in crew gradually returned to the crew room as they were replaced by fresh unruffled squadron members. There were drinks all round on the crew chief as he forked out for the coffees and teas for us. No alcohol or other stimulants, just a cup of hot tea or coffee!

CHAPTER 13

VICTOR TANKING

Stewart Waring, Adrian Richardson

This chapter has stories of the underpowered Victor K1 tanker by Stewart Waring and then the much improved Victor K2 tanker by Adrian Richardson.

__Stewart Waring__ spent a tour on the Victor K1 tanker with 214 Squadron. He was a co-pilot and gives a very good account of what it was like to be one for a whole tour. He started training on the Victor simulator which was a very early device with no visual or motion. When he finished his tour he had a period at HQ No. 1 (B) Group at RAF Bawtry. His high point there was when there was an exercise simulating the destruction of Strike Command and HQ required 1 Group to take over the control of the V Force. He was on duty when he had to broadcast to all the bomber stations: "Attention, Attention, This is the bomber controller for Strike List Alpha; Scramble Scramble". Four minutes later he could hear the QRA Vulcans from Finningley departing and very understandably he was especially proud at that moment.

Following completion of 26 Course on the Gnat at RAF Valley I was posted to Victor tankers at RAF Marham. First there was a comprehensive ground school course at RAF Finningley before starting the simulator and flying training with what was then the Tanker Training Flight. Before starting this course I flew several trips in the back of the Victor, which gave me a lasting appreciation of the airborne world inhabited by the two navigators, radar and plotter, and the air electronics officer.

Around thirty hours were spent in the simulator, a very basic device by today's standard with no motion or visual. Today it would probably be classified as a cockpit procedures trainer. However, it gave the opportunity to see and deal with the many possible malfunctions of the complicated fuel system, which was the responsibility of the co-pilot.

One of the co-pilot's duties was to calculate the performance and speeds for each flight. This involved entering a series of graphs in the operating data manual with the required information, and extracting the stop, go, unstick and emergency maximum braking speeds. Another speed required was the emergency maximum brake parachute stream speeds which varied not only with the aircraft's weight but also the number of times the chute had been streamed. At 180,000 lb a chute with less than five streams was 143 kt, but one with over six streams, max 24, was 136 kt. As related later take-offs could be critical. There was a good two hours work required by the crew before a quick snack in the 'aircrew feeder' and out to the aircraft.

On 26 April 1967 I did my first instructional flight with Flt Lt Les Ketcher in XH615 and although the Victor had not been my first choice of posting it was impossible not to be impressed with the aircraft. My third flight, on 2 May was as co-pilot to the station commander designate, Gp Capt David Roberts on his 'first solo'. At the time I was unaware of the fact that he had dropped the second British hydrogen bomb on Operation Orange Herald but was immediately aware that he was an excellent pilot.

The course ended in June and I was posted to 214 Squadron. Straightaway I found myself dispensing fuel to Lightnings and other Victors. Sorties two and three on the squadron were 'max weight transfers', where fuel was passed to the receiving aircraft up to maximum weight, I recall this as 186,000 lb. Then roles would reverse and the fuel passed back.

As experience was gained the job became really interesting as the calculations required to ensure giving maximum fuel for the receivers and leaving us enough fuel to get home with adequate reserves could be complex. 214 Squadron had three-point tankers (except for one two-pointer) and several of the procedures and techniques were still being perfected. Other calculations were required to uplift fuel on the ground. On the ground, and away from base the co-pilot was often responsible for ensuring the right fuel amount was loaded, not too much, not too little. A mistake or delay in closing a valve could result in too much being taken on and thus, in the worst case, making the take-off impossible. De-fuelling was most unpopular and, in this event, so was the co-pilot.

A good proportion of the flying was helping the Lightnings get around, involving multiple tankers refuelling each other and then proceeding onwards with the Lightnings in loose formation. Some of the sorties were Marham-Marham, but soon I found myself in Akrotiri for the first of many enjoyable visits. Then, as now, the French air traffic system presented interesting challenges as they demanded that re-fuelling only took place in certain areas. If all the fuel required had not been passed it was important to keep the fighters in contact, even outside the area, and the French would ask if we were complete etc. Sometimes they sent Mirages up to check if we were telling the truth.

To fulfil the basic training requirements every month, there was a requirement to carry out a minimum number of landings, emergency drills, navexes and so on. The navexes included celestial navigation legs and the co-pilot would work with the nav plotter with the timing. Long trips right around the UK, mostly at night ensured a high standard of this now dead art. However, there was not a lot of flying, forty hours being a good month's total.

On 2 April 1968 the crew flew non-stop from Marham to Offutt AFB, Nebraska for a flight time of 9 hours and 35 minutes, re-fuelling from another tanker over Goose Bay. This trip was memorable in that I met a pretty girl who lent me a car, a Ford

Mustang. When I arrived with this machine to meet the rest of the crew they thought I must have stolen it as it was felt that no sane person would lend a car to a co-pilot. We returned to Goose and the following day tanked another Victor who was flying direct Offutt-Marham.

On 10 April I was on an air test of XH667, following a tailplane change. This aircraft, a B1A, was the least popular one on the squadron, being plagued with problems, a lot of them associated with the flight controls. There was an intermittent restriction in the elevator control which defied diagnosis or remedy.

Flight line at Marham, dawn sometime in 1969. Note the C-130s and Argosy in the background so it must have been taken on the first day of a deployment. Note the vital metal ration box. (Stewart Waring)

On 5 July, returning from Akrotiri we failed to get 'three greens' on selecting undercarriage down. The weather at Marham was just on or slightly below limits so we diverted to Manston to make a landing on the foam strip. With great good sense the captain, Flt Lt Adrian Farlam did not re-cycle the gear as had he done so the right main would have stuck up. The night landing on the strip went well and denied the waiting fire crew the pleasure of chopping their way into the cockpit as they dearly wanted to do. Just before touchdown I looked back to see the three rear crew, plus the crew chief on the sixth seat cradling bottles and demijohns of duty-free against any possible shocks.

At that wonderful time the RAF had commitments right round-the-world and it was possible to experience the pleasures of Malta, Cyprus, Bahrain, Masirah, Gan in the Maldives, Singapore and Darwin. The tanker force had gained a well-earned reputation for playing hard and all in all it was a very satisfactory lifestyle.

However, as an aircraft the Victor 1 was underpowered and at some overseas bases it was not possible to get airborne with a full fuel load. At heavy weights the 'go' and 'stop' speeds could come up in the wrong order. This meant that having passed stop speed it was no longer possible to stop in the remaining runway available, but not yet able to go in the event of an engine failure.

At Akrotiri early one afternoon following a delay from our original take-off time, the ground roll was calculated at 8,900 ft on a 9,000 ft runway with the stop and go speeds the 'wrong' way by 15 kt. Our captain, the squadron commander Wg Cdr Colin Preece, to my amazement (and the crew's) gave me the take-off which was really critical.

Fifty-nine seconds after brakes off we staggered off the end of Akrotiri's runway, the Armstrong Siddleley Sapphire engines giving their all at their limit of 101.5 per cent.

In January 1969 I completed an intermediate co-pilots course which enabled me to fly in the left-hand seat. During April 1969 the bulk of the tanker force deployed to Goose Bay and Loring AFB for the transatlantic air race, Operation Blue Nylon. Each day at noon a decision was made regarding whether the crossing would be made the following day. If the answer was no, then there was at least thirty-six hours before a flight was possible. With at least ten tankers at Goose Bay, and nothing domestic to distract the crews it was a lot of fun.

Eventually we got airborne, filled up to the brim from another Victor and set off across the Atlantic with Sqn Ldr Graham Williams joining us in the Harrier. There were many re-fuelling brackets and everything performed as planned. Our Victor had the wing re-fuelling pods removed enabling us to cruise at Mach.88. Near Dublin the Harrier left us for the final high speed dash for London. The Victor/Harrier combination won the prize from London to New York, 'our' Harrier was narrowly beaten by a Royal Navy Phantom, also Victor tanker supported.

In March 1970 our crew was awarded command classification, the highest possible.

GOOSE BAY. TRANS ATLANTIC AIR RACE, MAY 1969.

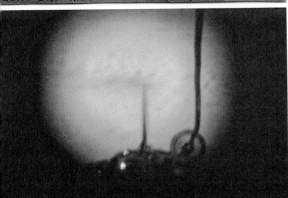

I'm sure that this was mostly due to the rest of the crew led by Wing Commander Preece.

On the flying side it was extremely professional. The V Force was, and was seen to be, an elite and the tanker force, although not always popular with the snooty Transport Command VC10 crews who were forced to share facilities etc. down the route, prided itself in getting the job done.

On the serviceability/flying side we had the usual things happen. The most dramatic was a really really close air

Top: Victors at Goose Bay for the transatlantic air race 1969. Note no underwing tanks. *(Stewart Waring)*
Bottom: Harrier XV744, Sqn Ldr Graham Williams, through the periscope somewhere over the Atlantic 9 May 1969. *(Stewart Waring)*

XH670. Victor B2 stored at Radlett, photographed on 11 February 1970, a few days before Handley Page folded. Ferried up to Woodford and converted to a K2. *(Stewart Waring)*

miss with a F-100 at night, which went over the cockpit and I don't know how it missed hitting the tail. We also had a moment during night re-fuelling trials assessing various combinations of lights on the tanker, and in contact with the hose. Suddenly the brightly lit, stark white planform of the tanker disappeared into total darkness as a switching 'problem' occurred.

On one trip we required an engine change at Akrotiri; the new engine arrived and was dropped, damaging it. A few days later another arrived with a notice 'This is the last serviceable Sapphire, do not drop'.

There were some wild times in the RAF during the sixties; it was not at all up-tight about people enjoying themselves. On the last night of a detachment to Darwin at a farewell party I exchanged most of my uniform with that of a Northern Territory police officer. This proved a big mistake as we had then to stage back to the UK through Singapore (Tengah) Gan, Bahrain, and Akrotiri and I had no uniform worth the name. My captain, Wg Cdr Preece was understandably unimpressed.

Stewart went on to fly all sorts of different aircraft commercially and finished up flying for eleven years with the Shuttleworth Collection and amazingly managing to fly twenty-seven of the types there. We can't resist listing them:

Bristol Boxkite	*Tutor*
Avro Triplane	*Paxmere Elf*
SE5A	*Spitfire GC*
Bristol fighter	*Vega Gull*
Sopwith Dove	*PA Swallow*
DH51	*Hawker Hind*
DH53 Humming Bird	*Gloster Gladiator*

DH60 Moth	Hawk Speed Six
DH86 Rapide	Cierva Autogiro (taxi)
DH87 Hornet Moth	NA Harvard
DH88 Comet Racer	Hawker Cygnet
DHC1 Chipmunk	Hawker Tomtit
DHC60X Hermes Moth	Puss Moth
Magister	

Adrian Richardson joined the RAF in 1965 and flew the Argosy C1 and the Dominie T1 before joining the Victor K2 tanker fleet between 1976 and 1991 taking part in the Falklands Campaign described in a later chapter. From 1993 to 1995 he flew coun-ter-narcotics operations in the British Virgin Islands on loan to the FCO, then a variety of parachute-dropping aircraft at Weston on the Green and Netheravon before flying the BN2T from Northolt. He retired from regular service in 2002 at 55 and then flew for three further years as a reservist in the Royal Auxiliary Air Force. He now lives in East Anglia.

Bubiyan and Failaka

A detachment of RAF Victor Mk 2 tanker aircraft had been operating from Muharraq in Bahrain since the autumn of 1990 following the invasion of Kuwait by Iraq on 2 August. The purpose of this was to 'work up' with the various receiver aircraft already in theatre as part of the defence of Saudi Arabia and to establish base operating and engineering facilities together with administrative accommodation which may have become necessary in any possible future conflict. The US designation for this phase was Operation Desert Shield. The aircrew and ground crews had been rotating into theatre with their counterparts from RAF Marham in Norfolk which was the long-established home-operating base for the Victor. I had not been involved in these preparations as I was occupied at the time with other activities back at Marham.

Around Christmas 1990, I was notified that I would be taking a crew out to Muharraq shortly before New Year, since it was becoming less likely that Saddam Hussein was going to comply with the United Nations resolution which demanded that he withdraw his occupying forces from Kuwait. This necessitated bringing our elderly Victor fleet up to full strength. The deadline for this withdrawal was initially supposed to be 15 January 1991, although Operation Desert Storm did not commence officially until two days later.

My crew was allocated to me as follows: co-pilot – Flt Lt Dave Attwood, a recently qualified captain in his own right. He was a man of outwardly serious disposition and a dry wit, whom I had first met many years previously. It was not long before he picked up the nickname of Captain Mainwaring within our crew. Navigator – Fg Off Rich Cooke, a young first-tour navigator, not long out of the OCU and recently married, who proved

Adrian Richardson at work. *(Adrian Richardson)*

himself to be a very capable operator indeed. Apart from being the youngest member by some way, he was also the best squash player on the crew. Finally, and to my great delight, my AEO was to be Flt Lt Tony Angell, a delightful, even-ly-balanced man with a wicked sense of humour who was highly experienced in his role. We were impertinent enough to give him the nickname 'Dad', although in reality, he was only a little older than me. By this time, I had been flying the Victor tanker on and off since the beginning of 1977, including the Falklands War, and I was now the pilot leader on 55 Squadron and an aircrew checking officer (ACO), which allowed me to fly as captain in either the left or right-hand pilot seat. My agreement with Dave was that we would alternate seats for each sortie, until, if ever, the fighting started, in which circumstance I would move permanently into the left seat. We travelled to the Middle East by VC10 transport, with stops at an unknown airfield which was packed with USAF F-16s, possibly Abu Dhabi, and another at Al Jubail in Saudi Arabia, before eventually arriving, rather tired, at Bahrain.

According to my flying logbook, we flew our first training sortie on 1 January, refuelling F3 Tornado fighters on a 'towline' (refuelling area) designated as Mango Low. The American term for our refuelling areas was 'anchors'. By the 15th we had completed nine training trips, refuelling mainly Tornado GR1s, although there was one sortie refuelling Jaguars. Our initiation into the conflict was on 17 January, (Day 1), when we carried out an 'olive trail', which was to accompany Tornado GR1s, armed with JP233 area denial weapons, to their 'cast-off point' on the Iraq border en route to delivering their munitions to one of Saddam's airfields. We flew several more missions of this nature during the next couple of weeks.

This story, however, deals with a specific sortie flown much later in the conflict on the night of 16 February. We had been tasked to provide AAR support for Canadian F-18s on a towline designated as 'puller'. As the name implies, it was designed to cater for aircraft which were returning from their missions over Kuwait and Iraq and which were either short of fuel due to excessive combat requirements or as a result of battle damage. Due to this requirement, it was located reasonably close to the Kuwaiti coast and inside its associated towline, 'pusher', whose name should make its function self-explanatory. Since the coalition forces had by this time successfully suppressed the Iraqi air force and the vast bulk of its air defences, any residual threat to us in this position was absolutely minimal. Initially, we shared the towline with a USAF KC-135 tanker which was above us with 2,000 ft height separation. Presumably, he was there to cater for US aircraft which required to use the boom and receptacle system of in-flight refuelling, (F-15s and F-16s), although we could also cater for the US Navy receivers such as the F-18, which used a compatible system to our own. After a while, he either ran out of transferable fuel or was advised that his presence was no longer required and departed to the east, leaving us quite alone in the dark. The weather that evening was clear at and above our altitude of around 7,000 feet, although the surface was not visible since there was an unbroken layer of cloud between us and the sea, which I would estimate as having been between around 1,000 ft thick with the tops being about 4,000 ft. This was a nuisance as we had become used to watching the various entertaining blue and orange flashes from the areas of combat which could often be seen from quite long distances. Possibly the most expensive fireworks display ever witnessed. Apparently things had gone well for the Canadian aircraft, since we followed our racetrack pattern in total isolation, quite bored, with absolutely nothing happening.

Suddenly, the whole sky below us lit up from horizon to horizon with a very bright orange glare refracting through the cloud. Night literally became day and to my ever-lasting shame, my first reaction was that someone had let off a nuke. Accompanied by the usual aircrew expletives, within a second or two, logic took over as I knew that in those circumstances I would have been blinded. The luminescence began to die away after several seconds. It must have been even more exciting for the boys in the back of the cockpit who only had a couple of small portholes and whose world had just changed from very dark to bright orange without any warning. I began a turn back to the north of the towline. Halfway around, I could see that a huge fireball had appeared through the cloud tops some distance to our north-west and was continuing to rise. Eventually it dulled and then disappeared. A short while later as we were discussing on the intercom the possibilities of what had just occurred, it happened once more. This time it was not quite so bright, perhaps because our night vision had already been affected and if anything, it appeared to have originated further away than the first. Nevertheless, it still lit up the whole sky. We remained on task until our allotted time without having received any trade at all and then high-tailed it back to Bahrain.

On landing at Muharraq, it was the standard practice to attend a debriefing by the intelligence staff. We could not wait. Squadron Leader Ted Gregory, himself a former Victor AEO, met us and we enthusiastically passed on details of the evening's events. He disappeared into the inner sanctum of the intelligence office for a few minutes and then returned beaming. It seems that notification had been received, probably after our departure, that the 'Blues Brothers' were about to clear the Kuwaiti islands of Bubiyan and Failaka of Iraqi troops. This information in isolation would probably have had little meaning for the intelligence staff in any case and would certainly have held no tactical value for us. Presumably these enemy forces were a threat to any likely attempt by the Allies to recover the islands to Kuwaiti control, however, I seemed to recall from previous

Adrian Richardson's crew complete thirty missions.

(Adrian Richardson)

briefings that these islands had also been associated with Silkworm anti-shipping missile launch sites and could therefore be considered a threat to any coalition vessel which would come within range without possessing suitable defences. They would also therefore pose a significant obstacle to any proposed landings on the islands by the US Marines Corps. The 'Blues Brothers' was a coded nickname for a US special forces group who specialised in the use of a fearsome new weapon called the fuel/air bomb. This anti-personnel munition, about which I knew nothing in those days, is apparently dropped from one or more C-130 transport aircraft, and detonates above the surface, killing every form of life within a wide area beneath it. We had seemingly witnessed the initial use of these devices from a grandstand platform. I believe that this weapon, or an advanced development of it, was later used to considerable effect in the initial stages of the fighting against the Taliban in Afghanistan a few years later.

By 28 February, the 'Cessation of Offensive Hostilities' took place, despite widespread scepticism in the ranks. It had been a privilege to fly with my crew and together we had completed thirty-four operational sorties as part of Desert Storm with a further nine having been flown in Desert Shield. That represented nineteen hours of training and ninety-nine hours of operations. The role of 55 Squadron in that conflict is adequately summed up by the words of Group Captain Andrew Vallance, a director of Defence Studies RAF:

> "The Victor detachment for example – despite having ancient aircraft – completed every one of the 299 tasks that it was allocated. Indeed it was not unusual for our tankers to fly across the border to ensure their receivers had all the fuel they needed to reach their targets and return safely. And they did this in spite of the considerable potential threat posed by Iraqi SAMs and fighters against which they had virtually no defence."

CHAPTER 14

FALKLANDS FRIENDLY FIRE

Adrian Richardson, Steve Biglands and Crew

This is a story of a friendly fire occurrence during the Falklands Campaign in May 1982 which fortunately didn't cause any damage. There is no intention in the chapter to attribute blame because in wartime friendly fire is always likely to occur. However, it is considered important to record the facts so that lessons can be learnt rather than hide any undesirable events.

The incident we are describing has for some unaccountable reason not been reported in any books recounting the annals of the Falklands Campaign though there is a very brief mention in Rowland White's Vulcan 607. *The facts are that two Victor tankers returning to Ascension Island were the targets of two launched live Sea Dart missiles when close to part of the Bristol naval group south of Ascension when the group was on the way south to the Falklands.*

*We have accounts from the captains of both Victors, starting with **Adrian Richardson.** He tells a fascinating story of his Victor being tracked by naval radar and then being illuminated by fire-control radar after missiles having been fired. Understandably, he is very concerned about the detailed accuracy of the story and the exact date due to the difficulty of keeping accurate records during the campaign and would welcome any more details if they become available.*

I intend to recount this tale to the best of my ability and with as much accuracy as I am able to apply to it considering the intervening passage of time and taking into account that one individual's perspective often varies from that of another. I will therefore be more than happy should anyone reading this article be in a position to correct or adjust any of the details. It has remained, for a long time, an itch which I have wanted to scratch and now seems to be a good opportunity. From my own recollections and from the information which is still available to me, I believe that the essence of the story is correct, but some of the conclusions are based on hearsay and circumstantial information, therefore it may be unwise of me to state categorically that the following events occurred exactly as recounted.

Unfortunately, I cannot be certain of the precise date on which this event occurred as our flying logbooks were by necessity completed on our eventual return to the UK.

The authorisation sheets, from which all flight details are derived, were in heavy demand by all aircrew hoping to get home for a break, therefore an element of haste may have contributed to inaccuracies. Some irregularities will have inevitably crept into the records of even the most fastidious of documenters. However, I am sure that the date will eventually be corroborated by one or more of the many parties involved who will no doubt also correct any false observations and assumptions which I may have made. I have cross-referred some details which are outside my range of expertise against the information contained in the excellent reference book *Falklands, The Air War*, compiled by a collaborating group of five authors who must have spent many difficult hours searching through official combat reports, etc. Not all of these appear to match up with my information, however, which gives me some cause for concern. The authors would, of course, have had no access to the kind of information contained below.

Around the middle of May 1982, a Victor tanker operation was launched from Wideawake air base on Ascension Island to support a Nimrod reconnaissance sortie in the South Atlantic. This was one of several which took place around that time and although the tanker crews were not included in the briefings as to what the Nimrod task specifically was, most of us could hazard an educated guess and consequently had a pretty good idea that they were operating much closer to the Argentinian coast than could generally be considered safe. Brave chaps, all of them, but sufficient fuel to conduct their operations was critical and even the Nimrod required much more than it could possibly lift on take-off in order to transit the vast distances each way and still be able to loiter on task. Therefore, staggered formations of two or three Victor K2s from either 55 or 57 Squadrons were flown along the same route, transferring fuel between themselves so that finally the remaining tanker could rendezvous with the Nimrod at a specified time and position and then transfer the maximum possible fuel load to it, only retaining enough to return to Ascension with a minimum of reserves.

The sortie in question was flown mainly in daylight, a reasonably rare and welcome event, which, if my logbook is accurate, makes one of the more likely dates to be 22 May. The five other sorties of a similar nature in which my crew took part and which I have

Victor K2s lined up on the ramp. *(Adrian Richardson)*

entered into my logbook during that period, were recorded as predominantly night flying, although an error on my part is perfectly possible. I have zero recollection of the initial part of the trip, partly due to the almost thirty-five years since it happened and probably because it was routine and unremarkable. I was the pilot of the number two aircraft to a Victor flown by Flight Lieutenant Steve Biglands (Biggles), a lovely man and a respected and experienced Victor tanker captain. I met him in passing a couple of decades later at RAF Leeming where he was flying as a civilian instructor on the University Air Squadron.

My own crew consisted of Ron Miller, my constituted co-pilot, whose additional function other than to fly was to manage the complex fuel systems. I remember him as a pleasant, quiet and studious young man of considerable intelligence with whom I unfortunately lost contact when he left the tanker force a year or so after the Falklands. My 'rear crew', also known as the society of directional consultants and allied trades (SODCAT) were in the order of nav plotter, nav radar and air electronics officer, Tim Timbers, a particularly competent and skilled operator, who I understand achieved great things professionally when the tanker force evolved beyond the Victor; Dave Taylor, who controlled the refuelling of receiver aircraft and who was also responsible for many of the aerial photographs which appeared in subsequent press articles covering the conflict; and finally Tom James, a sturdy and reliable Welshman who was the mastermind of the tanking operation, since apart from operating the communications equipment and keeping the elderly aircraft systems working correctly, he was the one who interpreted the very complex formation plan and kept me in the right place at the right time. Tom and I also shared accommodation, as at the time we were both 'billeted' in a salubrious car port in one of the bungalows in Georgetown, the 'capital' of Ascension.

It is likely that we would have transited southbound in formation as a pair at about flight level 330, which would have been the norm. We were also aware from the outbound intelligence briefing that significant elements of the naval task force were also steaming south as part of the Bristol group. This was of considerable importance to us, as should something have gone badly wrong and we had been forced to abandon our aircraft, a vessel of the Royal Navy or Fleet Auxiliary would have been our only hope of salvation, although we were all very aware that even this was a pretty long shot in the South Atlantic during their winter. Unfortunately, mainly due to the justified security philosophy of the RN, which occasionally appeared to us to be paranoid but which was actually essential for their own protection, we never really knew where the ships were, and probably would not have believed them if they had told us. In the early stages of the conflict, we all operated under radio and radar silence anyhow, with any electronic emissions being minimised to those which were essential for operational reasons or for safety.

Some way into the sortie, at which I now estimate to have been a very approximate position of 26°S and 33°W, roughly 1,650 nautical miles south-west of Ascension and shortly before I was due to receive an uplift of approximately 25,000 lb of fuel from

Victor about to be refuelled from another Victor.

(Adrian Richardson)

Biggles, Tom advised me that he had just received a recall message on our long-range HF radio, caused by the fact that the Nimrod had broken its refuelling probe during an attempted refuelling contact on the previous tanker rendezvous and was now in the process of returning to base. At the same time, Terry Anning, the AEO in the lead Victor, having received the same broadcast, had passed the information to Biggles and I followed in loose formation as he turned gently to the right through 180° returning towards Ascension Island. I expected the Nimrod to be behind us somewhere in our proximity and following a similar track but probably at a lower altitude. I let Biggles get ahead of me by a couple of miles and followed him home in a comfortable astern position so that the return journey would be less tiring. Although close formation in the Victor was in essence the bread and butter of the pilots, due to the appallingly restricted visibility from the cockpit, loose echelon formation was even more difficult and certainly more arduous for the pilot. We only discovered after the Falklands War that the Victor was the most difficult large aircraft to fly into contact with a refuelling basket due to the unconventional flight control system and its high tailplane which was normally affected by the turbulent wake of the tanker in front.

In particular, the 'feel' bellows, which synthesised the feedback from the effects of control column movements (sometimes very poorly as in the case of XL191, an aircraft which I used to dread being allocated), could develop flat spots on the many rollers and bearings which comprised this elderly, although innovative, mechanical system. This, together with worn and slightly loosened connecting levers through wear, had the effect of developing 'dead spots' in the reaction of the flight controls. In routine flight this was only a minor concern and was generally barely noticeable, although a clue to its presence was that when the autopilot was in use it tended to 'hunt' around the lateral axis. However, in the instances when this problem did exist and the aircraft was being flown manually and in close proximity to another aircraft while the pilot was attempting to hold a precisely steady position, it added an additional and unwelcome degree of difficulty to what was otherwise a physically testing and mentally challenging task.

Something like half to three quarters of an hour had passed since turning back when Tom said on the intercom that he was picking up a search-type radar from the front right quadrant. At this point I should explain that the Victor was fitted with, as standard, a passive radar warning receiver (RWR). This equipment was known as ARI 18228, which was rather old and somewhat limited in the range of signals it could detect. However, by chance, as I later discovered, my aircraft, possibly XL163 although it could have been any of them, was fitted with an uprated piece of equipment known as ARI 18235, as by good fortune was Biggles' jet. I think in those days there were only a few aircraft in the Victor fleet which had been fitted with this upgraded kit and luckily we both had one. After a short discussion, Tom was fairly sure that the radar he had detected and was continuing to monitor belonged to the Royal Navy and probably emanated from one of the Bristol group heading south. Since this was a quite routine occurrence and there was no apparent threat to us, no action was called for.

However, a short while later and in a much more animated voice, Tom said that we were now locked up by a fire-control radar in our forward right position and an immediate 90° turn to the left was highly advisable. Since this is not the time to argue with your AEO, I complied immediately and with considerable enthusiasm. As I rolled left onto a north-westerly heading towards Brazil, I could see Biggles carrying out the same manoeuvre two miles to the north-east of me. An alarmed and expectant silence followed as we waited to see what might happen. We had no defences, jamming or otherwise which may have been effective against a situation of this nature. After what seemed to be a rather long intermission, when we again spoke, it was clear to me that the westerly track had avoided the threat, but somehow we had clearly managed to ruffle a few feathers. The modes one and two of our IFF were transponding the correct wartime codes which had been passed to the navy and should therefore have identified us to them on their search radar as friendly forces and more specifically as two RAF tanker aircraft. Admittedly we were out of our expected timescales due to the recall, but it seemed unlikely that this alone could trigger that kind of reaction. Both Tom James and Terry Anning in the lead aircraft had been AEOps on Nimrods in a previous existence and the one thing that they were both exceedingly good at was ship radar recognition. Therefore, the use of a fire-control radar against us was a fairly ominous phenomenon.

Our track continued westwards for what was probably only a number of minutes in order to allow us to avoid whoever's missile engagement zone (MEZ) we had been about to infringe, albeit in total ignorance of its position. I saw that Biggles, now in my three o'clock position, was in a starboard turn back onto a heading for our base and the fuss appeared to have died down. Generally, in all the Falklands air operations, due to the endemic shortage of fuel, which was husbanded to the utmost degree in order to pass the maximum available to our customers, deviation from the direct track between points was avoided at all costs. This was fortunately not a consideration for us since we had not transferred any of our precious cargo to a more deserving cause.

We had rolled out onto a north-easterly track for barely a minute or so before the fire-control radar again illuminated us. This time, there was no consultation necessary. I went as hard left as the Victor would allow and applied full power to accelerate away from the threat direction, in the process of which I lost sight of Biggles' aircraft. Once again the only sound on the intercom was that of laboured breathing as we waited in anticipation for something to happen. Fortunately, nothing did. However, this time there was no hurry to return to the north-easterly heading, since to provoke further unfriendly activity was highly inadvisable and after all, apart from the direction of one unknown vessel, we had been briefed that there were others in the vicinity, who to the best of our knowledge by now may have had equally aggressive intentions. Following a considerable detour to the west, I can recall seeing some islands ahead, which I think Tim identified as belonging to Brazil and which may well have been the Trindade and Martim Vaz Archipelago. We turned north-eastwards well before reaching them and then reverted to the original plan of returning to base. Nothing further was seen or heard by us from Steve Biglands' aircraft, but they landed safely back at Wideawake not long before we did.

In essence, that is the end of the tale as I can recall it from my own experience, and I would be most interested to see how it compares to the memories of the others who were directly involved. However, the story does not stop here. While RAF aircrew in this kind of situation are notorious for 'letting it go' and a preparedness to 'put it down to experience', despite the temptation to mentally file it away for future use as good crew room war story or even for after a few beers in the mess bar, more information began to filter back to us. That evening, while I was enjoying a relaxing bevy or two in the Exiles Club on the island, which had reluctantly welcomed this massive influx of strangers into their otherwise cloistered existence, Tim arrived to join us and he was in what I would describe as an unusually sombre mood.

It transpired that he had just met up with one of the Nimrod crew, an old mate of his, who had asked him if we realised that the ship in question had fired two Sea Dart Mk 1 missiles at us. Seemingly, the Nimrod had, as expected, been following behind us at an unknown range, but probably between thirty and sixty nautical miles. I suspect that with their sophisticated equipment, they were well aware of the various radar emissions which were in progress. However, the Nimrod, or certainly this particular one, would have had the highest specification of kit on board for war operations and it was also fitted with the relatively new 'Searchwater' radar, which was renowned to be extremely capable, although details of its performance were highly classified. According to Tim's mate, the Nimrod crew had actually tracked missiles on their radar from the unidentified ship towards our vicinity on two occasions. Subsequently, this vessel was informally identified to us, I hope correctly, as HMS *Cardiff*. Despite a natural tendency to take everything with a pinch of salt, (no pun intended), we mentioned the events in passing to our superiors and to the resident intelligence officer. Assuming that things had occurred as described, a repeat of the performance could have represented an additional and quite unacceptable threat to our air-to-air refuelling operations.

Evidently something did perhaps get through to the upper echelons of command, since a day or two later, a signal was reputedly received on Ascension from the commodore of the Bristol group, of which HMS *Cardiff* was a component, apologising for one of his ships ranging its radars on us. Presumably, the same signal would have been copied to Maritime Headquarters at Northwood in London and perhaps to even higher authorities. This was a gallant and open act by this senior officer, which of course, could also be interpreted as conveniently helping to smooth over any indignation being subsequently expressed by the boys in blue. Since none of our aircraft had been reported as missing by that time, it was a reasonably safe thing to do, but therein lies a further problem. The Sea Dart Mk 1 was a beam-riding missile which tracked on its intended course under a directed beamed signal and then used infrared detection for its final homing and detonation. For those who may not be familiar with the implications of this, the 'lock-on beam' is not activated until the missile has left the rails and it then 'tracks' under radar guidance towards the position and altitude of the target in order to achieve a precision 'kill' by using a final IR homing with proximity fusing on a big warhead. What we had received was the tracking signal, which in simple terms means that the missiles had already been fired.

I have had to rely for this information on the advice of many former colleagues who are much better versed in these affairs than I am, since my function was simply to point my aircraft in the desired direction. Therefore, in order to have received the signals, which both aircraft did, it is virtually impossible to avoid the conclusion that HMS *Cardiff* had fired two Sea Darts at us. However, the fact that *Cardiff* had missed two Victor tankers, possibly the biggest and easiest flying targets around, initially in my own mind, appeared to make the whole series of events and certainly my initial conclusion, just a little bit unlikely. Why they should have fired on their friendly air force comrades was not only a mystery, it defied any logical explanation. This conundrum was only resolved at a much later date and then only with the advantage of a finer understanding of the surrounding events. A subsequent discussion with Biggles' crew revealed a parallel experience to our own, with the only difference reportedly being that they had continued with a spiral descent to much lower levels following the second lock-up while jettisoning a small quantity of 'window'. This had been fitted to their wing refuelling baskets as an experiment to cater for the possible occurrence of a similar event, although, when originally conceived it had been anticipated that Argentinian fighters would have been the perpetrators.

Some weeks later, I was tasked with recovering one of our 'sick' aeroplanes to the UK. The serviceability rates which our engineers achieved from these elderly airframes was little short of miraculous, particularly since they were, in aircrew terms, 'being hammered'. For the purposes of 'spares in theatre', this beast, although airworthy for transit purposes, had nearly all of its navigational equipment removed along with anything which we could 'live without'. This trip may well become the subject of a separate story in the future, but it did give me the welcome opportunity, at very short notice, of taking part in the No. 1 Group RAF Golf Championship at Stoke Rochford Golf Club near Grantham. One of the participants was an officer with whom I had played previously and during the course of a conversation about what was going on on Ascension, I mentioned the

Post-conflict; my crew from 57 Squadron discussing our wartime AAR activities with an officially sanctioned journalist outside the medical tent on 17 August. Shortly afterwards it was renamed to 112 MASH (55+57). From left to right: *Lynn News and Advertiser* journalist, **Tim Timbers (nav plotter), Dick Smith (AEO, who had replaced Taylor (nav radar)), Ron Miller (co-pilot), Adrian Richardson (captain), unknown newspaper man.** *(Adrian Richardson)*

events which I have detailed above. To my surprise, he admitted that he was aware of them. I believe that one salient piece of information I received from him was that the IFF on the radar of HMS *Cardiff* may have been unserviceable at the time.

I am therefore led to believe that what had occurred was as follows: On the day in question, HMS *Cardiff* was sailing south towards the Falkland Islands as part of the Bristol group, named after the capital ship, HMS *Bristol,* which was the flagship. The role of HMS *Cardiff* was to provide picket defence, which in layman's terms is that the ship was riding shotgun for the formation, since it was a dedicated missile destroyer. Apologies to my nautical cousins as my terminology and classification in these matters may leave something to be desired. At some stage, the ship's search radar detected two high level contacts heading directly towards them and in accordance with their rules of engagement they prepared their armaments, which primarily included getting a Sea Dart Mk 1 anti-aircraft missile onto the rails ready for firing. They were able to distinguish on their search radar that both possible targets were about FL 330 and the lead aircraft was being followed by another with about a couple of miles separation. Since these radar contacts did not correspond with the intelligence that they had been given with respect to the Nimrod refuelling operation which was in progress, they were clearly suspicious right from the start. However, it appears they had no way of conclusively identifying these contacts as friendly. It was certainly too far from Argentinian territory for any realistic prospect of enemy combat aircraft to be a threat and courtesy of the work of our Nimrod friends they could also be sure that these were not carrier-borne aircraft since the *Veinticinco de Mayo* was known to have remained in shallow local waters for fear of attention from Her Majesty's submarine service.

In view of the demise of the cruiser *General Belgrano* at the hands of HMS *Conqueror*, this was probably one of General Galtieri's better decisions. Unfortunately, intelligence had recently been passed to the fleet that the Argentine air force was known to operate at least one modified Boeing 707 in the maritime reconnaissance role. This was a confirmed fact and these particular aircraft could have posed a severe threat, not only to the whole of the Bristol group but possibly to the ultimate success of the British Forces' efforts to relieve the Falkland Islands should early detection have been achieved by the enemy naval and air forces. *Cardiff's* tacticians eventually deduced that since there were two contacts, the lead aircraft was likely to be a returning lone and empty Victor tanker, which would under normal circumstances have been the case, but they then assumed that it was unwittingly being stalked by one of the aforementioned 707s. Thus the scenario was set.

Around the time that the lead Victor entered the MEZ, the first missile was fired at the trailing aircraft – us! It appears that it only failed to hit its intended target because it had been on the rails for so long that the cooling mechanism for the infrared homing detector, which apparently is activated as the missile is loaded, had run out of compressed nitrogen by the time it reached us. We were both then seen to deviate rapidly to the north-west, which had taken us out of their MEZ and accordingly out of the parameters of their missiles. Shortly afterwards, however, another and final opportunity was presented to the gunnery crew when we returned to our original track and skirted the western edge of the MEZ. They then fired their second missile, but this time we were just out of range and by the grace of God, the missile fell short. Thank Christ that they did not have the upgraded Mk 2 version of the Sea Dart.

There is little now to add to this unfortunate saga and although 'all's well that ends well' appears to apply in this tale, there was at least an interesting post script. I am led to understand that the gunnery officer on HMS *Cardiff* was moved sideways as a consequence of this action and his career in the Royal Navy suffered accordingly. This was not because his superiors had got it wrong and had targeted a friendly aircraft, but because once the decision to fire had been made, he had failed to take us out! While I have some sympathy for the poor chap, that's the Royal Navy for you.

The events which I have recounted here are not intended as any form of criticism of anyone concerned. These are simply components of a story, which, until it is officially sanctioned as historical fact, a particularly unlikely departure for the MOD or any British government, it will remain as nothing more than just a story, which I hope has at least provided you with some entertainment. There are no heroes or villains involved, only dedicated members of HM Armed Forces trying to fulfil their duties to the best of their abilities, under considerable strain and often considerable discomfort. The 'fog of war' is regularly quoted in the media, but it is a fact that in stressful and dangerous situations, mistakes will be made and some decisions will not be perfect. We now, of course, have the benefit of hindsight. I remain most grateful to whichever deity may have intervened to allow this story to be recounted and I suspect that Steve Biglands and his crew may hold a similar view.

Steve Biglands guarding the town.

(Alan Bruyn)

As Adrian Richardson has narrated, **Flt Lt Steve Biglands,** *Biggles to his crew, was captain of the other Victor K2 being 'attacked' by Sea Dart missiles and based on Ascension Island during the Falklands campaign. Steve remembers the occasion described by Adrian but clearly not in such detail.*

During the Falklands War my crew completed some 236 hours on thirty-seven sorties on Operation Corporate. One sortie of note was in support of a Nimrod reconnaissance well south of Ascension Island. The period leading up to the sortie was that HMS *Sheffield* had been sunk by Exocet and HMS *Bristol* and HMS *Cardiff* task force were steaming south towards the Falklands. Our pre-flight brief gave a position of intended movement for the group and we were squawking codes of the day on the IFF. The sortie involved taking on fuel with a couple of night prods of some 60,000 lb.

After refuelling a Victor our route would take us clear of the HMS *Bristol* group on return to Ascension. Our Victor radar was switched off and no external lights were on. During the return journey the AEO, Terry Anning, said that we were being 'looked at'. I selected to listen to the signal on the intercom box, as I did so there was a continuous tone of weapon acquisition. I told the nav radar, John Foot, to start firing the chaff cartridges through the Verey pistol. The aircraft was put into a step descending turn and weapon lock was lost. The H2S radar was fired up and a group of surface contacts some forty-plus miles seen. We tracked away from the surface contacts.

The next day Ascension Ops informed us that HMS *Cardiff* had sent a missile report for the previous evening firing on an unidentified aircraft. Although I did not make a note of the date I flew a Nimrod sortie on 22 May.

Steve Webley, now a captain on Virgin 747-400s, was Steve Biglands' co-pilot and he has also written down what he remembers of the incident.

Having joined the RAF in 1978 I went through the training machine and was posted to 57 Squadron at Marham in 1981 in the rank of flying officer. I had been on the squadron for ten months when Argentina invaded the Falklands and was crewed up with Steve Biglands as captain. Also in the crew were an experienced trio of Flt Lts Terry Anning, John Foot and Al Bruyn.

On the night of 22 May Steve Biglands' crew and the crew of Adrian Richardson had briefed in the operations tent at Wideawake airfield, Ascension Island (ASI). The intelligence officer was in attendance and had shown us the satellite photographs taken earlier that day and which showed us the significant vessels of the Argentine navy docked in port. Basically, we were assured none were at sea.

Our mission that night was to depart as a pair, with us (the Biglands crew) leading and Flt Lt Richardson following. Adrian was to top up his tanks from us at a pre-determined point. We would then return to Ascension and Adrian would continue south-westwards to rendezvous with a Nimrod which had departed ASI earlier.

Our Victor K2 aircraft had been hurriedly retrofitted with 18235 radar warning receivers, (RWR) in the days after the Argentinian invasion of the Falklands. Fortunately, our AEO, Flt Lt Terry Anning, had previous experience using this tool.

After our uneventful departure and join up with Adrian's aircraft we settled into the cruise to await the next bit of action. I cannot remember how long into the flight or what our approximate position was, but after a while Terry announced that there was an X-band radar out there somewhere scanning. A short while later, I think it was after Adrian had started his fuel onload, Terry told us that that radar had gone into sector scan, this he could tell from the higher pulse repetition frequency (PRF).

The refuelling bracket must have lasted about 10 to 15 minutes and just as Adrian had completed his bracket Terry yelled, "Take any evasive action you want, that radar has locked us up".

We had, as a wing, discussed what we could do in event of a missile engagement. Bundles of chaff had been placed around the drogues on the wing hoses so that if the hoses were set to trail and then wind again, the chaff would be ejected and form a cloud. So we immediately started a left turn, Adrian in the other Victor being on our right, and increased the bank to 60 degrees and started a descent at 300 kts. Meanwhile, the nav radar, Flt Lt John Foot, selected our wing hoses to trail and wind.

Terry called that the lock was broken and shortly afterwards that the radar had a lock on again. Finally, the RWR stopped its high pitched warning and we proceeded back up to a cruising level to return to ASI. Upon arrival, we announced to the ops officer what had happened and he seemed quite underwhelmed; "after all," he said, "we know they've got no ships out there. There were no squadron 'wheels' about as it was very early morning so we went to bed and pretty much forgot about it."

A day or two later I heard that a 'misrep' had been received from the Bristol group, reporting that two Sea Dart missiles had been fired at unidentified targets/target on the night of 22/23 May. I don't know whether our captain, Steve Biglands had seen this report or indeed whether he spoke to our squadron boss about it.

Some years later in June 1991, I was in Diego Garcia with a VC10 tanker of 101 Squadron and there happened to been a type 42 destroyer, HMS *Gloucester,* paying a visit. We were asked if we'd like to come aboard for a few sundowners one evening and

I got chatting to one of the helicopter pilots. He said he'd heard about HMS *Cardiff* and HMS *Bristol*, during the Falklands War, both wanting to fire upon an unidentified aircraft; *Bristol*, being the group leader, took the honours.

I should add that although on the night we were emcon silent, we were given squawks and the RN was told of our movements and those squawks.

My logbook from the night of 22 May shows that our crew flew an 8:10 sortie which included twenty minutes of day flying so we arrived back at ASI at dawn.

The Biggles crew spent much of their spare time exploring the island. This was taken on their way up to the mountain peak. Steve Webley didn't join them as he was not as keen on the activity. *(Alan Bruyn)*

*We were also able to question Steve Biglands' nav plotter **Alan Bruyn** and he replied:*

I can't remember whether we were reserve or primary crew on the night you are asking about but I'm pretty sure we were on a middle slot and after completing our tanker/tanker offload were just turning to return to Ascension when Terry our AEO reported that we were being illuminated by a scan missile control radar track. I forget the terminology but Terry reported that he was getting indications that a missile had been fired. Biggles put the aircraft into what passed for evasive action in a Victor and Footy fired off chaff from the Verey pistol. After a while it became apparent that the missile had missed and we resumed our flight home.

I remember hearing that the missiles had been fired from HMS *Bristol* which was joining the fleet late from Gibraltar. Her captain was a renowned press-on merchant hurrying to get his share of the gongs. I also remember that he denied firing any missiles but the tanker rep at Northwood allegedly looked up the expenditure records for *Bristol* and discovered that he had fired 'practice' rounds at the time. But what do I know?

Terry Anning, Biggles' AEO, also searched his memory.

I saw that some weapon missile guidance radar had acquired our aircraft, at first at its edge of scan. I quickly realised its significance and made my intercom alerting call. Biggles reacted instantly and instinctively. He initiated his first of several steep turns within the parameters of our operating flying envelope.

John Foot, our navigator radar, immediately initiated the deployment of the defensive multi-frequency wavelength-sized types of foil strip from its stowed positions near the Whitcomb Bodies where it was packed and held by the refuelling drogues. John then proceeded to very bravely clamber away from his total safety and survival systems in his seat to start to fire multiple cartridges via the through-hull Verey pistol in the roof. This required individual 'making and breaking' then reloading with each cartridge taking perhaps five seconds with each reload. The cartridges could be either of infrared type or chaff deployers. They were colour coded red or green if I remember correctly and they were contained in large round tins perhaps containing twenty cartridges.

The attack radar was partly defeated in going into its acquisition and lock on modes by our manoeuvres and deployed systems as indicated by the calls and part indications on our basic radar warning receiver display system screen. The missile guidance radar momentarily gained one brief moment of fire mode.

The final turn and climb away, from the low descended height reduced the missile guidance radar to weak acquisition attempts and during the times of our turns there were calls of two lights and illumination of some kind that were seen passing to our starboard. I twisted vigorously in my flightdeck seat but did not manage to see these lights. We then regained our required track for our return to Wideawake airfield, Ascension Island.

Quite clearly from these five crew members from two Victors, virtually in formation, there can be no doubt that two Sea Darts were launched towards them. The naval situation at the time of these accounts was that the Royal Navy with HMS Bristol *was shepherding the Bristol group of ships steaming towards the Falklands and were south of the latitude of Ascension Island where the Victor tankers, Nimrods and Vulcans were based. The* Bristol *was armed with Sea Dart missiles as was one of the ships guarding the vessel HMS* Cardiff, *a type 42 destroyer; the Sea Darts were capable of engaging targets out to at least thirty nautical miles over a wide range of altitudes.*

As a result of the information from Victor crews we have tried to establish which ship actually fired the Sea Darts at the Victor and it appears that at the time of the incident the naval ships in the group going south had concerns that they were being tracked by Argentinian air force Boeing 707s and the following is an extract from The Royal Navy and the Falklands War *by* **David Brown.**

Day Two – Taking Breath

At least two of the 707s were out on 22 May and both very narrowly missed disaster. In the early hours one approached the northern entrance to the Falkland Sound, presumably to see if there were any shipping movements. At the time, the only ship offshore was the destroyer *Coventry,* about ten miles north-east of Pebble Island and waiting to be joined by the *Broadsword,* with whom she would team up to act as a missile trap to break up raids approaching from the west. The *Coventry* waited for the 707 to close in to twenty-five miles and then began the Sea Dart acquisition process, illuminating the target with both Type 909 tracking radars. All went well with the sequence until a flash-door failed safe, preventing missile loading on to the launcher. As the target did not wake up to the fact that it was in imminent danger until it was five miles closer and the fault could not be rectified before it was well out of range, there was bitter disappointment in the ship that the Coventry had been robbed of success against such a high-value target.

This near-engagement, which occurred at 3.00 a.m., was followed, five hours later and 1,800 miles to the north-east, by an actual firing. The Bristol group, which had been joined on 21 May by the *Tidespring*, hastening forward after getting rid of the South Georgia prisoners, detected what was undoubtedly not a civil airliner, for the track plot took the form of a series of loops and curlicues which brought the aircraft in from over 200 miles to thirty-five miles, its closest point of approach.

Sea Dart and launcher on HMS Cardiff. (Ken Griffiths)

Captain A Grose RN, leading the group, ordered the *Cardiff* to drop back and altered the disposition of his ships to disguise her disappearance. The 707 duly obliged by coming within extreme range of the Type 42, which fired a Sea Dart salvo at about 1230Z. One of the missiles was seen on radar to have burst close to the target, which promptly broke away and dived to low level. Whether or not the warhead exploded close enough to damage the Boeing and cause the loss of cabin pressurization, as was suggested at the time, the crew was certainly aware of the very narrow escape and the few 707s that were subsequently detected remained well beyond the range of all weapons.

Clearly one possibility was that the Cardiff *fired the Sea Darts at the Victor thinking the ship's radar return was an Argentinian 707. However we have the comments from the radar operator of the Cardiff and clearly they were convinced that they were firing at an Argentinian 707.*

Ken Griffiths, *ex-radar operator, HMS* Cardiff, *1982 (see footnote on page 181).*

With regards to the Boeing 707 incident on 22 May, we had been closing the TEZ with the Bristol group and had been alerted to the fact that an Argentine 707 was airborne (I think *Coventry* had tried to engage it earlier that day, but had a problem with her

FUERZA AEREA ARGENTII

TC-92

22 May: Vice-Comodoro Otto A Ritondale (far left) and his crew pose in front of the Boeing 707 before take-off on the reconnaissance mission which so nearly ended in disaster when they found the Bristol group, 1,400 miles (2,600 km) east-north-east of Buenos Aires. Only violent evasive action when the *Cardiff's* Sea Dart missile was sighted at the last moment saved the aircraft and crew. *(FAA via J C D Odorico)*

launcher). We picked up the 707 radar and eventually the aircraft on radar. I couldn't believe it, they were flying right towards us at 20,000 ft plus, it was a 'down the throat' shot. We asked *Bristol* if we could engage and got a 'Hold Fire' response, for some reason her captain was not happy about the ID. Our captain was absolutely 'gobsmacked'. The 707 closed to inside thirty miles, had a bloody good look at us then skirted around the group keeping around thirty miles plus distance. Our captain had seen enough and turned *Cardiff* 90° to starboard and stopped. The 707 was now opening on a reciprocal heading to the group. The group sailed on and when they were about 10 nm away and the 707 was now about 40 nm, it turned back in and closed. At 35 nm it appeared to turn slightly to starboard. That was enough for the captain so he ordered two Darts away. As soon as we launched the first Dart they turned away sharply and the 909s recorded a rapid decrease in height, and we watched the missiles on our radar open towards the target at amazing velocity. The first one exploded (you can see this on radar) about three to four miles astern of the target. The second, by now being very verbally urged on by the lads, seemed to merge and explode.

It is very likely the crew saw the first missile launch and the pilot initiated an almost suicidal dive for the sea. This manoeuvre and the fact we fired at extreme range saved the aircraft and her crew. They would not have survived if Captain Grose had not been so cautious. By the way whilst all this was going on HMS *Bristol* fired two Sea Darts at two closing contacts, this turned out to be interference from other 992 radars in the group and was a problem at that time. Was *Invincible* reacting the same?

The engagement took place in the afternoon on a bright crisp South Atlantic day. As the 707 approached our upper deck gun crews called "Aircraft Visual Green", meaning they had sighted the 707 on the gun deck platform through this bit of kit (photo taken at a later date). Ok, we can see them, albeit through a special bit of kit, so maybe we could be seen by them when a Sea Dart is launched. We have to assume the crew were well motivated to keep a good look out for a missile launch.

With these statements on public record it would seem quite clear the Cardiff *thought it had fired on an Argentinian 707 but it is hard to believe that the smart telescope shown in the picture could identify an aircraft type at thirty-odd miles; it seems impossible not to rule out that the aircraft could have been a Victor. However, we know nothing about the firings of the* Bristol's *two Sea Darts. Interestingly Alan Bruyn the nav plotter remarked that he thought that it was the* Bristol *that did fire the weapons. It is relevant to requote Ken Griffiths's comment: "By the way whilst all this was going on HMS* Bristol *fired two Sea Darts at two closing contacts, this turned out to be interference from other 992 radars in the group and was a problem at that time."*

Air War South Atlantic *by* **Ethell** *and* **Price** *records the Falkland campaign day by day and the last entry for 22 May was:*

> Elsewhere the only real excitement was far to the north of the Falklands, where a convoy of British ships bringing reinforcements was approached by a Boeing 707 of Grupo I on reconnaissance. Two of the escorts, *Bristol* and *Cardiff*, engaged with Sea Darts at extreme range, and only by diving away at high speed was the aircraft able to make good its escape.

In an internet discussion on The Aviation Forum[6], there is the following response relating to a question about the Bristol *firing.*

> '...my research into the Sea Dart engagements might be of interest.
>
> 'First of all, *Bristol's* engagement was unusual as there was no incoming threat; the launches were ordered when *Cardiff* Type 909 radar interference was mistaken for a contact.
>
> 'Salvo firings were used to increase likelihood of a kill. There were numerous salvo firings but this has never been recognised because of a rather embarrassing situation which existed at the time. There was a software

Device that was apparently used to view the Boeing 707 on HMS *Cardiff*. (Ken Griffiths)

bug in the Sea Dart system which meant that if a salvo firing was attempted with too quick an interval the second round would fail to guide. This phenomenon was first noticed during *Bristol* trials in 1976, but had not been resolved until June 1982. What I find incredible is that the captains of the Sea Dart ships were unaware of this problem until after they had received the software update which fixed it. Quite a few Sea Darts were needlessly expended as a result of this issue.'

There can be little doubt that either HMS Cardiff *or HMS* Bristol *launched some Sea Darts at the Victors. Unfortunately it has not been possible to contact any of the* Bristol's *crew to hear why they fired the Sea Darts. However, based on the report from the* Cardiff *radar operator and other comments it seems probable that it was the* Bristol *that launched the Sea Darts that acquired the two Victors, luckily with no adverse effects.*

CHAPTER 15

NUCLEAR WEAPONS AND QRA

Mike Keitch

This chapter tells the story of how the RAF managed the nuclear weapons that were programmed for use by the V bombers. The fundamental theme that comes through from this unique account of handling atomic and hydrogen bombs is how safety dominated every aspect of bomb management from storage through to weapon loading. **Mike Keitch** *spent his whole RAF working life dealing with nuclear weapon issues and his expertise was clearly recognised in the RAF by his steady promotion through the ranks from junior technician to squadron leader.*

V Bomber World – An Armourer's Story

I graduated in December 1961 from No. 1 School of Technical Training RAF Halton as a junior technician (JT) armourer after three years of technical training. I came high enough in the ninety-first entry to get accelerated promotion to corporal technician after twelve months instead of the normal three years. All of us went to V bomber bases which were growing as more and more of these aircraft were entering service.

Five of us, me, Dave Andrews, Ainslie Cruickshank, Mick Pine, and Roland Guilmoto, went to RAF Honington in Suffolk. Honington had Victor Mk 1A bombers (55 and 57 Squadrons) and Valiant tankers of 90 Squadron. On our arrival in January 1962 we were marched into OC armament engineering squadron's office – Sqn Ldr Gus

Victor B1 bomber in anti-flash finish. *(Mike Keitch)*

Payne – for our arrival interview. His first question was to ask which of us had graduated the highest in the Entry. Like a fool I cheerfully said, "Me sir". He then told Flt Sgt Jennings to distribute the other four between second line (the maintenance bays) and first line which was where guys worked on the actual aircraft. As the others left for their new work places I was told to wait for transport to the 'special area'. Eventually Cpl Tech Ginge Rye (another ex-apprentice) arrived from what I quickly learned was officially called the supplementary storage area (SSA) but more conveniently called 'the site', to collect me. The SSA was the nuclear weapon storage and maintenance site and, supposedly, only very bright armourers were sent to work there.

The Weapons

At Honington we had Yellow Sun (YS) Mk 1 which was replaced from 1962 onwards by Yellow Sun Mk 2. Both were megaton fusion weapons then known as hydrogen bombs. Megaton meant anything with a yield of over 500 kiloton. Both types weighed a nominal 7,000 lb and had the same size and shape. Only one weapon was carried per aircraft. YS2 had been tested to a maximum yield during British nuclear tests to 1.5 megaton. YS1 had replaced

Yellow Sun 2. *(Mike Keitch)*

both Blue Danube (BD) which was the UK's first fully operational nuclear weapon and Violet Club. Violet Club never became fully operational and only a handful were produced. YS1 entered RAF service in the late 1950s and I saw the last one leave Honington in 1963. We also had Red Beard (RB) Mk 1 and Mk 2 which were tactical weapons in the kiloton range. RBs were nominally 2,000 lb in weight and were carried by Canberras, RN aircraft such as Buccaneer and Scimitar as well as Valiants, Vulcans and Victors.

Unexpected Events

We were continually moving weapons because of the QRAs. This was the real thing and was the main reason for our existence. Security, safety and meticulous compliance with procedure was the order of the day. But it didn't always happen as it should.

The procedure for conveying a weapon from the SSA to first line for aircraft loading was quite involved. In the SSA the controller, usually a chief technician, would decide which weapon was to be used. With the Yellow Sun selected the team would prepare it and its carrier, including fitting the electrical harness (for connecting to the aircraft power systems) and, on the YS1, fitting its electrically heated blanket (yes, honestly!), then tow both out of the building on special trailers (standard airfield bomb transporter later replaced by the L-type trolley) to the site gates. The rules required two armourers to escort the tractor driver (we used ancient David Brown tractors with no cabs – there was nothing sophisticated about nukes!) plus an armed RAF police escort. All aircraft and other vehicle movements on the airfield would cease until the weapon was safely delivered to the loading team inside the secured aircraft parking area. Entry to this was controlled by the RAF police. The convoy commander, e.g. me the corporal technician, would sign the weapon over to the loading team leader in the presence of an RAF policeman who confirmed both identities. The team would then proceed to load the weapon following very precise procedures.

The tractor driver had little protection from the elements. If he was lucky he might have a wartime duffle coat otherwise it was his RAF raincoat, beret and woolly gloves. Sometimes when I was the nominated driver I would get to the SSA gate to await my police escort only for them to say they were too busy and so I would have to do without an escort. No problem. One day in November the airfield had ceased flying due to a heavy freezing fog. The police with their unheated Land Rovers, as usual, declined to come with me. So being an intrepid soul I set of on my own towing a YS2 (the megaton bomb). Passing the runway intersection and frozen to the bone I decided to take a short cut across the runway. Surely no one would see me in the fog? Wrong! The intersection came out right under the ATC tower and I was spotted. An irate senior air traffic control officer demanded my presence and I suffered an almighty bollocking for ignoring red lights, crossing an active runway without permission and numerous other infractions. But surprisingly the lack of a police escort never raised its head.

On another occasion in the dreadful winter of 1962/63 Senior Aircraftman (SAC) Checkets who was our resident MT driver was tasked to drive the tractor as all the SSA armourers had wimped out of driving in freezing conditions. As usual, the RAF police declined to join in thus leaving poor Checkets to his own devices. The lying snow was thick. Now, the YS2 was over four feet in diameter with a flat front, no pointy bomb was this. On V bomber bases there were several refuelling areas positioned off the taxiways. Fuel came through a nationwide underground pipeline and each refuelling point had a hydrant system which could be connected direct to the aircraft. I never saw them used. One of these points was on the corner where the road to the SSA met the main taxiway, Checkets decided to save time (who would blame him in that weather?) by cutting the corner. But these areas were never cleared of snow. The flat front of the bomb on its trailer, which had only six inches ground clearance, became a snow plough in its own right. Eventually the piled-up snow caused poor Checkets to come to a halt. Meanwhile the loading team leader was going ape demanding to know at regular intervals from the SSA controller where his bomb was. Things got a bit heated between the two sides. Eventually my chief, Jack Dorrell recognised something had gone wrong. We had no walkie-talkies in those days and mobile phones hadn't been invented. So I set out on the second tractor and eventually found Checkets bravely digging out a 7,000-lb hydrogen bomb with his bare, frozen hands. I went back for a couple of spades and some help. This time the police did get a serious reprimand and from then on escorted us every time.

On another occasion we lost a YS2. Twice each day every weapon storage building had to have its temperature and humidity checked. The buildings were climatically controlled. The two SSA armourers on that duty would draw a box of keys and proceed to each building in turn. They would have the identity details of each weapon in each building. An RAF policeman would provide the armed escort. One day when I was on this duty with Dave Tyndall we entered a building – it was empty! A quick check with the controller confirmed which weapon was supposed to be there. He quickly got in a panic. His records clearly showed that building to be occupied. Being a wit and never taking such things very seriously as an airman, I advised him to tell our CO that we had lost a hydrogen bomb. He didn't think that was very funny. We checked every other building to see if it had the correct weapon. Yes, they all did. After about an hour of panic (by the controller not me) we found the missing YS2 in the RB maintenance building where someone had put it there temporarily but forgot to tell the controller.

Inspections

Every aspect of the nuclear world was examined periodically by the MOD weapons standardisation team – the dreaded WST. Every unit, however minutely involved in the nuclear world from the V bases, would undergo periodic WST inspections. In later years the nuclear weapon activities on American airbases in the UK were also checked by the MOD WST. On the V bases and the maintenance units at Barnham and Faldingworth inspections were every year. Checks covered every maintenance and rectification task carried out on every nuclear system on the aircraft, the weapons themselves and the transportation and support equipment. Every tool and item of test equipment was checked for correct function and serviceability and up-to-date modifications.

WST also checked that all personnel involved in such work were up-to-date in their training and certification, that any supervisor involved was similarly authorised, that the repair, maintenance and operating schedules used by ground crew and aircrew were up-to-date, and that nothing was present in the buildings or vehicles or tool sets which was not an authorised item. All procedures such as weapon maintenance and loading, aircrew and ground crew operations, firefighting and medical responses, RAF police security, firearms training etc. had to be 100 per cent correct in every detail. Personnel would have to demonstrate their relevant proficiency in their particular responsibilities in exercise incidents such as a fire or a security problem. All buildings inside the SSA were inspected for the minutest defect, and checked that their maintenance was done at the prescribed intervals by correctly trained and authorised personnel. A WST inspection could take up to two weeks. The inspection would be followed up by a lengthy debrief of all the various departments involved and senior unit staff. A grading score would be given by the team for each activity and an overall score given to the unit. A no-pass score would have serious repercussions for the unit's management.

Road Convoys

Road convoys were a pain. The RAF had three types of trailers for use on public roads. The A-container, basically an 11-ton fire-proof safe suspended between two bogies, was used to convey a Yellow Sun 2 warhead.

The Z-container was a 20-ton steel coffin-like box suspended between two huge bogies. It was used to convey live YS1 and YS 2 weapons less their tail units. I have never been able to track down a picture of a Z-container.

The Pantechnicon was a 44-foot trailer with lighting and heating and was used to convey a complete live weapon on its transporter trolley.

All units had at least one or two Pantechnicons which would normally only be used in wartime at V bomber dispersal airfields to house a weapon that had to be removed from an aircraft. They could

Top: **A-container.** *(Mike Keitch)*

Bottom: **Pantechnicon trailer.** *(Mike Keitch)*

also convey a complete weapon which had no warhead or explosive component in it.

One day I was summoned to Flt Lt Bill Kitchen's office for a special briefing. I was to take a convoy of four Pantechnicons each carrying an inert YS2 to a secret destination. Inert weapons only simulated shape, size and weight and were used by armourers for weapon-loading training. They were painted white and were basically steel and concrete. As they were classified only as 'restricted' the task could be safely given to an NCO i.e. Cpl Tech Keitch. There were no motorways and few by-passes in those days and at over seventy feet in length the Pantechnicon and its towing vehicle was unusually long for the 1960s. So four of them in convoy would be an impressive sight. On the due morning I met my four drivers and the RAF policeman who was to be the escort, for a briefing. My orders were in a sealed envelope – the only time in thirty-five years in the RAF I ever had sealed orders. My policeman on his ancient RAF 250 cc James motorbike, wearing a white helmet, a long trench mac and leather gauntlets looked more suited for *Dad's Army* than escorting a nuclear convoy across England. Our destination was the Aircraft and Armament Experimental Establishment (A&AEE) at Boscombe Down, nearly 200 miles away in Wiltshire. The 1944-era ten-ton Leyland Hippos struggled to get much over 30 mph at the best of times let alone when hauling a loaded Pantechnicon. It was going to be a long day.

We headed out with me, as any true leader would be, in the front vehicle. Our brave policeman would clear the way for us as in those days RAF police could control civilian traffic. All was well until we got on the A11 towards Newmarket when I became puzzled as to why every so often, Cpl Edwards, my elderly (well, he was to me), driver kept standing up to put his face close to the windscreen. Turned out he was long sighted so couldn't see the road clearly in front of him. A good start! Going through St Neots, it was market day so the main street was full of stallholders. You can imagine the chaos we caused getting through that lot with stallholders cursing us left right and centre and shopkeepers having to wind in their awnings. All was well after that until we reached Bedford when our policeman was knocked off his bike by a motorist who was frustrated at our slow pace. Luckily he was OK.

The next crisis was somewhere (I forget where after all these years) which had a hill. To my dismay the traffic going up it was at a standstill. A truck had had break failure at the top and then slid backwards into a wall closing half the main road. A local policeman was at the scene directing traffic. I couldn't allow my four vehicles to stop on the hill let alone get separated as even in their two mph crawler gear it would be a nightmare getting them up the hill from a standing start. So I jumped out of my vehicle, raced up to the policeman and tried to explain that I had a secret RAF convoy with four huge vehicles which could not stop on the hill. The copper just shrugged and said we'd have to wait our turn. I rushed back and told my RAF police escort to tell the drivers to go past the queue of traffic on the inside and just keep going – right through people's front gardens! Luckily, for us if not for the house owners, the gardens were all open plan. The damage was horrendous. I gave the traffic policeman an MOD damage and accident claim form which all military vehicles carried, and the relevant MOD phone number and just left him utterly speechless. I never heard any more about it.

Later, as darkness began to fall, one of the Hippos sprung an oil leak in the middle of Newbury. Those trucks took nearly four gallons of sump oil. So now we were blocking the middle of the town so I sent my intrepid RAF policeman to the nearest military establishment – the army apprentice school at Arborfield. He had some trouble explaining our predicament to the guard room with a cock and bull story about four huge RAF vehicles on a secret mission stranded in Newbury and that we needed a jerry can of engine oil. With his *Dad's Army* outfit they must have thought he was joking. But they eventually called the orderly officer who decided to see for himself what this secret convoy looked like. Remember, I was just a corporal in charge of this lot which impressed the army officer! We eventually got going again and limped into Boscombe Down some twelve hours after leaving Honington.

The Cuban Crisis
In November 1962 came the Cuban crisis. We all knew from the news that international tension was high but we little thought how it would affect us but on the Friday of that

critical weekend the sirens went off. On a Friday afternoon it wasn't unusual for Bomber Command to test V bases with a no-notice exercise. But the Tannoy kept referring to Operation Mickey Finn instead of Exercise Mickey Finn. In the SSA we assumed that it was a mistake by the announcer until our controller chief came into the crew room in a panic to say that this was the real thing! Suddenly the adrenalin kicked in. We were preparing for nuclear war. Our job was to prepare live weapons and get them to the aircraft pronto. Meanwhile, aircraft were rapidly returning to the UK from wherever in the world they were and those in the hangars had to be made available urgently. They could be dropping nukes within the next few days or even hours. We armourers just joked that at least we wouldn't have to download them again and we probably wouldn't be seeing another Monday morning either. Very cynical military humour. No one was allowed off base, gates were closed and all personnel off duty were called back.

We worked our socks off preparing the weapons sleeping and eating when and where we could, and providing additional teams to load all available aircraft. All eight V bases which had the bombing role were doing the same thing. As the weekend went on we all became more serious about our role. It is still difficult to realise that I was one of those who prepared and loaded Britain's nuclear bombs to be dropped on unknown targets in the Soviet Union. But by late Sunday Khrushchev had relented and agreed to withdraw the missiles from Cuba. An interesting question – why didn't the RAF V bombers disperse? Mickey Finn required all available aircraft to be 'generated' i.e. made serviceable for flight, and loaded with live nukes within specified time-scales prior to their dispersal across the UK. But we didn't disperse. Later it became apparent that Harold Macmillan – a wily very experienced prime minister – was convinced that the Soviets would back down so by allowing the V bombers to fly to their dispersal airfields the British public could be unnecessarily panicked with unforeseeable consequences. As a result, few people realised and probably still don't, that this was the nearest the UK came to joining in a nuclear war.

Quick Reaction Alert

All V bomber bases except Gaydon had two or four aircraft ready armed at fifteen minutes warning. Despite popular belief, the aircraft often seen in photos of that time sitting at the end of the runway ready to go (the famous four-minute warning concept) were not always the real QRA aircraft. Often they were positioned there for exercise alerts. Normally the real QRA aircraft would be parked inside a secure area away from the runway. Any aircraft loaded with a nuclear weapon would have the strictest security around it, barbed wire fences, armed RAF police etc. but many photos purporting to be of QRA aircraft do not show any of these mandatory security measures. At Honington we loaded QRA aircraft in secure areas off the taxiway and the only time they moved to the operational readiness platform on the end of the runway was when Exercise Edom was called. Edom was a regular test to see if the base could meet the QRA alert times.

Wherever an aircraft loaded with a live nuclear weapon was located it would be surrounded by barbed wire security barriers and guarded by armed RAF police often with dogs. Only authorised personnel with the appropriate security clearance were allowed past the barriers. I have never found a photo of real QRA aircraft in their secured parking areas so maybe none were ever taken. Duty ground crews were housed in cabins close by. They were on QRA standby duty for seven days.

An Exercise Edom alert could be called by HQ Bomber (later Strike) Command at any hour of the day or night. A favourite time was on Christmas or Boxing Day and it wasn't unusual for an alert to be called (by means of sirens and Tannoy broadcasts) twice in twenty-four hours just to keep us on our toes. I was on QRA duty on one occasion when an Edom was called on Christmas Eve and another on the following day when the duty crews were recovering from their Christmas lunch. When the alert went off, aircrew and ground crew would race to their respective locations. The various tradesmen would check their part of the aircraft, engines started up, clearance given for the aircraft to go to the declared readiness state –fifteen minutes or less. They would taxi to the end of the runway with engines running, then go to four minutes warning, then two then 'scramble'. At that point the aircraft would simulate a take-off, maybe taxiing down the runway before returning to the secure area. On one alert when I was on duty the police had pulled aside the security barriers to allow the aircraft out of the secure area but one aircraft took the corner leading to the taxi way too sharply. The port undercarriage sank into the grass not only preventing that aircraft from moving but blocking the second one behind it. It was quite a pantomime to get the aircraft level so the weapon could be downloaded and the aircraft checked for damage. Luckily such incidents were extremely rare and didn't involve any danger to the weapon or personnel.

Weapon Loading

Weapon loading was done by specially trained teams of armourers from first and second line. We armourers in the SSA were nearly two miles from first line on the far side of the airfield but we were also trained to load aircraft. A load team would be 'constituted' which meant that it would always consist of the same personnel as far as possible. The Victor bomb carrier for the Yellow Suns was a large item about 2.5 metres long by 1.5 metres wide. The Red Beard carrier was much smaller and was fitted to the bomb before leaving the SSA. Carriers were prepared for use in the

Yellow Sun inert weapon ready for moving under Victor bomb bay.
(Mike Keitch)

T-building then they and the weapons would be taken out on special trailers to the waiting aircraft and handed over to the load team leader who was never lower in rank than sergeant. The operation would be supervised by an armament officer or warrant officer, called the weapon loading supervising officer (WLSO) and he and the team leader would be armed. We were never sure if that was so they could shoot an attacker or us if we made a mistake. The carrier and then the weapon if it was a YS would, in turn, be manoeuvred under the bomb bay.

Only a single British weapon was carried by all three V bombers although there had been a plan to arm the Valiant with one Blue Danube in the bomb bay and one on each wing. All the V bombers were designed also to carry conventional weapons – the Valiants and Vulcans could carry twenty-one 1,000-lb bombs but the mighty Victor carried thirty-five – the heaviest bomb load of any British aircraft. But even though bases also held conventional HE bombs these were only dropped in anger twice – during the 1956 Suez campaign by Valiants and in the Falklands War by Vulcans.

VIP Visits

One day in 1963, Chapman Pincher, the *Daily Express* defence correspondent at the time, made an official visit to a V bomber base – Honington. Secrecy was so sensitive in those days that very little about the nuclear weapon world had ever reached the media so Chapman was especially privileged. I assume he was first shown round an aircraft and had a briefing from Honington's senior hierarchy, He then came to visit the SSA – or so he was led to believe. When his visit report was published in the newspaper it included a picture of Chapman standing by a tarpaulin-covered bomb-shaped object on a trailer with his hand resting on it. The caption read, 'Under my hand is one of Britain's H-Bombs'. Except that it wasn't! He wasn't even in the SSA. He had been taken into the conventional explosives storage area (ESA) (then called 'bomb dumps') and the object was an American E-weapon training round made of steel and concrete which had been left behind a few years earlier from when the RAF temporarily leased USAF weapons before receiving British weapons. You couldn't fool the press so easily these days. Chapman also claimed that he had been into an underground weapon storage bunker. During my RAF career I visited every nuclear weapon facility in the UK and even beyond. I never came across any underground weapon bunker.

I think it was in 1965 that the Queen paid an official visit to RAF Honington. As with all royal visits to military establishments the stops were pulled out. The whole station had to be spick and span and on first line (which I had joined by then) we had to do our bit. The Yellow Sun weapons had very large tail units which were prevented from moving inside the bomb bay by an aluminium bracing frame called a 'tail steady'. Flt Sgt Jenkins in charge of first line often had us respraying them silver. The grass outside first line therefore had silver-coloured patches. In preparation for the Queen (even though we were not going to see hide nor hair of her) he had us spray the grass green. All the kerb stones along her route had to be painted alternate black and white and on the morning of the visit fresh grass cuttings were spread to cover the patches where folk had worn paths for short cuts on the grassed areas. I wonder if Her Majesty noticed such fine touches.

Escape to First Line

In 1964 Honington deployed Victors to RAF Tengah in Singapore to act as a deterrent to Indonesia which was threatening to attack the Malaysian Federation which then included Malaya, North Borneo, Sarawak and Singapore. I desperately wanted to see some action so I applied to Sqn Ldr Gus Payne to be let out of the SSA to join the deployment. But I had to gain experience on first line working on the aircraft at Honington first. He agreed so I finally escaped from behind the wire.

So after a few months on first line I flew out to RAF Tengah in Singapore to join the 57 Squadron Detachment. I was put into the bomber armoury with my two-man team where I was responsible for the servicing of the Victor ejection seats, bomb carriers, and the bomb release and arming units. There was one QRA aircraft fully loaded with 1,000-lb bombs at Tengah and another one at the Royal Australian Air Force base at Butterworth on the west coast of the Malaysian peninsula opposite the island of Penang.

One Saturday at Tengah there was a huge air power display exercise to show the Indonesians what the UK had available to defend Malaya and Singapore. This involved RAF Hunters, Javelins and Canberras, RN Scimitars and Sea Vixens, RNZAF Canberras, and Tengah's QRA Victor. All morning wave after wave of aircraft took off carrying live ordnance to drop on the bombing range in the Malacca Straits. The exercise command centre was the aircraft carrier HMS *Eagle* with various observers on board. One of these was the command armament officer (CarmO) from HQ Far East Air Force, a very experienced squadron leader. After several hours the exercise concluded with the single Victor coming out of the clouds to drop its impressive load of 35 x 1,000-lb live bombs. Except it didn't! As each bomb was released automatically, a doll's-eye indicator in the cockpit, one for each bomb station, would change from black to white showing the crew that the bomb had dropped. When the aircraft dropped its load all thirty-five doll's eyes showed that it was a full release. But as the aircraft climbed to head home, the CarmO had an emergency message relayed to the crew to say that only thirty-four bombs had dropped. Despite the pilot's insistence that he had thirty-five white doll's eyes the aircraft was told to return. As the bomb doors were opened again out fell the thirty-fifth bomb.

I was sunbathing by the swimming pool at the time when I got an urgent message to report to the armoury. All hell had broken loose after the aircraft's return. An investigation found a lot of damage inside the bomb bay as the loose bomb had rattled round after it had shaken loose from its carriers. It had suffered what armourers called a 'hang-up'. In theory one bomb release unit could not receive its electrical pulse to open it until the lower bombs had been released in turn. But for some reason the release unit holding the renegade bomb had not opened but all the rest had. It was discovered that the jaws of the release unit had opened sufficiently to allow the electrical pulse to continue to the other units but not sufficiently to allow the jaws to open completely to release the bomb. As the corporal in charge of the servicing of these units I was hauled before the inevitable inquiry. One of my team had serviced the faulty unit but I had over-signed his work. I realised that as the corporal in charge I could be facing serious trouble. Had the aircraft not returned to drop the renegade bomb in the sea but landed normally, the armourers would have checked that all thirty-five doll's eyes were clear and opened the bomb doors. A live, armed 1,000-lb bomb would have fallen onto the concrete floor with potentially lethal consequences. But ultimately I was not held responsible.

It was eventually discovered that when the bombs were fitted to their carriers in the explosives storage area they were left on the trailers in the open for up to twenty-four hours. This was so that in the event of a QRA aircraft having to be replaced urgently there would be a ready prepared bomb load. In Singapore's humidity that was enough to cause corrosion on the jaws of the release unit causing it to stick momentarily. Did I heave a sigh of relief after that one! Interestingly, the detachment armament officer who did the investigation, Pilot Officer Peter Symonds, years later as a group captain interviewed me at the MOD for a liaison job attached to the USAF. He remembered me and the incident but I didn't remember him. For a while I was puzzled as to how he knew so much about me as an airman until he eventually let on that we had met all those years earlier.

On another occasion in Singapore I was driving past a line of parked aircraft when I noticed a fully bombed-up Victor with a very short set of servicing steps under one wing. As I got closer I realised it was the standard RAF 6 ft stepladder but the top two feet were inside the wing. The armourers who had loaded the aircraft hadn't noticed the steps and with a full weapon load the Victor could sink nearly two feet due to the extra weight. A very expensive repair was the result.

New Horizons

From Honington I was commissioned into the Engineering Branch but the postings people never forgot my nuclear background. I did my officer training at RAF Feltwell and engineering officer training at the 'college of knowledge' – RAF College Cranwell. Then in 1967 as a shiny new flying officer I was posted to 92 MU at Faldingworth as a convoy commander to take charge of the dreaded convoys that I hated as an airman. The commanding officer there then was Wing Commander Macro. As a Supply Branch officer he had little knowledge of weapons or even the convoys since Sqn Ldr Reg Rayden, the senior engineering officer had these responsibilities on a 'need-to-know' basis. Macro was one of the last 'gentleman officers' in that he had a private income and the RAF was little more than a pastime. A lovely man nevertheless, he was a big buddy of Burgess and McLean of spy fame. Their activities and resulting defections were big news in 1967/68. Macro had met them when he had served in a British embassy somewhere in the Middle East. He often went home on a Thursday to his house in Surrey returning to work the following Monday. He had little idea of, or even interest in, what convoy officers did. One cold, foggy November Monday morning I was getting the convoy ready for a pick up at RAF Finningley near Doncaster. With a maximum speed of the Hippos of not much more than thirty miles per hour it took five days to go from Faldingworth to Finningley, to Aldermaston/Burghfield, then back to Finningley and finally home to Faldingworth. All the convoy vehicles including the escort Bedford twelve minibuses that I and the RAF Police and others travelled in were not only slow and unreliable but cold and uncomfortable without modern luxuries such as radios. The job was pretty boring most of the time.

Macro suddenly appeared one morning and to my surprise asked, "What is the convoy doing today?" I had to bite my tongue to politely explain to my own CO what the major part of his unit did as a routine job. He was most surprised to hear that we did the same thing week in, week out but he never volunteered to come out on a convoy. Years later, when Faldingworth's role became public knowledge a rumour grew locally that there was a seven-mile secret tunnel to RAF Scampton which had been used by our convoys. I was told of this only recently on a 'down memory lane' visit to Falding-worth, now long since closed.

One of the few perks as a convoy officer was the overseas trips. The RAF had Red Beard weapons in Singapore and Cyprus and these had to be periodically replaced from the UK for various reasons. I flew as the escort and custodian in Britannia cargo aircraft and we carried up to six RBs at a time. Later the flights were done by the new Hercules transport aircraft. Every stopover was at an overseas RAF station of which there were many at that time. First stop was RAF Luqa in Malta for refuelling, then RAF Akrotiri in Cyprus. If we were going to Singapore the next stopover was RAF Masirah off the Arabian Peninsula. Then it was RAF Gan in the Maldives before reaching RAF Tengah. Of necessity these flights were secret. But they still had their moments. The very strict rules required the aircraft to be met by fire vehicles manned only by RAF UK nationals and guarded by RAF police who also had to be UK nationals. I had this in my official instructions for the trip. But on Gan the RAF employed locals as firemen and police. On my first flight arriving at Gan, I refused to hand over the aircraft to the RAF Provost officer, who would secure it in my absence, because he had only locally recruited Maldivian police and firemen. This caused quite a stand-off as he was senior to me, until an order came from Gan's commanding officer for me to back down. I wrote up this incident in my end-of-trip report which went to my boss then onto HQ Maintenance Command which had responsibility for Faldingworth and RAF Barnham.

A few months later on my next arrival at Gan I was met by a very frosty committee consisting of the CO, Far East Air Force's Provost marshal, the command armament officer and sundry others and asked to explain my nerve at putting complaints about RAF Gan in my report. In those days, overseas RAF Commands were virtually air forces in their own right; Maintenance Command's writ did not extend halfway around the world to

WE177 weapon. *(Mike Keitch)*

Gan. So it was the sort of meeting that I, as a very junior flying officer, wished my mum was there to rescue me from. But when you are nearly half a world away from your boss without any direct communications you have to just grin and bear such difficulties.

My next return to the nuclear world was in 1978 in the dying days of the V Force to RAF Scampton as the squadron leader in charge of the armament engineering squadron. The old weapons had long been replaced by the much smaller WE177 (originally intended for the ill-fated TSR2 aircraft). Everything had changed, tighter procedures, better and more modern equipment and vehicles and more intensive training in all the various activities associated with nukes.

At Scampton I had all the WE177s on my 'personal charge'. Everything in the military has to be on someone's 'charge'. Owning several dozen nuclear weapons was quite a responsibility. I also had a secondary duty as one of three officers responsible for planning and running station alert and response exercises. This was great fun as the CO, Group Captain Clive Herbert gave me carte blanche authority to introduce the most elaborate incidents possible such as nuclear accidents, terrorists attacks, air raids etc. which would test the whole station and not just aircrew and ground crews. He let me run exercises over three days which meant that I could set up very realistic events stretching over long periods. The exercises mainly tested the station's response to a WWIII scenario. Planning these exercises in secret took many weeks. I would select a team of trustworthy and imaginative SNCOs who would each be given an incident to arrange. This could range from an aircraft crash or a bomb destroying the communications centre to a full-scale terrorist attack. When the sirens, including those in RAF housing areas in Lincoln itself, went off usually at some godforsaken hour of the night (known as 0h, 0h dark-thirty to military folk) all personnel would be recalled for duty, all aircraft brought to flying condition and loaded with nukes against prescribed timings. When I had taken over my married quarter at Scampton, I had failed to notice the siren attached to the wall just outside our bedroom window. My wife was none too pleased whenever it went off in the early hours of the morning. Over the three days that I was given to run an exercise, I kept everyone on their toes as they would not know where my team was going to hit next.

As the end of each exercise drew near with the inevitable air attack pending, the station would go into nuclear lockdown with only essential personnel such as the RAF police guarding armed aircraft still in the open. We were getting near the end of one of these exercises and an air attack was coming. All the Vulcans, twenty-four of them loaded with practice nuclear weapons, had been scrambled. As the aircraft taxied in turn towards the runway I had already briefed one crew that their aircraft would develop a simulated fire in the bomb bay. The crew, air traffic and RAF police and the fire crews were also briefed that one aircraft was going to have an emergency. At the given signal the chosen Vulcan came to a halt, one of my sergeant armourer assistants rushed out, opened the access panel in the bomb bay and put a non-flammable smoke flare inside. As smoke poured out the crew declared an emergency saying they were shutting down engines and evacuating the aircraft. Air traffic, fire crews, medical teams, nuclear response teams all went into action as expected. The operations centre reacted to what was to them a completely unexpected incident as best they could. But what I had missed in my planning was to tell the crew in the following aircraft that this was an exercise. They just saw pandemonium in front of them with fire vehicles, ambulances, and police all rushing to the scene therefore they assumed it was for real. So they also promptly shut down their engines, declared an emergency and evacuated their aircraft. It soon got out of control as the following crews were very confused as to what was happening. About twenty Vulcans were now backed up on the taxiway with nowhere else to go and the scramble was going to pot. But order was quickly restored and the aircraft continued their scramble take-off.

On another occasion the aircraft had all taken off and the airfield was under attack from Buccaneers. Everyone was in their respective air raid shelters and I had armourers setting off simulated explosions along the runway and other areas. We always lost WWIII but how to signal the exercise finale? The army used nuclear explosion simulators for their training exercises but because they looked so realistic they were only used on military training areas where the public wouldn't see them. I had one of my best SNCO scroungers obtain by various means a couple of these simulators to use to indicate the end of one of Scampton's three-day exercises. They looked spectacular as they went off on the airfield – complete with miniature mushroom clouds. Unfortunately motorists on the A15 which bends round the end of Scampton's runway were mesmerised by what looked like real nuclear explosions. Several motorists with their attention well distracted missed the curve and came off the road. Luckily there was no serious accident. Although HQ Strike Command were somewhat displeased about the whole affair Scampton's CO, Clive Herbert congratulated me and my team on a very realistic and valuable training exercise.

More Nuclear Postings

My next involvement with nukes was as the RAF armament liaison officer at the USAF 3rd Air Force HQ at RAF Mildenhall in Suffolk. There my responsibilities were to ensure that everything the US forces based in the UK (USAF, US Army, USN, USMC and others) did that involved armament ranging from cruise missiles, firearms, explosive ordnance disposal (EOD), weapon ranges to nuclear weapons, mines and torpedoes was done to accord with UK armament regulations and safety procedures. The Americans were highly

Top: **Heavy duty cargo transporter for nuclear weapons.** *(Mike Keitch)*

Bottom: **Convoy in the early 1990s.** *(Mike Keitch)*

professional in everything but I had more problems with their attitude to firearms than anything else. I could write a small book about the many incidents that this created. The cruise missiles, which of course had nuclear warheads, at Greenham Common and Molesworth were an interesting aspect of my work at 3rd Air Force. Contrary to what the CND crowd and the media sometimes put out, not one cruise missile ever left the bases from the time they arrived in the UK by transport aircraft to the day they left the same way. All cruise missile launch vehicles seen on British roads were always empty of missiles. The day the last missile was flown out of Greenham Common with lots of VIPs such as the US ambassador and senior MOD and American officials present plus the cheering CND crowd, we in our office at Mildenhall smiled. The last missile had been flown out quietly several days before and only an empty launcher was on that last aircraft.

My final nuclear posting in 1994 was to the RAF Armament Support Unit (RAFASUPU) at Wittering as OC Engineering and Supply Squadron. There I was responsible, among other things for planning and running nuclear convoys for the RAF and Royal Navy in the UK and overseas. But the vehicles, equipment and training and procedures were a world apart from the early days. The load-carrying trucks costing £1.5 million each, had every conceivable safety and security protection device you could (and couldn't) imagine.

From the first RAF nuclear convoy in 1953 to the last one in the late 1990s there was never an incident or accident which posed the slightest risk to the public or indeed the convoy personnel. Even serious incidents, of which there were very few, did not result in any weapon becoming hazardous.

These days the convoys are the responsibility of the RN and operated by the Atomic Weapons Establishment (AWE) Aldermaston. The weapon-carrying vehicles are driven by civilian drivers – which would have been inconceivable in my day. But nuclear convoys still make an impressive sight if you are lucky enough to see one. I retired from the service in 1997 just before the RAF gave up its nuclear role in 1998. I can claim that at that point my involvement with RAF nuclear weapons stretched back probably longer than anyone else in the air force. It's a world rapidly disappearing into the past so I hope these few words will give a taste of what that world was like.

I have often been asked what it was like to work on nuclear weapons and whether I had any moral dilemmas. My answer has always been that you can't judge the rights and wrongs of historic events by applying today's morals and ideas. As a young newly qualified RAF technician over fifty years ago I, like all military personnel, did whatever I was required to do. One's personal views about nuclear weapons, if one even had them which most if not all of us didn't have, were not relevant. To us, the weapons were just items of equipment which we armourers and others were required to work on. So what was life like as a nuclear weapon armourer? The aircrew had all the glamour and publicity which was understandable as they knew the targets and had the responsibility of dropping the things in a real war. But RAF armourers have had little mention in all the various books, media articles, TV programmes etc. about their role in the Cold War so this narrative will hopefully go some way towards rectifying this.

CHAPTER 16

617 SQUADRON CREW CHIEF

Bob Martin

Bob Martin joined the RAF in 1958 as an apprentice engine fitter, which took three years full-time training. Not surprisingly his early career was associated entirely with engines and he got involved with the Olympus Engine and the Vulcan. In 1973 Bob Martin became a Vulcan crew chief. He left the RAF in 1982 and emigrated to the States where he worked on the Gulfstream and then the AV-8B. He was engine manager for seven years on the Goshawk team with a fleet of 100 aircraft in Meridian, Mississippi. He is now retired living in Florida.

After my crew chief training I wangled a post to 617 Squadron Scampton in 1975 where I spent seven happy years as a crew chief. We did a lot of things but some happenings stand out. In 1976 there was a lone ranger to Abbotsford, British Columbia. Wg Cdr Warrington, 617 Squadron commanding officer was slated for a special ranger (off the normal ranger route) with myself and chief technician Mike West as his sixth and seventh seats. Mike and I were asked to choose an aircraft for the Abbotsford trip. Fortunately for us XL392 had just returned from a major inspection at RAF St Athan and was resplendent in a new livery. Unfortunately for us it had recently had an emergency abort on the main runway; I was the crew chief who had recovered it. Several days went by and no problems were found.

The aborted take-off was claimed by Flt Lt Ford; he had a history of some famed occurrences. There was the time when flying low level in Italy (we were on deployment to Luqa) he diverted into Istrana reporting a canopy seal failure, it was flapping on the outside of the canopy. After he had talked with the squadron commander I asked if the door seal stayed inflated, he said it had, I suggested that it was not the canopy seal at fault but maybe the weather strip. At this the squadron commander threw his hat on the ground and stamped on it. Flt Lt Ford was then instructed to have the offending strip cut off and to proceed on his way. Then there was the Eagle incident, just after take-off from Goose Bay he reported an eagle attacked the cockpit, he performed an emergency landing with max fuel load saying the aircraft performed erratically right after the incident. I guess he flinched and pulled on the stick. Anyway myself and Mike were very suspicious of the aborted take-off of XL392 and decided to take it to Canada.

We performed the ranger prep, collecting seven winter survival packs, a tail brake chute, a set of wheels etc. Away we went.

Our squadron commander was a great story teller, so too was Mike West and throughout the ranger they swapped stories putting myself and the rest of the crew in stitches. The reason for this will become apparent as the story unfolds. We arrived at Goose Bay on our first leg; this was very normal and the wing commander said we should get down to Offutt ASAP and spend several days there awaiting to go to Abbotsford. So far the trip was proceeding very well, we had no maintenance to perform except for the routine before and after-flight servicings. After arriving at Offutt AFB, we noticed that the port rapid start air system was empty, a leak had occurred on the Goose Bay-Offutt leg so we were limited to probably three engine starts using the starboard side rapid air system. Ground starts using the Palouste air starter were not affected. We spent three lazy days at Offutt AFB before getting airborne for Abbotsford.

We arrived at Abbotsford in the midst of a terrific thunderstorm, were marshalled to a display point and told to shut down our engines. We deplaned the crew and crew chiefs lowered the 4,000-lb pannier with spares and tools and prepared to perform the after-flight servicing. A runner appeared on a moped. He told us we had been parked in the wrong spot and we needed to move the aircraft. Wg Cdr Warrington and a couple of the crew, the AEO and co-pilot, got in and fired up the engines using a rapid start and a seventy per cent cross feed and with me on the short lead plugged into the nosewheel bay talked the aircraft to its pre-located parking spot on the other side of the taxiway.

Mike and I sent the crew away to a reception party for all display attendees at the base armoury while we performed the after-flight servicing and put the aircraft to bed. We then joined them at the party to which a C-130 captain and co-pilot challenged us to a game of shuffleboard. We were told if we lost they wanted our flying suits. We started in great style, winning several points. However the Americans then decided to start the game again after calling us ringers. As a result, Mike and I agreed we would deliberately lose the game. This we did, and at the end of the game we stripped off our flight suits.

I then told the C-130 team to strip off their flying suits and give them to us. They argued that it wasn't part of the game. We told them to strip or be stripped. The captain was considerably smaller than I and I had trouble getting into his suit, however a nice lady helped shoe horn me into it. Next thing we knew was that Wg Cdr Warrington had two Americans on a table giving them drill instructions, he wound up having them sing Rule Britannia and using brooms as rifles. We had a rousing welcome to Abbotsford.

After the party one of the not so drunk crew members drove us to our hotel in downtown Vancouver. We retired to our rooms, rested, showered and changed to meet up in the wing commander's room for pre-dinner drinks. Our captain always carried a portable bar on rangers. We met and all members were asked to chip in $5.00 for entertainment for the co-pilot, our youngest member. The plan was to hire an escort for him. The call was made, during dinner a young man arrived with a large photo album under his arm. He took the co-pilot aside to show him the girls. In the event he didn't select any of the young ladies and we all got our money back.

The next day with a thirteen per cent fuel load, XL392 performed its display using a rapid start, leaving us with maybe one start left. We quickly negotiated with the American Thunder Bird team the use of their air starter. The Thunder Birds were scheduled to display immediately before the Vulcan and were situated next to us on the taxiway, so it was an easy task to go and push the starter over to the Vulcan after the eight or nine Thunder Birds had started. Mike and I then learned the Thunder Birds were leaving early in the morning after the displays. We decided not to mention this to the rest of the crew.

At the next display we were waiting to go, the Thunder Birds had started their engines then they abruptly shut them down. Mike and I went and got their air starter, when the runner from air traffic appeared on his moped. He told us that a P-51 had landed wheels up on the only working runway. There was a much shorter secondary runway in a considerable state of disrepair that ran alongside of the air show crowd. This runway, which had grass emanating from cracks, was used for visiting light aircraft. He asked the wing commander if the Vulcan could take off from there and the response was "of course we can". So we crewed in and started the engines when a runner came over from the Thunder Birds asking if we knew about the closed runway. After saying we did, the runner asked, "well how are you going to take off?" to which Mike indicated the short runway. The runner went away shaking his head and saying "you're nuts". The Vulcan took off and the crowd were elated. I have never had to sign so many autographs.

Then we had to think, as the Vulcan certainly could not land on that runway, if the P-51 had not been cleared. We would have to divert to Vancouver international, which would mean Mike and I taking the tail brake parachute in a Land Rover and replacing the parachute. But as luck would have it, when the Vulcan turned finals to land the P-51 was being shoved off the runway; our bacon was saved.

One other amusing incident, we had a friend at Offutt AFB who asked us if we could bring him a case of Molson. I asked the bar tender in the armoury, he said sure and immediately began taking the tops off the bottles, How was I going to transport a case of beer to Offutt with the tops removed? He told me that he wasn't allowed to sell it without removing the tops. Then he told me to back my car up to the back door and not to mention where I got the Molson from.

Our wing commander got wind of the Thunder Birds' planned early departure and decided he wanted to leave early too so we could use their air starter. Mike and I looked at each other disappointed as it would have taken three or four days to get a starter from Offutt AFB. Oh well. We departed Abbotsford after a great time treated like royalty. We then rested up at Offutt AFB for three days, before flying to Goose Bay, to perform an air display there. Mike and I were entertained that night by the Goose Bay maintenance

617 Squadron in 1978 with awards won during Exercise Double Top.

team. They wanted to have a competition, where each in turn would tell a joke, if it was a good one everyone except the story teller would down his drink, if it was a bad one the story teller would down his. What dummies! We had been on the road for two weeks listening to the biggest story tellers in the world; by 2.00 a.m. the whole team (eight of them) were fast asleep and Mike and I were virtually unscathed. Then we flew to St John's Newfoundland where we were to appear at a prize giving for 617 ATC Squadron, once again treated like royalty. I had friends in St Johns so I purchased a couple of lobsters and my friends cooked them for me. The next day in the hotel I decided to have a Newfoundland breakfast, whatever that was. It turned out to be a pound of smoked cod broiled. Oh well you live and learn.

We crewed in for the final time and shot off for home – a truly memorable trip with enough memories to last a lifetime. However there was more to come.

In the spring of 1978 I became involved in Exercise Double Top. This was a bombing and navigation exercise involving all Vulcan squadrons and the Boeing B-52s of 2nd Bomb Wing 8th Air Force (USAF). The crew chiefs would prepare the aircraft along with the ground crews and launch them on their missions. 617 Squadron performed exceptionally well and took the vast majority of the awards offered. The exercise took the better part of a week and involved take-off times at all daylight hours. Crews were particularly excited for a chance to beat their American counterparts.

Another story that comes to mind concerns Dave Patterson and crew. They were on a ranger to Malta, Dave was nearing the end of his Vulcan tour, with only his swansong to Hickham AFB Hawaii left. While in the officers' mess at Luqa, he was harassed by the F-4 Phantom 'Jocks' while flying in the area . The Phantoms became such a nuisance that he decided he was going to teach them about the Vulcan.

On leaving Luqa he asked air traffic for clearance to do a low level pass over the airfield, in the event he flew low level over Malta for a considerable distance which was strictly forbidden. He came over the Phantom flight line at about 50 feet, scattering the ground crew and some say a flight sergeant broke his leg. Mechanics jumped off wings and a general kerfuffle ensued.

Phantom pilots requested permission to give chase to this cheeky fellow. Two Phantoms scrambled to give chase. Vulcan going through 20,000 ft heard the Phantoms ask him to slow down to give them a chance. The reply was "not a chance" and the Vulcan left them in the dust.

Back at base a welcoming committee was waiting for Dave, it consisted of the station commander, wing commander tech and 617 Squadron commander. I don't know what was said but I do know that Dave's swansong to Hawaii was changed to a Goose Bay/ Offutt ranger. I was his crew chief and Chief Fitzsimmonds rode seventh seat.

We did our ranger prep for the Offutt trip; our aircraft was the one I held the inventory for, XL426. I called my girlfriend Sara from the sergeants' mess to tell her I was on my way to Offutt and would see her in the Ramada Inn in Belle Vue Nebraska. Sara was a nurse in Bossier City, Louisiana. She called a friend and they set off to drive the 700 plus miles to Belle Vue.

We arrived two days later, having performed our survival training in Goose Bay, sending the crew to the hotel, while myself and Fitz, together with the detachment guys performed the after-flight servicing. We arrived at the Ramada just as the girls were checking in.

We crewed in for the first flight of three, the aircraft taxied and lined up, the engines were set to max. and the take-off run started, then at close to unstick speed there was silence as all four engines were brought back to idle, the parachute was deployed and Dave turned off the runway at our intersection and taxied back to his allotted position on the ramp. Brakes were red hot, fire section was called we stood back and waited for the brakes to cool. A PFC warning had illuminated causing the aborted take-off. There had been a cold air unit oil leak, when the brakes were applied and the oil from the cold air unit drip tray was shot all over the avionics suite in the nosewheel bay. So we had eight wheels to change, eight brake units to change, a TBC to repack and change, a rudder powered flight control unit (PFCU) to change and an avionics suite to replace. It suddenly dawned on Fitz and myself we were going to be in Offutt for a considerable time. Three days later we were disappointed to see taxiing in a Vulcan en route from Waddington to an air display, his 4,000-lb pannier carrying all the equipment we needed.

So on day four of our ranger Fitz and I started work, we left the wheels and brakes to the detachment and we started on the more complicated tasks. Day five we unpacked the rudder PFCU and as I lifted it I fell about laughing. Fitz asked me what was so funny, I said look at this thing. The unit had been heavily damaged, all the pipework was bent and broken – it had obviously been dropped before it was packaged. Someone somewhere was in for a roasting.

Giant Voice team 1977. The flight ramp of Barksdale AFB, Bossier City, Louisiana. Bob Martin is back row in flying kit, second from left. *(Bob Martin)*

We finally got a replacement PFCU on day sixteen, and Fitz and I installed it and tested it. Good to go. In the meantime Dave and the crew had mailed a postcard back to the squadron CO Wg Cdr Stephenson Oliver, thanking him for the aircraft. Dave was engaged to the wing commander's sister. A fast response came back, get the aircraft serviceable and get back home. The result was an eighteen-day ranger with no flying except for arrival and departure and a good time was had by all. Thank you very much.

In 1977 I was part of the Giant Voice team that went to Barksdale and again in 1979 I was lucky enough to be nominated along with crew chief Dick Abrahams for exercise Red Flag. This involved a flight from RAF Scampton to Nellis AFB, Las Vegas, Nevada.

The RAF had been requested to test the USAF air defences and the Vulcans and Buccaneers had been set targets in the desert. The Vulcans were launched at their targets and two USAF F-15s attacked them. As the Vulcans peeled away four Buccaneers appeared one from under each Vulcan wing. They proceeded to target unhindered.

My time on 617 Squadron finished in 1982 when the squadron disbanded and I reckoned I had been very lucky to have been on the squadron all those years.

ROYAL AIR FORCE SCAMPTON

No. 617 SQUADRON

DISBANDMENT PARADE

REVIEWING OFFICER
AIR CHIEF MARSHAL
SIR KEITH WILLIAMSON
KCB, AFC, RAF
AIR OFFICER COMMANDING-IN-CHIEF
STRIKE COMMAND

TUESDAY 22nd DECEMBER 1981

IT WAS ALL BULL

Monty Montgomery

A lot has been written about Black Buck 1 and this is an addendum showing the muddle over the correct name for the operation. **Monty Montgomery** *was detachment commander of the Vulcan Detachment at Ascension Island in 1982 for the duration of the Falklands Campaign and captain of the reserve crew for Black Bucks 2, 5, 6 and 7.*

In 1982, communications between Ascension Island and the UK were, at least initially, limited to a secure voice system that had the clarity of Donald Duck on dope. Later, a secure teleprinter link was established which improved the clarity and speed of transmissions dramatically.

The first attack on Port Stanley was launched on 30 April. Of course, reaching this point had taken an enormous amount of effort by a great number of people in the UK and, latterly, on the island. However, as with all RAF sorties, authorisation was required and this ritual – indeed a legal requirement for any Royal Air Force flight – was just about the last item undertaken before the crews departed for their aircraft. The *final* act before boarding the bomber was somewhat more functional. Authorisation of a sortie is an important event: it is the legal order to the crew to carry out a sortie and the statement of understanding by the aircraft captain that he understands and accepts the requirements and limitations of the sortie. In the controlled mayhem preceding the launch, there had been some doubt about the name allocated to the mission. 'Black Buck' did not (at least then) sound right and, consequently, the two sorties were entered on the authorisation sheet by me as 'Black Bull'.

The next afternoon, the error was spotted and a clumsy correction made. Clumsy was the right word for this. An early instructor of the authoriser – who had earned an AFC in another Avro product dodging Lisbon Harbour bridge – had once said to him, in a very strong South African accent, following his entry in the authorisation sheets many years previously: "Montgomery, did you not go to one of them fancy universities?" "Yes Sir" *"Well, they did not teach you to write too good!"* As a consequence, the sheet was neatly re-written and signed up correctly. Don't believe this? Look at the photographs of the original authorisation sheet.

As an aside, the 'sortie description' of a peacetime Vulcan sortie in the authorisation sheets usually filled about ten lines detailing every aspect of what, where and when; here, as you can see, 'as briefed' was quite enough and quite adequate.

Original authorisation sheet for Black Buck 1 sortie with close-up below.

EPILOGUE

This book brings to an end the first-hand accounts of operating the three V bombers. I have been incredibly luckily to get so much help and so many inputs but I would never have managed at all without John Reeve who captained Black Buck Two and introduced me to so many Vulcan aircrew, Dick Russell of Black Buck One who was the backbone of *Victor Boys* and of course Anthony Wright who co-authored *Valiant Boys* and this book. He also helped enormously with *Vulcan Boys*.

The books have covered all three V bombers with which I was very much involved during my test-flying years. First the Valiant which I first flew in 1956 until 1963 when the metal fatigue problem was finally recognised. Then the Victor starting with Johnny Allam, who developed the Victor through to K2 development, which I flew initially, the aircraft continued in service until 1992. Finally, the Vulcan, which I first flew in 1956, ending its RAF service in 1984. It was then reborn in 2007 before eventually finishing in October 2015.

I believe the books are important as I have remarked before because they give first-hand accounts of what was involved operating the aircraft and providing the UK's deterrent in the Cold War to the threat from Russia. It is quite clear from the books that the aircraft were very effective and kept the threat at bay until the Royal Navy could take over with Polaris.

I am very pleased that helped by Grub Street, our publisher, we have been able to demonstrate that the UK was able to provide a credible deterrent in its own right throughout the Cold War years and we all should be very proud of this achievement.

Tony Blackman
June 2017

ACRONYMS

AAPP	airborne auxiliary power pack	**GCA**	ground-controlled approach
AEO	air electronics officer	**GPI**	ground position indicator
AEOp	air electronics operator	**GSU**	Group Standardisation Unit
AEW	airborne early warfare	**H2S**	ground mapping radar
ANS	Air Navigation School	**HDU**	hose drum unit
AWE	atomic weapons establishment	**HTP**	high test peroxide
BCBS	Bomber Command Bombing School	**ILS**	instrument landing system
BCCF	Bomber Command Communications Flight	**INCU**	inertial navigator control unit
		INMU	inertial navigator monitor unit
BNS	bombing and navigation system	**INS**	inertial navigation system
BSCP	Blue Steel control panel	**LCN**	load classification number
BTR	basic training requirement	**MBF**	medium bomber force
CCCF	Coastal Command CommunicationsFlight	**MEZ**	missile engagement zone
		MOTU	Maritime Operational Training Unit
DR	Dead Reckoning. Navigation estimate of position	**NBS**	navigation and bombing system
ECM	electronic counter measures	**NTP**	navigation termination point
EMRU	electromechnical release unit	**OCU**	Operational Conversion Unit
ESA	explosives storage area	**PAR**	pilot-approach radar
EW	electronic warfare	**PFCU**	powered flying control unit
EWO	electronic warfare officer	**PPI**	plan position indicator
FTS	Flying Training School	**PRF**	pulse repetition frequency

QFI	qualified flying instructor	**TTF**	Tanker Training Flight
QRA	quick reaction alert	**UAS**	University Air Squadron
RAT	ram air turbine	**VTF**	Victor Training Flight
RBSU	radar bomb scoring unit	**WLSO**	weapons loading supervising officer
RPF	release point fix	**WST**	Weapons Standardisation Unit
RPU	rapid processing unit		
RS05	readiness in five minutes [relating to QRA]		
RS15	readiness in fifteen minutes [relating to QRA]		
RSO	range safety officer		
RWR	radar warning receiver		
SACEUR	Strategic Air Command Europe		
SAM	surface-to-air missile		
SDO	station duty officer		
SOP	standard operating procedures		
SRA	standard-radar approach		
SSA	supplementary storage area		
TACAN	beacon heading and distance indicator		
TDU	time delay unit		
TFR	terrain following radar		

REFERENCES
AND SOURCES

Chapter Two

"Blue Steel – The V Force's Stand-off Bomb", *The RAF Historical Society Journal*, 62, 1 April 2015, pp. 31-47

"History of Navigation in the RAF", *The RAF Historical Society Journal*, 17A, 21 October 1996, pp. 98-106

"The RAF and Nuclear Weapons", *The RAF Historical Society Journal*, 26, 11 April 2001, pp. 10-15 and 54-66

Allen J. E., "Blue Steel and Developments", Lecture to the Royal Aeronautical Society Historical Group, London, 23 April 1996

Francis R. H., "The Development of Blue Steel", *Journal of the Royal Aeronautical Society*, Vol. 68, No. 641, May 1964, pp. 303-322

Gibson Chris, *Vulcan's Hammer: V-Force Projects and Weapons Since 1945*, Hikoki Publications, Manchester, 2011

Meeting between the author and Professor John Allen, 20 March 2015

SD4766, RAF Servicing Document for Blue Steel – ASGW 16,000, HC No. 1

Chapter Fourteen

Brown David, *The Royal Navy and the Falklands War*, Guild Publishing, London, 1987

Ethell Jeffrey, and Price Alfred, *Air War: South Atlantic*, Sidgwick & Jackson, London, 1983

"Falklands Aircraft Kills", *The Aero Forum*, Key Publishing, 1 February 2007 http://forum.keypublishing.com/showthread.php?67322-Falklands-Aircraft-Kills. Last accessed 13 April 2017

INDEX